OFFICE HOURS

OFFICE HOURS
A Guide to the Managerial Life

WALTER KIECHEL III

LITTLE, BROWN AND COMPANY
BOSTON   TORONTO

FIRST EDITION

Library of Congress Cataloging-in-Publication Data

Kiechel, Walter.
  Office hours.

  1. Organizational effectiveness.   2. Office
politics.   3. Executive ability.   I. Title.
HD58.7.K52   1988   658.4'09   87-34242

          10   9   8   7   6   5   4   3   2   1

RRD-VA

Published simultaneously in Canada
by Little, Brown & Company (Canada) Limited

PRINTED IN THE UNITED STATES OF AMERICA

To my mother and father

Contents

Introduction

IN THESE DAYS of pervasive corporate enterprise, just about anybody with a college degree and a two-piece suit can insinuate him- or herself into a job as a manager, even if it's only running the local fast-food outlet. The real challenge is to make a satisfying career of managerial work. How to craft a life one can take pride in, at the end of the day and at the end of one's innings, when the perks are gone, the money no longer seems so important, and the old résumé is finally put away in a drawer, to be updated no further? This book represents a modest attempt to answer that question.

The managerial life entails constant, sometimes nettlesome interaction with others. Indeed, not-so-gentle readers of the pages that follow may be tempted to complain: "What we have here is essentially a guidebook to office politics, and yet you almost never use those two words. What's the matter, bozo? Too prissy to call a spade a spade, or, as may be more accurate in this context, to label it a gore-bespattered shovel?"

The author pleads guilty, but not exactly as charged. The trouble with the words "office politics" is what they connote to most people: nasty, sneaky, back-stabbing intrigue. Let's form a cabal to eliminate old Fred and get ourselves promoted. Let's wrap Helen, the new V.P. from outside, in a net of bureaucratic obfuscation, then roll her off a cliff. To be sure, plenty of skullduggery goes on in corporate America. But this book won't tell you how to commit same, for two reasons. It's my conviction, based on about ten years of looking inside companies, that such behavior usually doesn't pay off. And even if it does work in a particular instance, at what cost to the perpetrators?

There is, however, a higher office politics sufficiently honorable that it probably should not even be tarred with the name. Enlightened practice in this arena begins with the recognition that to get a manager's job done, much less to get ahead, you have to be able to work amicably with other people. Alas, something in the very nature of organizations conspires to make this difficult.

Babes new to the woods of business, including a surprising number of supposedly pre-hardbitten M.B.A.'s, often virtuously intone, "I'm not going to play politics." Sorry, when it comes to the higher variety, you don't have any choice. Wherever two or more souls gather together to accomplish something, there will be politics. When they gather together in large organizations, with different groups competing for scarce resources, such as budget money or the boss's attention, the give-and-take can become mighty complicated. Much of what follows is devoted to helping the reader parse these complications so that he or she can act effectively. Also honorably. *Office Hours* stands for the proposition that a successful manager can be humane, decent, wise, even funny. It isn't always easy, but it's possible.

One final, arguably perverse point by way of introduction to a book on career-making: perhaps the most common mistake managers fall into is devoting themselves so single-mindedly to their work that they neglect other aspects — and there ought to be some — of their lives. The reader will find this theme woven through the treatment of many topics in the book, accompanied by what the author hopes are useful ideas on striking the right balance.

The chapters below appeared originally in *Fortune* magazine. They were checked for accuracy by the same crack researchers who helped immeasurably in reporting them, and they have been revised for publication as a book. Still, the titles of some people quoted have almost certainly changed since we talked to them; welcome to post-restructuring corporate America. For these and any other errors that have crept in, the author assumes full responsibility.

❧ Part I ❧

LA TECHNIQUE

Beating the Clock

*Traditional advice on how to manage your time
doesn't comport with executive reality.*

TREATISES on how an executive should manage his time almost inevitably begin the same way: with the stern admonition that time is the one thing you can't get more of. Consider, for example, the first three sentences of Alan Lakein's *How to Get Control of Your Time and Your Life,* probably the most widely circulated guide to the subject: "Time is life. It is irreversible and irreplaceable. To waste your time is to waste your life, but to master your time is to master your life and make the most of it."

Businessmen and -women eat this stuff up. The hot gospel message raises the prospect of redemption — you can be saved if you learn to plan better, organize better — but only after it has strummed about every chord of guilt that can be sounded in anyone even moderately imbued with the good old American work ethic. Most executives feel they should be handling their time better. The lament of John Mowrey, American Motors' vice president in charge of product planning, is representative: "Time management is probably the major problem in my life."

The cruel irony is that much of this executive fretfulness is unwarranted. A lot of the guilt comes from measuring one's own seemingly miserable performance against ideals that, when examined in light of the best research on how executives actually get things done, simply don't hold up.

On its face, nothing in the conventional wisdom seems particularly exceptionable. You may know the drill. Decide what you want to accomplish and list what you'll have to do to reach these goals. Assign priorities to both goals and activities. Review the rankings constantly, making sure your daily what-to-do list is in accord with them, and then work hardest at the A items. Since you can't possibly get any serious work done in fits and starts, block out healthy chunks of time to single-mindedly address your major projects. Do everything that you can to avoid being interrupted, particularly during those half-hours or hours that you've set aside for heavy managerial thinking and decision-making. Your secretary can intercept telephone calls; the petty annoyances that they represent can almost always wait until later.

The only problem with this regimen is that you probably have to be what psychologists call an obsessive-compulsive to keep to it — in fact, an obsessive-compulsive working on another planet. A current joke accurately summarizes the typical experience of an executive trying to live up to such an ideal: he comes to work with a list of eleven things to do and goes home with a list of fourteen, including the original eleven.

In the mid-1960s, certain academics got the bright idea of looking at how managers in fact spend their time. Henry Mintzberg, now a professor at McGill University, did the pioneering work. What he discovered in a study of chief executives of five organizations was a hyperkinetically far cry from the big-blocks-of-coolly-deliberative-time model. Perhaps his most widely publicized finding was that the top dogs spent half their time on activities to which they devoted less than nine minutes.

These brief bouts of activity were not precious moments frittered away — they were often the time when executives accomplished the most. The research of Professor John Kotter of the Harvard Business School, summarized in his 1982 book *The General Managers*, explains why. After closely observing fifteen better-than-average general managers in action, Kotter concluded that his subjects got work done not by giving orders or churning out reports, but mostly by talking to people — asking questions, making requests, maybe prodding a bit. These conversations often consisted of nothing more than a two-minute encounter in the hallway or on the phone. The good manager sees opportunity where his lesser counterparts see only interruptions. Kotter found that his subjects did not plan their days in great detail; instead they reacted to events and people.

His research left the professor with some rather unconventional views on how to manage time. "The two biggest tools," he says, "are a good agenda — a clear notion of what the hell you're trying to do, not just today, but tomorrow, next month, next year, and how they all tie together — and a good network of relationships with the resources you need to implement that agenda." A list, he stresses, is not an agenda. "When you say, 'Make a list'—boom, you're bringing it down to the mechanistic." That's not the way these guys do it. An agenda, according to Kotter, is "more like a big, complex map, constructed over time."

Even if you are a rabid proponent of what is currently called management by wandering around — get out of your office, chat up the troops, listen, learn, and inspire (no, no, not your Patton imitation; your Omar Bradley) — there will probably come a day when you have to schedule a meeting or two. The secret here, savvy time managers say, is not to book too many on any given day. James Treybig of Tandem Computers is about as accessible a chief executive as you'll find — he usually has an open door and he keeps a calendar outside it that any employee can use to sign up for an appointment. He also goes home around six most nights, he says, taking no work with him. The key is maintaining a healthy amount of what Treybig calls, a little redundantly, "disposable free time." By booking only half the day with appointments, he leaves time for lots of interruptions and spur-of-the-moment meetings.

To avoid overbooking, it helps to schedule as far in advance as possible those meetings you know you're going to have to have next quarter or even next year. James Tappan, a group vice president of General Foods, plans all major events six to twelve months in advance. Tappan also always keeps about him a file with a list of all meetings for the next day, a schedule of all trips and appointments for the next two months, a schedule of the locations of all major events he'll attend in the next twelve months, a six-week schedule of staff activities, and a six-week schedule of what the other members of the company's operating committee will be doing. Mr. Tappan does not, as they say, mess around. He reports that he has plenty of time for unplanned interaction.

There are a few other tactics that a manager who values his interactive time can employ. Get help sorting out that atavism of the computer age, paperwork. John Mowrey of American Motors has his secretary do the triage for him, consigning anything that comes in to one of five folders — red for "hot," to be read immediately; orange for material that needs his attention today; yellow for what has to be read this week; white for weekend reading; and black for documents requiring his signature. If you discover you still need a little time for that seemingly precluded diversion, thinking quietly to yourself, try sneaking in early, before anyone else is ready to interact.

The co-worker who will really drive you crazy with his interactive demands — and most upset your management of time — is the workaholic, particularly if he or she is your boss. Blessedly, true workaholics, the kind who put in seventy hours or more and like it — however secretly — are rare.

Academics and psychologists offer this advice for dealing with a workaholic boss: as soon as it becomes apparent that he's going to routinely keep you there until ten or eleven at night, go to the misguided soul. Tactfully explain that his ways are not yours, that you value your personal life and can get your work done before the sun goes down. The problem with this advice: it assumes that the workaholic doesn't necessarily want you to grind away the same way he does. Indeed, workaholics sometimes say as much.

Don't believe it. While in the abstract he may applaud the value you attach to your life outside the office, what he in fact values is the work that's getting done. It is, after all, what he has chosen to give the bulk of his time to. H. Michael Hayes, a professor of business at the University of Colorado at Denver, admits that he was a workaholic in the years he spent in the employ of General Electric. Did it bother him when his subordinates failed to put in the same long hours that he did? "Yes," he confesses. "I'd think, 'What's the matter? They're not interested in the job?'"

Real live managers understand this. Their advice — the correct advice — is to decide whether what you'll get out of slaving away can possibly be worth it and, if it can't, to dust off your résumé.

If the workaholic is your subordinate, your alternatives are easier. At the magnanimous extreme, you may dispatch him on a mandatory vacation, as Treybig of Tandem says he might do. At the other extreme, you may have to think seriously about firing him, particularly if he has subordinates of his own. Sure, sure, he really turns the stuff out, but he may also keep everybody else — including you — from effectively managing time. The collective misery may not be worth his output. Philemon Marcoux is chairman of AWI, a start-up electronics company in Silicon Valley. Contrary to what you might expect at an entrepreneurial venture, he reports that he has no workaholics working for him and doesn't want any. "It's not healthy," he says.

What the workaholic has forgotten, and the would-be manager of time should always keep in mind, is what one might be doing outside the office. Possibilities include walking out in the weather of sunlit days and storm; watching the seasons change; seeing children grow and maybe even helping the process along; talking in candlelight, perhaps over a meal, with attractive persons, possibly including one's spouse; and being there to solace a troubled friend, or child, or aging parent. If you consistently choose work over these alternatives, then you really do have a problem managing time.

Getting Organized

*Shelling out $150 for a trendy organizer-notebook
won't do the job. The secret is, gulp, making decisions.*

GETTING ORGANIZED has become chic. Arbiters of popular culture such as the *New York Times* and *Time* magazine weigh the merits of different so-called organizers — notebooks cum planning calendars cum personal phone directories. Connoisseurs of the genre note, for example, that Filofax, an import widely believed to be the fashion leader, offers a year-at-a-glance calendar, color-coordinated blank sheets, don't-forget sheets, onionskin paper, pull-out grid paper, a credit card holder, and, just what you need for your next business trip to Akron, a map of the London subway system.

All this for a mere $150 for the basic black calfskin binding, though you can spend up to $550 if you're out to accessorize yourself with more exotic snakeskin, say, or shark. "Paloma Picasso has an ostrich Filofax," observes Helene Furst, vice president for sales of Londonhouse Corp. of Santa Monica, California, which sells the organizer in the U.S. She says Londonhouse expects U.S. sales of the books and inserts to go as high as $14 million this year, as against $10 million in 1985.

Sobersided business folk may not always be up on the latest giddiness, but neither are they immune to the organizer trend. Manufacturers say they sell a goodly number to people whose daily drill is likely to be hectic, particularly sales reps, entrepreneurs, and advertising types. Consultants in organizing, who typically get $1,000 a day to come in and help someone straighten out the mess in his office and on his calendar, say, too, that corporate executives are becoming more receptive to their pitch.

Why the mounting interest in getting one's act together? Attribute some of it to metastasizing careerism among baby-boomers, women, and artistic sorts; getting organized thus takes its place somewhere after training with Nautilus machines as the latest thing in self-development. Felice Willat, co-owner of Harper House in Culver City, California, which makes a popular series of organizers with names like Day Runner and Running Mate, describes her company's customers as people who "actualize their goals and get things done," who use the notebooks to "create more opportunities for themselves." Organizing consultants offer a less hip explanation for the trend, at least as it affects managers: everybody began to get religion when they saw what the Japanese, with their emphasis on productivity, could do.

Okay, so what's it all to untrendy you, twenty pounds overweight, unable to see over the papers on your desk, and still using a wall calendar provided every Christmas by your friendly home heating oil distributor? Even thoroughgoing slobbonies will be relieved and heartened by certain less faddish conclusions reached by the organizing experts. First, organized is not necessarily neat. So your office looks as if it was just ransacked by a motorcycle gang; if you can still find the report you want, you may well be as organized as you ought to be. Indeed, the consultants say that some people need a measure of clutter around them to get their productive juices bubbling.

Second, as Sunny Schlenger, head of the consulting firm Schlenger Organizational Systems, puts it, "Being organized is no longer a moral issue." Yesterday's careless, lazy bum has become today's unproductive drag on the team's effectiveness. Finally, for all of the winds of fashion that gust around the subject, the necessary equipment remains remarkably unchanged and simple. Almost to a person, the consultants say you don't need a fancy organizer.

What you do need is the ability to make decisions — constantly, and sometimes on what might seem the most trivial of matters. What shall you do about this memo that just hit your in-box? How do you want to respond to that invitation? Consultant Stephanie Winston, author of *The Organized Executive*, notes that her clients consider incoming paper their biggest bugbear. "Anyone can get organized who can assign priorities, categorize, and allocate places," she insists.

Proper organization begins with deciding what's most important for you to do. This can be trickier than it sounds. Experts on the management of time routinely counsel people to think about what they want to be doing in five years, break this down into concrete goals, and then figure out the steps to achieve each one. For most corporate apparatchiks, however, it's probably at least as important to understand what the boss wants.

You may think you know, but don't be too sure. Superiors aren't always wildly communicative on the subject, and plans and priorities change, sometimes with head-spinning speed. If you're lucky enough to have an approachable boss, you can ask what should be on your A list, and what on the B. Failing that, consider a brief, friendly memo or conversational gambit along the lines of, "I'm giving top priority to A, less to B, and still less to C, unless I hear to the contrary from Your Worshipfulness."

Also consult your subordinates. Scott D. Cook, president of Intuit, a California software house, says that in his years as a brand manager at Procter & Gamble he learned to hold weekly meetings at which each member of his team would discuss his goals for the past week, how far he had gone toward achieving them, and his goals for the coming week, in order of importance. The leader's priorities help determine the subordinates', and vice versa. Scott notes that there's a motivational kicker built into the system: since people almost invariably overestimate how much they can get done, they're constantly spurring themselves on to make up for last week's shortfall.

With a hierarchy of priorities firmly in mind, you should be able to decide quickly how much attention to give each blip that appears on your managerial radar screen. If you're a tightly wired type, compelled to make a list of everything you have to do, your hierarchy will at least enable you to differentiate A items from B's and C's. Try chucking the C's in a drawer, figuratively or literally; if they don't have enough moxie to fight their way out into your ken again, you probably can forget them.

Constantly update your pecking order with the subordinate most instrumental in keeping you organized: your secretary. It will save you lots of time if she knows which fires you want put out immediately and which you're willing to let burn awhile. Richard Cheney, vice chairman of the Hill & Knowlton public relations firm and a man known to get caught up in the occasional takeover battle, reports that he spends five or ten minutes every morning talking with his secretary about what he has to do. It helps him set priorities, he says, and enables him to "get a grip on the day."

Most managers seem to be able to get by with a simple planning calendar, one or two pages for each week, or, if they're hyperkinetic, a page for each day. If an executive makes his own appointments, it makes sense for him to keep the book himself; if he entrusts the choreography to his secretary, she may. The most important physical specification is that the calendar fit in a briefcase so the peripatetic manager can take it with him on the road. Beware the possible complications inherent in having two planning calendars, or a desk calendar along with an organizer. Consultant Ronni Eisenberg tells of a client who scheduled a breakfast meeting on one calendar, and another meeting with somebody else at the same time and place on another calendar. Breakfast was crowded.

To cope with the tide of paper that courses into your office every day, be guided not by the old saw that a good executive touches any given piece of paper only once, but by another maxim: every time you pick up a piece of paper, make a decision about it. If this seems daunting, bear in mind Stephanie Winston's insight that you basically have only four options, which you can remember with the handy mnemonic, TRAF: throw it away, refer it to somebody else, act on it, or file it.

Your best opportunity to toss the new arrival comes right after you first pick it up and read it. If you don't dispose of it then, but just lay it down to think about later, it's likely to become part of the permanent collection drifting around your office, picked up and put down again and again. Come on now, you ruthless decision-maker, do you really need to keep this one? Won't the information be available somewhere else?

If you refer the matter to someone else, do so not in the spirit of getting the monkey off your back and onto his, but because he can handle the matter better than you, or, by some miracle, might actually be interested in it. If you truly do want him to attend to it, and not to lose it or refer it to still someone else, indicate on it that you'd like it back by a certain date. And if you're deadly serious about it, make a note in your calendar to remind you when it's supposed to be returned.

If you're going to take action, do so immediately. Should an act of

God intervene to prevent this, again make a note in your calendar indicating when you'll get on the matter, and, if you have to keep the paper, put it somewhere you can find it.

Which brings us, as too much paper inevitably does, to filing. You can organize your files by subject (don't be overprecise, or you'll end up with a thousand extremely thin files), by the action you intend to take (read, answer, pay, take revenge), even by the week or day you will deal with the matter. Ideally your system should somehow incorporate your hierarchy of priorities: read immediately (pertains to an A project); read within the next three days (B priority); maybe read this C stuff sometime. Finally, try hard to get back to the file when you're supposed to. That's being *really* organized.

Working with a Liberated Secretary

Your secretary knows quite clearly what she wants from the job.
To get the best from her, you should know, too.

IN THE REVERIE of an ambitious junior executive still dependent on the typing pool, the secretary of the future has a complex job indeed. Just having a private secretary would, of course, signal his arrival as a manager: his words deemed of sufficient weight to be taken down and transcribed quickly, his time of such value that he should be spared the trivial interruption. She would be his buffer against the unwanted telephone call, the incompetent reservations clerk, the annoying subordinate. And that's not all. His secretary would be a respite from the managerial challenge — not an employee to be carefully supervised, but rather someone to get along with on more human terms. She would be loyal to him, an appreciative audience for his displays of enlightenment or flair, a witness to his progress, a fan . . .

It's not a job description that fits many applicants, especially in the last fifth of the twentieth century. Changes in the work force, in the technology of office work, and in male-female relations — all but about 1 percent of secretaries still are women, and most bosses still are men — have even led some to worry, or hope, that the traditional secretary is an endangered species. In fact, the outlook is for evolution, not extinction.

The clamor over "liberated secretaries" has died down considerably since 1977, when Diana Becker, an employee of the Waterloo, Iowa, community school district, refused to make coffee, was fired, and promptly sued on grounds of sex discrimination. By 1980, Hollywood could treat the issue as fodder for farce. The movie *Nine to Five* cheerfully depicted the response of three female clerical workers to their churlish male boss: elaborate fantasies of murder, a kidnapping and bondage, ultimate triumph. Audiences laughed, some perhaps less comfortably than others.

This is not to say that the battle for secretarial liberation is over — far from it. The conflict has evolved so rapidly that a manager still worrying about who makes the coffee has come to seem rather like a mounted cavalryman plotting tactics to stave off a panzer assault.

Contentious factions on the secretarial side have made up their differences. When in 1973 Gloria Steinem intimated that no girl-child should learn to type and others suggested that all clerical work was demeaning, an angry cry went up from women who had labored proudly as secretaries all their lives. "They wanted everyone to be a brain surgeon," recalled one old-line secretary recently. The feminists quickly came around. A past president of the National Organization for Women, Karen DeCrow, publicly apologized for her and her sisters' mistake.

The result has been a consensus on the respectability of being a secretary, a consensus that has made for less noise — and greater change. Early in 1981, in San Francisco, Professional Secretaries International held its first annual "secretary speakout." Over three hundred secretaries from across the country, half of them there at their employers' expense, addressed questions of image, productivity, and pay.

The convocation was remarkable in a number of respects, not the least of them that Professional Secretaries International had chosen to stage such an event. By and large, PSI draws its membership from the secretarial elite, typically women who have worked at such jobs for years and regard themselves as professionals. The organization has been no friend to unionizing efforts. But here they were, the old guard, some blue-haired if not white-gloved, speaking out. "Ten years ago, if this had been proposed, we would never have done it," maintains Fran Riley, spokeswoman for the group. "It would have seemed akin to militancy."

Militant or not, the proceedings often took on the character of what the Chinese term "speaking bitterness"—criticism of others, interlarded with doses of self-accusation. Their salaries were too low, many suspected. "Suspected" because their employers discouraged them from comparing with others just how much they made, and they had gone along. They resolved to conduct a region-by-region survey of members' pay. Others complained of underemployment — sometimes too little work of any sort, more commonly too little of the right kinds of work. They wanted to understand what was going on at their companies, and to help the business along — freeing their bosses from minor administrative hassles, expediting truly important matters, using their brains. Not that they minded using their hands as well. Many enjoyed typing and took pride in the appearance of the finished document. (Filing was another matter, but even that held out the prospect described by one participant as "the ultimate thrill of retrieval.")

Gloria Steinem spoke, as did a covey of other experts, but the single standing ovation went to Barbara Rechel, secretary to the president of the Fairchild Republic aircraft company. Ms. Rechel's theme was secretarial power — the power of a heroic, ethical professional to get things done, and done more efficiently. Secretaries had power and could have more, she averred, but to achieve it, they would have to set their own house in order. Had they done enough to cast the mediocrities out from their profession? Were they as individuals guilty of deciding in advance how much they would give of themselves each day? Ah, but the secretary who had broken into the clear empyrean blue of full competence and professional responsibility — Ms. Rechel's idea, if not her phrase — was free to dazzle and cajole, to employ whatever wiles she had, to amass still more power. For the use of that power served not only her own good, but also her boss's and her company's.

Ms. Rechel and her colleagues in PSI obviously represent only one color on the spectrum of secretarial attitudes and aspirations, albeit a pretty bright color. The spectrum currently encompasses at least three types of secretaries. There are the professionals, women who see the job as conferring benefits and duties independent of a particular employer. There are what some companies call "progressive secretaries" — not necessarily more up-to-date, but looking to progress out of the clerical ranks into better-paid jobs. Typically younger than the pros, a progressive may have a college degree and a sad tale to tell about trying to find nonsecretarial work upon graduation. And there are the "rising clericals," often women from low-income homes and minority groups. They like the money, feel a little at sea, and may look to the other two types in charting their aspirations.

While no one keeps statistics, many who recruit secretaries have the impression that most newcomers to the field are rising clericals. Accordingly, the company that would assure itself a supply of crackerjack secretarial help through the 1980s and 1990s will probably have to find a way to bring the skill levels of rising clericals up to those achieved by the other types. This may mean raising their aspirations as well.

A good beginning is to recognize that all three types make many of the same demands: more varied work; information about what's going on; and visibility, in the sense of not being invisible. (One secretary's anecdote: She and two other women are at work in an open office bay. Coat-and-tie-clad manager walks in. Looking at them, he asks, "Is anybody here?")

These days secretaries of almost any stripe can make demands. Pick a frightening statistic from the ample menu — 90,000 more secretarial jobs open each year; a cumulative shortfall that may reach a quarter-million in five years; more job openings over the coming decade than in any of the 270 other categories monitored by the Department of Labor. "In the 1960s we saw over 100 secretaries a week," reports Robert Marcus, president of the Sloan Personnel Agency in New York. "Now we see fewer than 150 a month." Marcus has given up trying to fill secretarial positions — steno, typing, and two years' experience required — that pay less than $15,000 a year. In Washington, D.C., the same work may command a starting salary of $18,000.

If a competent secretary can substantially improve a $50,000-a-year executive's productivity, such salaries may not be too high. Moreover, the ways a manager should rearrange his and his secretary's work to improve his own efficiency are often precisely those that will make his secretary happy and less likely to bolt.

"Anyone who is not integrating his secretary into information-screening and decision-making is making a mistake," asserts Randy J. Goldfield. Ms. Goldfield, formerly the most senior woman in Booz Allen's management-consulting division, heads Gibbs Consulting Group, an offshoot of the Katharine Gibbs secretarial schools set up to help companies make better use of expensive office equipment and personnel. Her group preaches job definition, secretarial training, and no-holds-barred evaluation.

The catechism begins with a set of questions for the boss. Does his secretary know the nature of the business? Can she name his three most important clients, suppliers, buyers? Does she understand the structure of the company?

The manager must organize himself so that he can organize her. What does he want her to do? Write it down in a job description that she can add to as she learns new skills and takes on more duties. At the very least, such a mandate will orient the dizzy, gum-chewing temporary who occasionally takes her place.

It's also up to the boss to see that someone analyzes the tide of paperwork and phone calls that courses through his office, decides what's important in it and why, and educates his secretary in these mysteries. From such practice, good things flow — a stack of letters each morning, arranged according to their importance, each covered with a two- or three-sentence précis of its contents; artfully choreographed meetings; warmed-up superiors and flash-frozen foes. Before long, the illuminata may be composing letters, doing research, putting out small managerial fires, even haggling with hotel chains for the best rates if quarterly earnings are down.

She should also be taking it straight from the shoulder. According to Gibbs, formal evaluation is the only way for her to monitor her success. Not an evaluation of her, mind you, but rather of how she has done on each of the tasks delegated in her job description. "It takes the personal dynamics out of it," says Rose Lockwood, a senior consultant at the Gibbs firm, "and puts the matter back in context."

Who makes the coffee? The least expensive person available should perform the least skilled tasks, and those chores might even be written into the job description he or she agrees to upon joining up. If it's the secretary, so be it. What about running the boss's personal errands — getting a present for the wife, or whomever? "If it's done as a personal favor, all right," suggests Ms. Lockwood, "but it should clearly be the exception." Personal favors being a two-way proposition, the manager should presumably pick up *her* dry cleaning from time to time.

All that remains is for the boss to learn to say good-bye gracefully. Consultants, personnel-agency people, and secretaries agree that the prospect of another, more responsible, job probably constitutes the most powerful inducement for a secretary to do her job well, even if she doesn't jump at the first new possibility offered. So all that training went for naught?

No, the manager has helped her on her way to something better. Besides, if he hadn't trained her, she would have gone anyway, and probably sooner. "There's no longevity in secretaries left," according to Rose Lockwood. By these standards, the best, most efficient boss in years to come will not be the one with the fifteen-year "office wife" —a concept almost universally loathed by secretaries today—but rather the fortunate he, or she, who can look around the company to see five of his former secretaries in administrative, sales, or managerial positions. Even then he won't win the "International Boss of the Year" award, however. Professional Secretaries International, which used to hand out that accolade, abolished it in 1972.

❉ 4 ❉

How to Take Part in a Meeting

Know the different stages that groups go through.
And watch out for the guy sprawling in his chair.

MOST MANAGERS take it as a point of honor to dislike meetings, at least meetings called by somebody else. "If we didn't have so damn many," the standard complaint runs, "we might actually get a little work done." This is an unenlightened attitude. Handled properly, meetings represent probably the single most efficient mechanism for passing word down and, equally important, up the ranks. For the savvy underling, they also provide an uncommon chance to demonstrate one's talents to higher-ups.

But how to do it right? While there are plenty of tracts on how to conduct a meeting, most of them all too obviously unread, comparatively little seems to have been written on how to be an effective participant. Asked about the subject, real live managers tend to offer less-than-breakthrough insights like "Be on time." Fortunately, academic types, mostly professors of psychology or communications, have for years been studying human behavior in groups. They base their counsel on their research and on what they have seen consulting for business.

Cynthia Stohl, a professor of organizational communication at Purdue, says classical behavioral science taught that on meeting for the first time, groups typically go through a four-stage process. In the first stage, participants feel each other out and orient themselves. In the second, conflicts erupt between members, often over what the group is supposed to be doing. In the third, the group agrees on certain rules of behavior, or norms, to govern their deliberations. Finally, the assembly settles down to its assigned work. Academics summed up the model as forming, storming, norming, and performing.

Nowadays, Stohl says, she and her colleagues think there probably is no single typical or even desirable sequence, but rather that groups jump back and forth among the various stages. An effective group may, for example, experience some heavy conflict and then go back to orientation. What's important to understand is that groups do go through stages in a meeting, however unpredictable the order in which they occur. You should gauge your contribution accordingly, helping the group form when it is forming, not storming when the rest of the crew is trying to perform. In other words, don't yell, "Stop — we gotta change the rules" when the group is on the verge of a decision.

The experts have developed the taxonomy of meetings to a fare-thee-well. They break down the roles people play at various stages of a meeting into such categories as information giver, information seeker, coordinator, encourager, follower, and compromiser. In some roles participants try to help accomplish the group's assigned task. In other roles they just try to keep the group working smoothly together. While you need not learn the taxonomy by heart, do pay attention to the different parts meeting goers take on. Also bear in mind that in a meeting, as elsewhere, people strive to satisfy their psychological needs, conscious or unconscious. A member may act as an aggressor, say, or as a recognition seeker. While the same person may adopt different roles in different groups, when one group meets a number of times, he tends to stick with the roles he staked out in the first few encounters.

One should not have to say it to a manager scheduled to attend a meeting, but the experts insist: do your homework. "It is amazing how many people think they are too busy to prepare for a meeting," laments Leonard Greenhalgh, who teaches an immensely popular course called Executive Power and Negotiation at Dartmouth's Amos Tuck School of Business Administration. Find out what is to be discussed, even if it means calling up the convening authority who thoughtlessly left that little detail out of his announcement of the gathering. Think of the points you want to make and gather evidence to support them. If you suspect that your assertions on a particular subject may gore another participant's ox, or even nick it, tell him in advance that you are going to raise the issue. "This makes you an ally rather than an immediate enemy," says Greenhalgh.

Get there a few minutes before the appointed hour and, as others file in, start acting like what social scientists term a participant-observer. This stance, much favored by anthropologists, entails joining the natives in their ritual dance around the fire while making detailed mental notes on all that goes on. Pay attention not only to what is said, but also to so-called nonverbal behavior. Seating arrangements, for example.

If you are joining a group that has met several times before, you will probably find that most members have tacitly assigned themselves places around the table and expect to reclaim them each time. You do well to ask before occupying the accustomed seat of some high-ranking late arriver. Certain spots carry more clout than others. John Dovidio, a psychology professor at Colgate University, who specializes in nonverbal communication, notes that in a meeting held around a rectangular table, the leader almost always sits at the head and another dominant figure at the foot. All the better for everyone else to see their lordly selves. So strong is the aura of those spots, Dovidio says, that if people are randomly assigned places, those who draw the end seats will end up acting more forcefully than they usually do.

You will also be able to tell who is feeling dominant from their body language. Heavy hitters tend to sit in a relaxed, even sprawling, position. Not for them the chair pulled up to the table, the torso leaning expectantly forward. They shift position frequently, swivel a little if possible, and gesture with large movements away from the body. Anything to call attention to themselves. When speaking, they also look at people more than other participants do, and they avert their gaze more when listening.

The proceedings begin. At the outset your best contribution may be to help clear up ambiguities that remain about agenda or procedures. This may require only a question or two directed at the leader, or a brief statement along the lines of "I'm not exactly sure about what we're supposed to be doing with this." Don't be in a sweat to nail down every detail. If the group is still in the orientation stage, rushing in with a forceful statement that it must do thus and so may prompt it to freeze you out for the rest of the meeting.

The process of settling down to the group task won't take long if the group is one that meets regularly. When it does get down to cases, prepare to volunteer your substantial point. Listen carefully, then pick your moment. Andrew S. Grove, chief executive of Intel Corp. and author of a book entitled *High Output Management*, compares the challenge to jumping aboard a moving train. Jump too soon and the train may run over you; jump too late and you'll miss it. If you are confident about the point you want to make and have the evidence to back it up, raise it the first time it becomes relevant. If you are less confident about it, you may want to hang back a bit, waiting for a moment when it can be introduced as a helpful response to someone else's remark.

When you do bring up your dynamite idea, try not to present it as your 100 percent original drop-dead answer to the group's prayers, but rather as an outgrowth of the discussion, something the others helped you see and may now help refine. Make your point crisply, preferably with declarative sentences that quickly summarize your evidence. Listen carefully to the remarks that follow, answer questions, defend the idea without getting defensive, and be careful not to press prematurely for a conclusion. If the decision goes against you, shut up and let the matter drop without sulking or whining.

For an underling, probably the diciest moment in a meeting comes when he feels he must disagree with somebody else's point, especially if the somebody else is a higher-up, worst of all the person presiding. In expressing disagreement, be exquisitely conscious of the need for everyone to save face. Milton Hakel, a professor of industrial psychology at the University of Houston, suggests a couple of tacks. You might try going back to the purpose of the meeting, perhaps by asking questions: "Gee, how does that fit with what we set out to do?" Or you might suggest looking at the issue in a broader context: "I know we're only supposed to be studying this from a technical point of view, but I wonder how that solution might look if news of it got to the press?"

Other experts propose that you adopt the role of devil's advocate, announcing clearly what you are doing and raising your killer objections in that guise. If you are in a risk-taking mood, you might also consider a strategy suggested by Joseph A. Alutto, professor of organizational behavior and dean of management at the State University of New York at Buffalo: co-opt what the person you disagree with has said by embracing part of his view enthusiastically and restating the rest, slightly altered to fit your own view. It will then be up to him to challenge your restatement if your emendation is not to become the agreed-on version. Even "I'm sorry, Barbara, but you misinterpreted me" as a rejoinder can sound slightly nasty and put the person who says it at a disadvantage.

As the meeting winds toward a close, look for opportunities to sum up. As at the beginning, avoid forcing a resolution of issues the group clearly wants to keep ambiguous. You may want to volunteer to do the follow-up work on a particular matter. As the Tuck School's Greenhalgh notes, "That way you can report back to the people at the meeting with your information and also give yourself a good claim to the outcome," shaping it and getting some of the credit.

On leaving, do not mutter, "Maybe now I can get some work done." You just did.

5

The Big Presentation

*It's terrifying, easy to botch —
and an absolutely golden opportunity.*

LET US IN NO WAY MINIMIZE the opportunity, or the danger, involved. The thirty minutes an executive spends on his feet formally presenting his latest project to corporate superiors are simply and absolutely the most important thirty minutes of that or any other managerial season. The game isn't show-and-tell; it's gladiator time, career death or career glory, the Big P — for presentation.

"There are the people who do the work, and the people who present it," wryly observes the chief executive of one Fortune 500 company. "Often it's the presenters who get the credit, and the promotion." This is true, canny managers realize, even with respect to events regularly scheduled, such as the offering up of quarterly results. Kevin Daley, president of Communispond, a leading firm in teaching corporatchiks the rhetor's art, draws an instructive analogy: "If you're ushered in to see God every three months, He's still God each time."

While not viewing the matter on quite that lofty a plane, most businessmen do recognize the importance of the rite. How many of their other activities, one may ask, do they deem momentous enough to rehearse? When giving a speech to the public, too often the hard-pressed executive will look at the text for the first time ten minutes beforehand, then drone through a soporific reading. If the audience is his company's board, however, the same $100,000-a-year man is likely to come on like Ronald Reagan himself, the result of precious half hours devoted to shadowboxing with audiovisual aids before an array of empty chairs, nerve-racked minions, or a semi-interested spouse.

For all their preparation, though, many still get it wrong. There's the little problem of being utterly terrified, for starters — one survey of three thousand Americans found that what they feared most, even more than death, was speaking before a group. What probably trips up more managers, however, is misunderstanding the rules of the game. For example, what the board tells you it wants — a dispassionate explanation of the numbers — is almost always precisely what it *doesn't* want. But be of modest good cheer — once you grasp what's actually going on in presentations, it's often not that difficult to marshal the techniques that will leave them eating out of your overhead projector.

There are at least three reasons for the overweening importance of presentations in corporate councils and in the careers of the presenters. First, most executives prefer verbal communications. They hate reading the reports, memoranda, and letters that choke their in-baskets, hate reading the stuff almost as much as they hate writing it. One poll of executives found that 81 percent judged the quality of the written communications they received as either fair or poor. Not that most thought they could do better — 55 percent described their own writing skills as fair or poor.

Second, in making decisions, executives tend to give more weight to concrete examples, concretely presented, than to assemblages of fact abstractly pitched. What is more concrete than Smoking Joe Junior Executive up there really making the numbers come alive, peppering his presentation with telling details like the little lady in the Peoria test market who broke down and cried — I mean genuinely wept — when told she wouldn't be able to get any more of the new balsam-scented catbox filler product for a while?

The third, and perhaps main, reason for the importance of presentations, however, lies in their immutable hidden agenda, enduring since the days of the pharaohs ("Imhotep, we propose a structure roughly pyramidal in shape . . . let's look at the model"): the bosses want to size up the underlings. Size them up to see if their work is to be taken seriously. Size them up to decide whether they're to be entrusted with carrying out the project. Size them up to divine whether they just might be the future leaders of the enterprise.

True, true, presentations are not a substitute for operating performance. If the facts and figures indicate a palpable disaster and he's clearly responsible, even the most skilled presenter probably won't be able to talk his way out (*probably* won't). And, yes, sometimes a presentation can be more inspiring than the unadorned facts would be, leading to the wrong decision. Perhaps balsam-scented catbox filler isn't a good product, despite one consumer's tears.

But come at the essential principle from another direction. The arguments for a project look terrific on paper, the supporting evidence is there, and the author of this wonderfulness stands before you. Pigeon-toed, staring resolutely at the floor, fiddling with his grease-stained tie, he squeaks in a Truman Capote voice, "If the board . . . will only see fit . . . to vote seven million . . . and authorize me . . ." You figure out how likely he is to get the money.

The implications of all this for the manager about to make a presentation are fairly straightforward. You're not going before the Olympians to recite the numbers and the memorandum that you've already sent them. (Don't assume they've read the material. But also, particularly when anticipating questions, don't assume they haven't.) You're going there to tell a story and to reveal why you're the hero of the piece. "We saw that it was going to be a down quarter industrywide, and that we were going to have to cut costs. So we began to cast about . . ."

In this effort, you walk a perilous fine line. You want to inform, delight, animate, and impress. But, as Communispond's Daley notes, "if you're perceived as a showboat, you're dead." You want to be seen as a team player. But you also want to come across, like O. J. Simpson in his days with the Buffalo Bills, as "the franchise."

To bring this balancing act off, begin preparing early. All right, so you won't know what you're going to say until late in the game. For many executives, the words and ideas aren't going to be the problem — it's the body, that recalcitrant beast, that gets them into trouble. You end up standing there, pumping adrenaline, full of fierce energies with nowhere to go except into twitches, jerks, and nervous "uuhhs." Why not spend the early phase of preparation learning to do something more productive with that blue-suited retort of boiling emotions?

Niki Flacks and Robert Rasberry, consultants to speechmaking managers and the authors of a book entitled *Power Talk*, recommend an actor's technique called split-focus concentration. For practice, you talk about something, anything, while going through the motions of some physical activity — assembling a swing set, washing a car. When you're finally at the lectern, you'll be able to accompany your words with appropriate gestures. "Last fall, the division projected a loss *this* big . . ."

As the Big P draws closer, deign to give a little thought to what you'll be mouthing up there. Some of the conventional speech-making wisdom holds true for presentations, and some doesn't. Present from an outline — if you write out every word, you'll end up reading every word and coming across as the stumblebum messenger of someone else's glad tidings.

Don't get so caught up in the guts of your message that you neglect to add a grab-their-little-minds introduction and a send-them-marching-forth conclusion. The worst possible beginnings: "We wish we'd had more time to prepare this . . ." or "Bill here probably knows more about this . . ." The audience will rapidly conclude that, indeed, you didn't prepare much, or that Bill does know more.

The politician's favorite opener, a slightly self-deprecating joke, doesn't work. In the boardroom you won't receive the kind of flowery introduction that needs a bit of deflating. No, you're there, corporate worm, at the generous sufferance of the great. The experts recommend starting with something like "When the chairman asked me to be here today, he said he wanted me to tell you about . . ." This at once communicates that you have the big guy behind you, and also sets the bounds for questions.

While planning what you want to say, you should begin crafting your audiovisual magic. In doing so, remind yourself again and again that *you* are to be the centerpiece of this production, not some set of eye-popping transparencies or *Chariots of Fire* background music. This eternal verity suggests, for example, that you eschew 35-mm slides. To use them, you'll have to lower the lights — oh goody, nobody can see me — and that's the problem: nobody can see you or be bowled over by you.

The visual aid of choice for most businessmen today is the transparency employed with an overhead projector. These can be made up fairly quickly and cheaply, used with lights up, and handled by the presenter himself, who can continue to face his audience while laying those babies down. The standard rule is that each transparency should contain no more than one idea, and even that one shouldn't be fully understandable from the transparency alone—Mr. Wizard will explain.

Thinking of doing without visuals? If you anticipate a lot of off-the-wall questions that might get you off track, know that a stack of transparencies may be your best defense. Audience members will realize that you have to get through the whole deck. Also, so-called holdbacks—transparencies that you don't plan to use but can whip out in response to a question—can be lethal in impressing them with your thoroughness.

Two or three days before the big event, visit the presentation site. Will there be a lectern? Who will sit where? Members of corporate boards, it may be noted, show a remarkable proclivity to sit in the same seats at every meeting, even without place cards. Whoever is sponsoring your appearance should clue you in on the likely order. Kevin Daley of Communispond also suggests that your sponsor should help you be clear on who each member of the audience is, the interest each represents, the degree of influence each has, the ax each will grind with respect to your subject, the questions each is likely to ask.

The day of the Big P dawns. Gird up your loins with your broken-in business best. Thoreau, while no master of corporate presentations, put it well: "Beware of all enterprises that require new clothes." A brand spanking new tie will only make you more self-conscious, if that's possible.

When you're finally introduced, stand up and walk to where you'll be speaking from, keeping your eyes on your destination. Say nothing until you're in position, have made eye contact with at least three members of the audience, and have your hands at gesture height—somewhere out of your pockets and above your waist. Then, to the extent that your fully buttoned, M.B.A.-standard-issue three-piece suit permits, float like a butterfly, sting like a bee. Tell the story, make the point, have the answer. The worst presentation, corporate honchos agree, is the one that trails off with "Frankly, we just don't know what to do . . ." Finish on time. If you run over, it reflects on the competence of the person running the meeting.

They laughed. They sobbed. At the end, they cheered. But, uh, there are a few questions. No, the professionals say, you can't anticipate every possible query, but you can predict the four or five main issues and think about them beforehand. When someone sends a slightly off-point zinger your way, try rephrasing it, bending it around one of the key issues: "Well, what it seems to me you're really getting at . . ." Some old curmudgeon may counter with "Young man, I believe I expressed myself clearly; answer the question." As the blood drains from your face, politely ask him to elaborate. Besides buying time, this may let his small-minded animus become apparent to all.

One final note for when the battle is over, the transparencies put away, and lunch is being served to presenter and audience alike: the battle isn't over. Observes one veteran of many successful presentations: "You've got to keep selling them—over lunch, in the hall afterward, wherever." This may get in the way of your enjoying the corporate chicken salad, but then, that's show business.

6

Memo Punctilio

Writing memos can advance your career, or end it.
Watch out if the boss starts sending you missives.

MOST MANAGERS dislike memos. They dislike writing them. They dislike reading them. They complain loudly about how many they receive, and wax eloquent on how disorganized, wordy, and pointless these communications typically are. Advanced thinkers even condemn memo-writing as incompatible with modern notions of management. Harvard Business School professor John Kotter, whose latest book is entitled *The Leadership Factor,* observes: "The most effective managers tend not to be trapped in their offices reading reports and writing memos. They sit in on meetings, make speeches to the troops, and convey an influential message orally."

And yet, at company after company, the daily accumulation of memoranda continues unabated, drifting into in-boxes, piling up in drawers, weighting briefcases for the journey home. The coming of electronic mail should not change this. Indeed, almost everyone who has studied computer-screen-to-computer-screen communications within offices concludes that the new systems actually tend to *increase* the number of memos sent. It becomes so easy just to sit down at the keyboard, tap out your great managerial thought, and send it in an electronic blink to fifteen or twenty subordinates.

Why do managers persist in sending so many memos? The reasons range from the truly managerial, through the psychological, to the political.

The memo remains the best single device for communicating substantial chunks of detailed information to a co-worker. Particularly if what you are communicating consists largely of numbers, and particularly if you are going to need a record of the information. A caution here, however: committing a matter to writing may be dangerous. If your company is investigated or sued, some pesky lawyer for the other side may end up waving the document in the air before the arbiters of the dispute. Or you may get into trouble with your so-called superiors. Robert Swain, who heads an outplacement firm in New York, tells of one manager who was fired because in a memo to his boss and staff he told the truth about a poor corporate practice. The boss did not like seeing the criticism on paper; it meant that he had to do something about it.

The memo is the managerial tool of choice when you want to put out word to lots of people, more than you can conveniently assemble for an oral exhortation. Such communications have to be worded with exquisite care, particularly if they announce bad news for some or all—a turndown in business, a firing, someone's promotion over rivals in the organization. Recipients, usually unable to question the sender directly, are likely to pore over these bulletins from on high with the same energy that Kremlinologists apply to analyzing the list of pallbearers at a Soviet state funeral.

William Morin, chairman of the Drake Beam Morin firm—it specializes in "outplacement," ministering to the fallen executive—notes that memos announcing an executive's dismissal have become more concise, mostly for legal reasons. Companies fear that an old-style recital of the firee's many contributions may end up as ammunition in a suit alleging that the firing was unjustified. Morin recommends use of the standard form—"So-and-so has resigned from the company effective today to pursue personal interests" (or "other endeavors") with perhaps a few warm words if the parting is more or less amicable. He also heartily applauds the fact that companies have stopped firing people by memo. In the bad old days, Morin swears, bosses actually sent written communications saying such things as, to a woman being dismissed, "You have always talked about going home and having a family. It's now time that you did that."

Some managers use, and overuse, memos because they feel uncomfortable communicating face-to-face or over the phone. Kenneth Roman, president of the Ogilvy & Mather Worldwide arm of the big advertising agency, reports that when he comes in on a Monday morning, he typically finds ten memos from David Ogilvy waiting for him, even though the legendary adman, now in his late seventies, is supposedly retired and living in the south of France. Ogilvy is a terrific writer, of course, but he is also quite a shy man, Roman says. In his memos, Ogilvy apparently can give full vent to his feelings, whether of enthusiasm or asperity. An example, undated, directed to a subordinate: "I thought you promised to show me the Sears ads (with copy) last Tuesday. It is now three months since Struthers picked them. Longer than the period of gestation in PIGS. D.O."

Managers also send memos for political reasons, good and bad: to get credit for their ideas ("I would like to propose a new way to handle . . ."), cover their you-know-whats ("While I am not opposed to the project, I do have certain reservations . . ."), or even to set a trap for others ("Would you please send me your comments on the following proposal . . ."). By and large, a useless memo is rarely held against you, while a good one can advance your cause with the powers above. The chief danger here is that a self-serving ulterior motive — to catapult the writer into the attention of higher-ups, for example — may be all too transparent.

Memos may also convey more subtle political messages, if the recipient has the acuity to decipher them. Eric van Merkensteijn, associate dean of the Wharton School, notes, for instance, that if someone you usually communicate with in person or over the phone starts sending you memos instead, something has happened, and probably for the worse. "The ideal work environment is informal," van Merkensteijn says, "characterized by first names, direct expression, trust, honesty. Any step someone takes to bring formality into that environment is a negative." You should try to find out what has changed, and to remedy any problems, especially if the suddenly more distant individual is your boss.

Whatever your memo-making motive, try to write clearly. If you don't think that there is already enough bad business prose around, consider the following example from real life. Here's the first sentence from an executive of a high-tech company, assessing the market for a new technology: "The market that is near-term as to ability to move on into operational systems with requirements defined and suitable for this technology are the Government Agencies with environmental data requirements from remote and inaccessible sites where present low data rate communications circuits are not readily survivable."

When you sit down to write, make sure you have a well-defined purpose in mind. Who is your audience? What do you want them to do? If possible, find out in advance from the intended recipients what information they want.

Pick a format, and use it to organize your thoughts. Some companies establish a standardized format. "That sounds cosmetic and kind of dopey," allows Mary Munter, a professor at the Tuck School and author of a book entitled *Guide to Managerial Communications*. "But it's not, because it forces people to differentiate their major points from their minor points." For writers without guidance from their companies, Communispond recommends the following: a "To" line, a "From" line, a single line identifying the subject, a brief paragraph explaining the background of the memo, a clear statement of the memo's purpose (usually the announcement of some change or a recommendation), supporting information as necessary, and a concluding summary or statement of the action requested.

Do not, however, let slavish observance of a format get in the way of communicating your message. Probably the most famous stricture in corporate memo-writing is Procter & Gamble's requirement that such communications be no more than one page long. The result, according to people who have tried to decipher them, is often a single-spaced document with no margins, full of esoteric abbreviations. A company spokesman confesses that the one-page P&G memo is "more an ideal than an actuality."

When it comes to choosing your words, write the way you talk, sort of. Remember that you are trying to put an idea across, not to impress the audience with your deep learning or membership in a jargon-speaking elite. Keep sentences short, preferably twenty words or less, and watch your verbs — the fewer uses of the verb "to be," the better. Contrary to what virtually every writing manual tells you, though, there may be times when you ought to use the passive voice, for good political reasons. Say the boss has proposed another one of his Looney Tunes schemes, and asked you to find out what people think of it. If you can come up with seventeen killer objections, but nobody else can, are you going to say, "I would raise the following objections . . ." or, instead, "The following objections were raised . . ."?

Keep the memo short. At the end, tack on what the experts call a response mechanism, something like "I will call you next week to confirm" or "If I don't hear from you to the contrary, I will assume the changes meet with your approval." Then, once you've completed the memo, hold onto it a while before you send it out. JoAnne Yates, a professor at MIT's Sloan School, reports that managers using electronic mail run a significantly higher risk of getting angry and firing off a memo they later regret. Students of the phenomenon have even coined a name for it: flaming. Which word, used as an adjective to modify a suitable noun, like "idiot," is precisely what the recipient will think you are.

7

Getting Creative

Forget left brain and right brain.
The real problem starts when you come up with a new idea.

WHAT ARE WE GOING TO DO about Woofies? A solid No. 4 in the dry dog food category for years, the favorite of millions of mutts, our one seemingly unstoppable money machine, and then, suddenly, nowheresville. We tried reformulating them twice—"all natural" and "vitamin enriched"—changed ad agencies, even got that actor to do those commercials talking about how much his borzoi loved them —and nothing. Nuuuthing. What are we going to do about Woofies?

Every day, in businesses large and small across America, someone is looking for an idea. Of late, however, discouraging words have been heard suggesting that our traditional methods of conducting the search won't suffice any longer. Company chairmen proclaim the need for new ways of fostering entrepreneurship within corporations. Pundits slightly smattered with psychology complain that the average businessman permits the left half of his brain—logical, linear, analytic—to so dominate the right—the big-picture-seeing hemisphere, full of affect—that the poor devil hasn't a prayer of generating a fresh insight.

Even with your questionable, left-brained capacity to grasp the full gravity of the problem, you will be relieved to know that corporate America is taking heed of such alarms. For instance, James Bandrowski, a San Francisco–based consultant, not long ago surveyed twenty-five major companies to determine what, if anything, they were doing to spark greater creativity among their strategic planners. A majority of the companies, he found, had undertaken some sort of formal training in creativity within the last two years. Providers of such training for planners and others—consultants, educators— confirm Bandrowski's impression; they're doing lots of business these days, considerably more than a year ago.

The question, of course, is whether corporate America is getting anything for its money. Not that all purveyors of creativity training are charlatans — though the most rabid proponents of left-brain-right-brain theory at times come perilously close to greasing the sale of their techniques with snake oil. No, customers for these services — and they include such giants as Du Pont, Westinghouse, and Chase Manhattan — often report that in sessions with the trainers, their people have come up with promising ideas for new products, or interesting new uses for old ones. The real issue is whether a company can, with or without outside help, institutionalize a higher level of creativity among its employees. Can you, in effect, build in a creative approach to corporate problems?

Framing the issue this way is itself an indication of how far businesspersons have come in thinking about turning on those mental light bulbs. Harrison Gough, director of the Institute of Personality Assessment and Research at the University of California, posits three popular conceptions of creativity. According to the first view, the creative person is, if not actually insane, at least a bit weird. This corresponds to the corporate notion that "if we need creative people, we can always hire them," together with its unspoken addendum, "and then we'll isolate them, of course, so they don't mess up the rest of the operation." Keep the rocket scientists down in the skunk-works; our artistic director — or head of R&D, or marketing manager — is brilliant, but boy, you've got to be careful about how you handle him.

In the second view, the act of creation is held up apart from the person or persons responsible. Attention focuses on the mysterious process by which new ideas are generated. Let's form a task force to figure out precisely how we came up with the Model 360; that way we can repeat the drill next time around.

In the final, and arguably the most progressive, view, creativity is latent within everyone. It just needs to be brought out. As you would expect, this is the conception that most creativity-training types subscribe to. Corporations buying their services adopt it either consciously or by default.

Which view is correct or — if that's too left-brained for you — most productive? The answer is simply that we don't know. As careful students of the subject admit, neither psychology nor physiology has yet been able to provide a definitive explanation of how creativity works. The lack of such an explanation is a burden particularly for those who embrace the third conception. For their view to be taken seriously, they have to explain why, if everyone has the potential to be creative, so few folks seem actually to deliver on that potential.

Enter, bearing the answer before them, apostles of the left-brain–right-brain theory. Their rap, often suffused with a sort of oh-wow-the-mysteries-of-science enthusiasm, goes something like this: experiments with individuals who have sustained injuries to the left or the right side of the brain, or who have had the connection between the two—the corpus callosum to you—severed, reveal that we have not one, but in effect two brains. The left hemisphere produces language and speech, and carries out those mental processes we characterize as logical, analytic, and sequential. The right hemisphere, by comparison, traffics in emotion and recognizes patterns—it is "holistic," capable of seeing and understanding the whole, not just the parts.

In each individual, the story goes, one hemisphere is dominant. Businesspersons, schooled to be bloodless processors of facts and numbers, are typically left-brained. So much so, in fact, that like a right-handed person struggling to perform some simple task with his left hand, they are positively awful at using the ol' right hemisphere. What we need—here the rhetoric rises to a crescendo of exhortation, and the real selling begins—are techniques to put people in touch with the right side so that we can have whole-brained managers.

The pitch does have an appeal, a very old one. As William Francis, an assistant professor of psychology at Lawrence University, notes, "From biblical times there has been thought to be a duality in the left and right sides. The left side represents the darker impulses, the right, goodness and light." The only problem with the left-brain–right-brain duality is that it is, put charitably, an oversimplification of the scientific evidence.

Few practicing businessmen suffer lesions of the left or right brain or a severed corpus callosum. In the brains of normal people, the research indicates, there's a great deal of back-and-forth communication between the hemispheres, and many mental functions that both share in. In short — and remember, you read it here first — you already are whole-brained.

Responsible advocates of creativity training concede as much. For example, Dudley Lynch, a creativity consultant and the publisher of a newsletter entitled *Brain & Strategy*, says that he uses left-brain–right-brain as a "presentational device. . . . Most people with M.B.A.'s aren't comfortable with techniques aimed at bringing out creativity," he maintains. "If you talk to them in engineering terms, suggesting that one side of the head processes information differently from the other, you can lay a foundation, provide a context in which they are comfortable."

Whether by means of left-brain–right-brain or some other metaphor, a good facilitator — what else would he call himself? — can, it seems, usually get corporate groups to be comfortable with even fairly offbeat ways of generating new ideas. As companies increasingly realize, the real obstacle to building in creativity is not getting the folks to come up with fresh ways to look at problems. It is, rather, what happens to those insights when everyone goes back to the office.

Even if ideas suddenly rain down on your theretofore arid corporation, what do they avail if the company, because of the bureaucratic way it is, does nothing with them — doesn't draw them out, doesn't act on them, doesn't reward the people responsible? Students of corporate performance, most notably Thomas J. Peters and Robert Waterman, Jr., authors of *In Search of Excellence*, have found that certain companies excel at fostering new ideas and bringing them to market — Minnesota Mining & Manufacturing, for instance, or Hewlett-Packard. At each of these companies, a strong corporate culture — a set of shared values — treasures, nurtures, and protects creativity.

Two questions confront any company that would emulate their example. First, do we so want or need new ideas that we're willing to put up with all the agony that building a new corporate culture entails — the endless meetings proclaiming the new values, the constant, grinding attempt to alter behavior, the necessity to get rid of old-timers who can't struggle onto the bandwagon? Second, is it even possible to deliberately, synthetically change a corporation's culture much?

To their credit, most merchants of creativity training acknowledge that acceptance of the ideas they help engender is often a problem, even at the companies that hire them. Their response to the difficulty varies widely, however. Professor Michael Ray, who together with Rochelle Myers teaches a Stanford Business School course designed to help M.B.A. candidates unleash their inherent individual creativity — students chant mantras, consult the *I Ching,* and look for epiphanies in tarot cards — says simply, "To open up your own creativity is to become very resourceful. Part of this is coming up with the ideas necessary for implementation too."

In contrast, Synectics, with around thirty professionals worldwide probably the largest consulting and training firm devoted exclusively to creativity, takes the view that issues of implementation have to be built into the idea-generation process. The Cambridge, Massachusetts, firm got its start twenty-five years ago merchandising brainstorming — just let those ideas flow free; reserve any judgment of them until later. Now, however, it counsels clients to devote more time to developing ways to make ideas acceptable to the corporation than was spent coming up with the ideas in the first place. Only when an idea has been fiddled with and debugged thoroughly will it be presented to the management layer that passes on new projects.

It's all part of generating a situation that management psychologist Harry Levinson describes as "controlled craziness." Controlled because at least some percentage of what you come up with has to have a chance of succeeding within the company, and there's something in most companies that doesn't love too radical or fresh a proposal. Moreover, the people who generate the idea have to continue to abide by most of the organization's norms. Craziness because, even though we don't have a good psychological model of the creative act, most of us sense that there is inside us some kind of censor that doesn't normally permit many of our ideas to bubble up into the light.

Methods held out as likely to induce the appropriate craziness, whether in individuals or groups, are legion; few are new. Certain relatively straightforward prescriptions are common to most of them.

First, stop thinking of yourself as a machine programmed to accept certain inputs and spit out results according to an assembly-line schedule. Second, external stimuli often seem to help — music, pictures, almost any movement within your visual field, even the spray of shower on your head in the morning. Third, try to think in terms of analogies and metaphors — how is the problem you're trying to un- ravel like something else you already understand?

Fourth, try to put yourself mentally in someone else's shoes — how would my chief competitor think about this? Last, give full sway to dreams — whether daydreams, or those delicious thoughts that come between waking and sleeping, or the strange notions that may come to you while asleep. Dreams harness the wild horses of desire to pull ideas from the mental muck.

In short, act just like the person that your company, most of the time, probably tells you you shouldn't be — not very well scheduled or planned, but sensual, poetic. If you have to have some defense of this strange behavior to serve up to your corporate masters, one candidate might be the title of a story by the poet Delmore Schwartz: "In Dreams Begin Responsibilities."

8

How to Pick Talent

In interviewing job candidates, most managers talk too much,
listen too little, and ask the wrong questions.

ALL ACROSS THIS INDUSTRIOUS LAND of ours, in dormitory rooms, book-lined dens, and the offices of outplacement counselors, job seekers have been busy honing their interviewing skills. Parry and *thrust:* "My shortcomings? Well, my better half says that I work too hard, that I'm never home for dinner." Parry and *thrust:* "Problems on my last job? Oh, I guess sometimes I had so many projects cooking that I couldn't always give each the attention I wanted to." Parry and *thrust:* "Weekends? Ah, let's see. I guess that on an average Sunday I might get up, read the papers, play a few sets of tennis with the kids, make love to the ol' spouse a couple of times, maybe sneak downstairs to get a little work done. Then, of course, it would be time for brunch with friends . . ."

And whom do employers field to match the steel of these bravos? D'Artagnan it usually isn't. More likely a manager with all the finesse of Jack the Ripper. Experts on the subject — headhunters, human-resources types, and people who teach interviewing — report that while job candidates typically have become more savvy about verbal give-and-take, the line managers who interview them have not. This does not bode well for the acuity of hiring decisions.

Interviewing job applicants is a managerial art that executives should be trained in, or should train themselves in. John W. Cogger, who gives such instruction under the auspices of the Drake Beam Morin outplacement firm, offers two reasons. Hiring mistakes can cost a bundle, not only in severance pay and whatever it takes to find a replacement, but also to repair the damage that Mr. Wrong may do before he's found out. On a more optimistic note, the interviewing skills you acquire can also help you with other managerial duties —

counseling employees, talking to customers about their needs, maybe even giving, gulp, performance appraisals.

In conducting a job interview, Cogger says, you are trying to get answers to three basic questions. First, can the applicant do the job? Second, will he do it? Does he have the motivation? Third, and too often overlooked, will he or she fit into the organization? Is he enough like the people he will be working with to feel comfortable, and for them to feel comfortable?

Your first step: spend some time preparing for the interview, which means more than the customary thirty seconds looking over the candidate's résumé while your secretary asks him if he wants coffee. Part of your task is to persuade this possible hotshot that he should work for you or your company; a thoughtful, well-organized interview can help a lot. Preparation will also enable you to avoid two mistakes that most line managers make: doing all the talking yourself and straining so hard to come up with your next brilliant question that you neglect to listen to the candidate's response to the last one.

In getting ready, think first about the position to be filled, and in terms that go beyond the written job description. What skills does it require? How is it likely to change? Whom does it entail working with? Then go over the applicant's résumé, looking for evidence that he has what it takes, and making a note of questions you want to ask. Keith Johnson, corporate staffing manager at Hewlett-Packard, goes to the heart of the matter: "I want to know if there was something a person did in his previous job that can be applied to the job at H-P."

In these litigious times it might also be a good idea to call up your company lawyer or the human resources department to find out what you should *not* say in the interview. The list of subjects *verboten* to ask about varies from state to state, but in most places it seems to get longer all the time. In California, for example, you may not inquire about the applicant's age, birthplace, nationality, sex, marital status, family or plans for a family, race, height, weight, general health, religion, arrest record, military record, credit rating, or the name and address of a relative to be notified in case of an emergency. The lawyer should warn you, too, about making any promises to the candidate to get him to take the job. If he accepts but your company doesn't deliver, he can sue and collect the monetary equivalent of the moon, sun, and stars you promised him.

Comes the appointed hour, you will act the perfect host or hostess, greeting the candidate with a warm smile, showing him into your office, making small talk in the hope of putting him at ease. Of course, he's nervous, acting stiff, withdrawn, or cocky as a result. Your challenge — it being your show, and you so self-assured from all the preparation you have done — is to reduce that nervousness; the closer the interview comes to a friendly conversation, the more you will learn about the real him or her. Throughout the interview, make a point of nodding or commenting with approval whenever the candidate says something remotely on target.

After the preliminary informalities, you may want to go briefly over the nature of the job with him. Experts emphasize the "briefly" part — if you tell him too much, the smart candidate will simply tailor his answers to fit what you want to hear. Better to plunge quickly into the guts of the interview: your exquisitely crafted questions. Some authorities suggest that you follow a prescribed sequence of subjects — first job history, then education, outside activities and interests, strengths, and finally shortcomings, according to Cogger, for example. But almost all the experts agree that the form of your questions counts for more than the order you ask them in.

Questions should be open-ended, not susceptible to brief answers like "yes" or "no." Inquiries that begin with "how" or "why" usually qualify. Questions that telegraph the desired response do not. Michael Ahearn, manager of central staffing at Apple Computer, offers two examples of the answer-prepaid genre: Would you say that you have good interpersonal skills? Was getting your M.B.A. from Stanford a positive experience for you?

Some better questions:

On your last job, what was it that you most wanted to accomplish but didn't? Why not?

What was the best job you ever had? Worst job? Best boss? Worst boss? Why?

What do you pride yourself on?

You don't have to answer this: tell me about some important event in your childhood. How did it shape you?

That hardy perennial: why are you interested in changing jobs?

Listen carefully to the answers. Take notes. If you sense some reluctance or skittishness in response to a particular inquiry, probe further with follow-up questions, even if it makes for a bit of unconversationlike anxiety. And, of course, let the candidate ask questions himself. Observes Marcia Worthing, vice president of human resources at Avon: "Most candidates are prepared. The talented are really prepared. They ask tough questions that are not already answered in the annual report."

When you both have pretty much shot your bolts, put the cleanup question: "Is there anything else we should cover?" Even if it doesn't elicit any more information, it will give the proceedings a pleasing sense of completeness. Tell the candidate what he can expect next in the selection process and when. Thank him for his time.

Then closet yourself and mull. Recall your first impression of the candidate. And later on in the interview: Were you bored? Fascinated? Weigh these impressions, but weigh equally, or perhaps a bit more, what you learned in the course of the questioning. By thus checking and balancing, you can avoid some of the more common mistakes, such as hiring in your own image, dismissing a candidate for cosmetic imperfections, or what executive recruiter Robert Half calls "falling in love." As in, gush, "Gee, that guy just looks like an executive V.P." — or a banker, or an ace purveyor of chiropractic supplies.

You will make a better decision on the candidate if you can compare your evaluation of him with others' at your company. Smart employers such as Xerox and McKinsey & Co. have each applicant who gets past a preliminary interview talk with three or more managerial types, preferably in a series of one-on-one conversations. Then the interviewers are required to hammer out a consensus ranking of the various contenders.

The winners get their references checked. You should do this with anyone you consider hiring, even though checking is getting harder to do because disappointed job seekers increasingly sue employers who give them bad references. Andre Block, a vice president of human resources at Citibank and the president of the National Association of Corporate and Professional Recruiters, sums up the dilemma: "We tell our people not to give out any references, but not to hire anyone without them." Robert Half, author of the book *Robert Half on Hiring,* proffers a couple of helpful tips: The higher you go in an organization to check references, the more likely you are to learn something.

That is, from the human resources department all you may get are his dates of service with the company; but from the senior V.P. who was his boss, volumes. Half also suggests networking, you should pardon the expression—quizzing everyone you speak to about others you might consult.

If it all checks out, offer Mr. or Ms. Wonderful the job. He or she has met the test. And so have you.

9

The Managerial Mind Probe

Psychological tests are still used to weed out
executive candidates. Some tips for the testy testee.

IT'S ENOUGH to make you slightly paranoid. For a few hours a stranger probes your mind with questions and exercises attempting to lay bare patterns you may be completely unaware of. His report goes to your superiors and is used to grade you relative to others. In determining your future, the findings rank right up there with your years of accomplishment and whatever personal impression you've managed to create.

Something out of Orwell's *1984?* Fun and games on Dzerzhinsky Square, home office of the KGB? No, biz-sports fans, just another statistic in the dossier of corporate psychological testing.

It could happen to you. Estimates of the percentage of major corporations that use formal tests of some sort as guides to hiring or promotion range as high as 40 percent. Included are a number of not exactly flaky outfits — AT&T, IBM, Knight-Ridder Newspapers, J. C. Penney, Sears Roebuck.

If you should be afforded the opportunity to display your prowess on one of their little puzzles, there are a few things you ought to know. The tests themselves, and the uses companies make of them, take many forms. Some are distinctly more questionable than others. Thanks mainly to the Equal Employment Opportunity Commission, you as a test taker have more rights and prerogatives than you would have had, say, twenty years ago. But of course exercising those rights — challenging the validity of a particular test, asking to see the results — won't necessarily make it easier for you to get the job. It also seems to be getting harder to cheat on, or to use the modern term, to *game* these endeavors, particularly if you're put through something called an assessment center.

In offering you this experience, management is trying to predict how you'll perform in some new slot. This is tough to do. In matching candidates to managerial positions, a success rate of 75 percent — three out of every four picked turn out to be okay in their new spots — is spectacular and uncommon.

To achieve such success, proponents of testing claim, a company needs organized methods of gathering information about candidates and putting that information together. Testing isn't the only systematic means of getting the lowdown on someone. But, goes the siren song of the psychologists, it illuminates problems that may not show up elsewhere, furnishing that extra insight that (hushed, serious tones here) no careful decision-maker would want to do without.

If an employer asks you to take a test in conjunction with a battery of interviews, a detailed review of your career, and reference checks, be selectively skeptical but duly appreciative of his thoroughness. If the process consists mostly of your sweating through test questions and talking over the results with a psychologist brought in from outside, think twice about any job offer that may be forthcoming. If they just ask you to take a test, and that's it, run.

Once you've ascertained that your candidacy is not going to stand or fall solely on the basis of your response to Rorschach ink-blots, the next question becomes precisely which test, and why is it being administered to you. Four types of pencil-and-paper brain-teaser are typically administered to managers. They are intelligence tests, skill tests, interest inventories, and, the most suspect of all, personality tests.

Intelligence tests have been around since 1905, when Alfred Binet, in search of a device to cull retarded children from the general population of students in the French school system, invented the exercise that was eventually to become the IQ test. These days, retarded executives are culled with devices such as the Wechsler Adult Intelligence Scale, which has to be administered one-on-one and goes beyond mere pencil pushing, or the fiendishly difficult Miller Analogies Test. The latter—"a real ball-buster" in the professional estimate of one academic expert—begins with simple constructions like "Man is to woman as (a) fish is to bicycle (b) bull is to cow . . ." and proceeds to conundrums that would take a combination of Albert Einstein and Noah Webster to figure out.

Why, you may disingenuously ask, would anyone want to measure intelligence in selecting candidates for top management? As it turns out, according to John Sauer of Rohrer Hibler & Replogle, probably the best-known firm of psychological consultants to business, research indicates the single attribute that best predicts success at the highest levels of management is intelligence, though admittedly its predictive power isn't all that great. In middle management, so-called interpersonal skills seem to be more important, while on the bottom rungs of the managerial ladder, technical expertise appears to give the best purchase.

One small problem with all this: measuring adult intelligence is hardly an open-and-shut-your-head proposition. There is, for instance, the problem that tests may not take cultural differences into account. If before joining the ranks of management, you spent most of your life in the Kalahari desert happily speaking the !Kung language —"!" indicates one of four distinct clicking sounds, the other three being denominated "/," "//," and "-"—you're probably going to have extra trouble coping with the Miller Analogies, as much trouble as the typical Wharton M.B.A. wrestling with the subtle distinctions between / and -. You should cry !foul.

Similar kind things may be said about many skill tests. If the hiring organization has developed the procedure specifically to check performance on concrete tasks that an analysis of the job shows to be important, good, in general. A test of writing skill, for example, would not be out of place for a manager expected to churn out reports. This is not to be confused with the handwriting samples that German firms seem to require of Americans they're thinking of hiring—you know, big loops indicate creativity, a horrible scrawl a med-school education. But when the definition of skills fuzzily strays into areas such as the ability to manage others, paper-and-pencil tests of this type become debatable, to say the least.

With interest inventories, by comparison, the problem is not so much with the test itself as with the uses to which it's put. The most commonly administered of these babies, the Strong-Campbell Interest Inventory, asks you how you feel—"Like," "Indifferent," or "Dislike"—about some 325 items, such as repairing a clock or raising money for charity. From your responses, the test determines how you rank on "theme scales" such as artistic, enterprising, and conven-

tional. More interestingly, it also tells you how your pattern of answers compares with those of persons already in particular occupations. That's not to say that a 68 on the Funeral Director scale means
that you should become a mortician, or that you'll be a good one.
"What the inventory is useful for is to predict how long someone will
stay in a job," suggests Lyle Schoenfeldt, professor of management at
Texas A&M. Aside from its value to you in career planning, it
shouldn't be used for anything else.

The category of mind probe that probably shouldn't be used at all by
corporations is the personality test. Many of these — the ubiquitous
Minnesota Multiphasic Personality Inventory, for example — were
developed originally to identify severely disturbed individuals. What
they say about the great mass of the rest of us, sane by conventional
definition, is less clear. How many paranoid schizophrenics are considered for the job of senior V.P.-finance these days? (Senior V.P.-
marketing is, of course, another matter.)

Projective tests — where you have to tell what you see in ink blots
or drawings of shadowy, ambiguous human figures — are particularly
egregious. Sixty years after its invention, in the wake of hundreds
of studies of its validity, the Rorschach ink-blot test remains
controversial — some experts maintain there is no evidence to confirm that, say, perceiving human movement in the blots indicates a
rich imagination or fantasy life. Psychologists who use the Rorschach, on the other hand, maintain that the lack of validating evidence isn't important. In their view, the test is mostly an occasion for a
trained evaluator to tease revealing psychological information out of
you — his skill in interpreting your answers, and asking you follow-
up questions, is all-important.

When confronted with a Rorschach, don't immediately plunge into
tales of flowing fountains and benign flamingos. Exercise your rights.
Ask the person administering the test what kind of validity data he has
on its use in this context. Push him for an explanation of how it
satisfies the key EEOC requirement, job-relatedness.

Because conventional psychological tests have, in the final analysis,
proven not that wonderful as predictors of managerial success, many
companies have turned to an alternative known as the assessment
center. The German and British armies developed the forerunners of

these institutions several wars ago, and they were first used in the U.S. by the Office of Strategic Services — progenitor of the CIA — to pick folks who would make good spies. Douglas Bray, a renowned psychologist with AT&T, pioneered the use of assessment centers in the corporate world beginning in the late 1950s. Today they've spread to more than two thousand companies and governmental organizations, including the EEOC itself.

The underlying principle is that rather than test you for qualities that an employer thinks may be important in a manager, he will ask you instead to do those things — in an exercise — that he knows managers have to do. The people who evaluate your performance are quite often managers from your company, two or three ranks above you.

Typically you might begin on a Monday morning, together with five other candidates. The group is divided into three teams and given a financial exercise — much like a business-school case — that must be worked up, sometimes in consultation with other teams. In the afternoon each person is put through an in-basket test. It's supposedly Sunday morning at the office — no one is around for you to call or consult. Take three hours, go through this heaping in-basket, and decide what to do with the host of managerial problems you may find therein.

Tuesday morning it's time for a so-called leaderless group discussion. There's $25,000 of bonus money to be parceled out by the group among six fictive employees. Each assessee makes the case for one employee. Who gets the marbles? How? In the afternoon you might be required to give a presentation on the financial exercise. Maybe a pencil-and-paper test the next morning, and you — wilted — go home. The assessors remain the rest of the week, systematically sharing observations, grading each participant on such dimensions as administrative ability, leadership, even empathy.

Proponents claim a number of advantages for assessment centers over conventional tests. Their rate of predicting success seems much higher. They have greater "face validity"— for assessees, they simply seem a fairer measure of ability. Assessors can themselves learn a lot about management in the process. Moreover, it's supposedly less easy to cheat. How do you fake being able to analyze the contents of an in-basket? Coaching by people who've been through the drill doesn't help much, apparently.

From discussions with the experts, however, one can glean a couple of modest suggestions. On the in-basket exercise, first go through the entire pile — though only sappy employers these days pull the memo-at-the-bottom-saying-disregard-half-this-stuff routine — and group related items. Talking a lot seems to help boost your leadership score on the group discussions, perhaps a comment on what goes on in all those endless real-world meetings. But bear in mind the observation of William Byham, whose firm, Development Dimensions International, helps companies design assessment centers: "Timing is so important. On the leaderless group discussion, somebody will have been told that the thing to do is to call for a vote. He'll call for a vote four times, and be promptly voted down each time."

Disadvantages of the assessment center, from the employer's point of view, include cost — you've got to have a healthy number of candidates to amortize the start-up expense against — and the amount of managerial time consumed assessing. From the assessee's worm's-eye view, a possible objection is that the whole experience may be so stressful as to indicate little about how he would perform on the presumably slightly calmer actual job.

Assessment centers do, however, have one signal virtue. If they are designed for a particular company, and use company managers as assessors, they filter into the decision-making process a good bit of the ol' corporate culture — the way things are done here at Monolithic Enterprises. This is important, and reflects perhaps the major shortcoming of the alternative, send-this-guy-out-to-be-tested approach to hiring or promotion. As psychologist Harry Levinson notes, at least as important as your psychology in determining your success on the job is the mind-set of the organization and, in particular, the state of your boss's head. Maybe he needs the test, not you.

10

Picking Your Successor

*If you work in a large company, the choice
probably won't be left up to you, and for good reason.*

IT HAS all the inherent appeal, the sheer sexy come-hither, of retirement planning, making out a will, or investigating the latest options in life insurance. You know you shouldn't put it off. You're aware that the prudent, solid-citizen executives all labor over it intensely. But still . . .

Most managers don't seem to do a very good job of providing replacements for themselves, which is one reason why, increasingly, the matter isn't left up to them. While some businessmen retain the right to designate their successors — because they own the operation, for example — at most large, well-run companies, the practice is effectively proscribed. "I can't imagine a corporation where the incumbent has much control over filling his own job," observes Robert W. Eichinger, the corporate director of human resources at PepsiCo. Even the traditional exception — the chief executive — these days may find his prerogative hemmed in by a nominating committee of outside directors.

Why shouldn't the incumbent pick his own successor? Harry Levinson, the management psychologist, explains. For starters, the incumbent may be blithely unaware of changes in the world out there that may dictate that whoever occupies his job in the years ahead must act very differently. Even if the current jobholder sees big changes coming and a need to import an Attila-the-Hun type to surmount them, he may not be able to bring himself to do so. He owes too much to too many people in the organization to bring in someone to shake them up. Moreover, the deviousness of human psychology is such that the incumbent may elevate some marginal character, knowing full well, though not necessarily at a conscious level, that the new boy is sure to fail. How better to prove to everyone precisely how indispensable you really were?

If the incumbent doesn't choose the brave or bravette to fill his moccasins, who does? The answer from the best-managed corporations is clear: his boss does. After all, it is that worthy's fundament that will ultimately be, as they say, in a sling if the successor fails to perform.

Typically the boss gets plenty of advice along the way. The practice at most large companies is to hedge the selection process with institutional checks and balances.

The big differences in how well-run companies fill about-to-be-vacant managerial slots are mostly about defining the universe of people to be considered. The basic alternatives are the queue — which may have only one person in it — and the pool. Exxon uses the former — indeed, the oil giant has raised waiting in line to a height of systematization that even the military might find incredible. Whenever the presidents of Exxon's fourteen regional and operating companies get together with their principal subordinates to muse on personnel matters — which they typically do once a week for about two hours — the honchos have available a so-called replacement table. This elaborate document lists all the people who report to them directly, notes when those individuals are likely to be rotated to other jobs, lists by name the folks likely to replace them, estimates how long these managers will be left in their new positions, and sometimes even designates their successors by name — all this for the next five years.

The tables are revised and updated at least once a year, with the president of each company, advised by his vice presidents, making the final decisions. By virtue of this system, it is possible for management to know pretty clearly which job each executive will have five, and in some cases ten, years hence.

At PepsiCo, by comparison, in the upper executive regions it's everybody into the pool. In a sense, every promotable manager is in the pool of people who might be considered to fill a vacancy. The vice president for personnel of each of the seven divisions keeps the list of lower-level managers who make up that division's pool; the corporate V.P. of personnel, Roger King, keeps a sort of master list. "Mine consists of the top managers," he says, "the top 470 people. The president of PepsiCo knows them all." When an opening comes up at PepsiCo, the divisional or corporate pool is sluiced and a little pool of contenders drawn off. The boss then chooses among the contenders, with a little help from personnel and, if the position is a senior one, with agreement from the president.

Other large companies tend to be less formal about picking successors. Neither Procter & Gamble nor IBM, for example, has official queues or pools. A few practices are common to almost all the well-managed giants, though: they promote pretty much exclusively from within. The incumbent's boss chooses the successor. And at these companies, the push seems to be constantly on to make the criteria for selection, and the data on the candidates, objective — a word typically intoned in the most serious basso profundo that the corporate speaker can muster.

Objectivity in these matters is a tall order, perhaps an impossible one. Press a human resources executive even at a good company to tell you how well the formal performance appraisal system is working, and after sighing, he's likely to confess that it isn't working quite the way everyone hoped it would — doggone managers just don't seem to be willing to give anyone low marks. At supersystematic Exxon, for instance, the cornerstone of the appraisal system is a forced distribution of performance — only 10 percent of people in a given area can be evaluated as in the top category, only 25 percent in the next bracket, and so on. "No one really likes this," admits Scoop Tiedemann, Exxon's manager of compensation organization and executive development, "and everyone is always demanding a new format for performance appraisal. In the thirty years or so that I've been here we've had a host of different formats for evaluation."

Even if you could be objective, what are you going to be objective about? In picking your subordinate's successor — or your own, if you have the wherewithal and the pigheadedness to do it — what are you going to look at? Once you get beyond the bromides — a history of successful performance, proven leadership ability, no known criminal record — you quickly find that even the experts disagree on the criteria to be applied.

What you should be looking at is the candidate's behavior, in detail as rich as you can get. What precisely did he do to pull off his past coups, and how did he act in the course of them? Get at his psychology the only way it's useful to you: as demonstrated in conduct on the job. But get beyond the merely historical. Reed M. Powell, a visiting professor of management at California's Claremont Graduate School, observes that people who didn't do all that well in middle-management jobs sometimes do better as top executives — the skills required in each stratum can be different.

You will, of course, already have thought hard about the job that the candidate is to fill. If you're not the incumbent, you will have talked to him or her about what it requires. Truly bright successor-pickers go on to ask the people who report to the incumbent about what they think the job entails, particularly in dealings with them. If you're seeking a replacement for yourself, such information may help you be a bit more clinical and detached — the point is to avoid cloning yourself unthinkingly. Once you have in mind what the experts call a behavioral job description, you can go out looking for the best two-legged package of behavior to fit it.

Interview the competing packages. As an opener — one too often neglected — you might ask the candidate if he wants the job. You might also try to get at what the experts call team fit: how will this candidate get along with others, particularly the other candidates, if he does get the job, or — which may be just as important — if he doesn't? In this regard, you might use a question that Reginald Jones, the former chief executive of General Electric, employed in interviewing candidates to succeed him: you and I are riding in a company plane, and, unfortunately, it crashes, killing us both. Who should get the top job, and why? (In making the choice, it can help to know that if A gets the job, B and C will probably quit the next day.)

Probably the most important question to ask is, what would you do with this job if you got it? What the would-be executive-maker should be looking for is a capacity to envision the future, to anticipate in some detail what the job will require over the next few years, and the ability to formulate an adequate organizational response to what may be coming. Elliott Jaques is a British psychoanalyst, the director of the Institute of Organisation and Social Studies at Brunel University in Uxbridge, and an eminent student and thinker on organizations. His thirty-plus years of research have turned up the interesting fact that jobs at different levels in an organizational hierarchy almost inevitably require different capacities to think ahead — to conceptualize and plan for the future. The shop-floor worker need worry only about what he's going to do in the next hour. The chairman, if he's doing his job right, is thinking ahead years. You scoff? At Japan's Matsushita Electric they're already working on executing the third twenty-five years of the two-hundred-fifty-year plan laid down by founder Konosuke Matsushita.

For the job you're trying to fill, the time span the jobholder must be able to envision is probably considerably shorter, but it may still be longer than he's used to, or capable of. Ask the candidates for their scenarios. Test these with questions: What if this key assumption fails? What if that contingency occurs? When you get the answers, you'll be in a position to choose Mr. or Ms. Right.

Of course, he or she may still turn out to be The Incredible Mistake. Don't worry unduly about that. Veterans of the process of selecting a successor are almost unanimous that even after you've assembled all the best information available, you still have to make a leap of faith. Happy landings.

11

Managing Innovators

Give them space, money, time, and trust.
Slowly but surely strip away the excuses they can hide behind.

THEY ARE THE HOPE of corporate America, at least according to their press clippings. They will rebuild our sagging companies from within. They will stave off the Japanese challenge. They will be home for breakfast.

Call them innovators, creative types, or brilliant mavericks. They march — though not in formation, of course — under banners emblazoned PRODUCT CHAMPION, NEVER KILL AN IDEA, or, from a sweatshirt popular with Apple Computer employees, I WORK 90 HOURS A WEEK AND LOVE IT. Many conventional corporate people are suspicious of them. Robert Sternberg, a professor of psychology at Yale, studied how intelligence, creativity, and wisdom are perceived by different professions. Only business executives, he found, believed that the creative are not wise, nor the wise creative.

Fortunately, more and more managers seem to be wising up, looking beyond both old suspicions and new hype to realize that there may be something to this idea of tending the creative flame within a company. "Innovation is too important to be this year's fad," says William H. Weltyk, vice president of technology at Borg-Warner, a big Chicago-based equipment manufacturer. Drawing on his experience managing research in an industry a long way from Silicon Valley, Weltyk adds, "There are many people who could be more innovative than they are." The drums of creativity beat even in smokestack country.

The problem — or, for all you go-getters out there, the challenge — is that these creative types apparently have to be managed differently from your average wage slave. Or so says just about everyone who has tried to harness their distinctive energy. Some standard managerial wisdom on how to go about the task is beginning to emerge.

First, you have to figure out who the innovators are. Don't be misled, veterans of the exercise caution, by half-baked philistine folk wisdom: creative people do not necessarily wear plaid flannel shirts, handcrafted earrings, or loud ties. Their manner may not be flamboyant. Indeed, according to Lester C. Krogh, who heads R&D at that citadel of innovation, 3M: "Many of our creative people lead daily lives that would appear to an outsider to be exceptionally dull."

Not by their style but by their fruits shall ye know them. The only way to spot genuinely creative souls, the veterans say, is to notice who consistently comes up with good ideas. If you have sufficient managerial self-confidence to express an interest in doing things in new ways, and then — what's even harder — can keep your mind open to the suggestions brought to you, you shouldn't have much trouble distinguishing the innovative goats from the plaid-flannel sheep. Consider the variation among those poets of the new age, the authors of software. David A. Boucher, the president of Interleaf Inc., which produces software for work stations, observes, "The best programmer produces literally fifty times as much as a bad programmer. The best ones produce work that mediocre people can never produce."

Once you have identified the good ones, give them lots of room to maneuver. The first principle that virtually everyone who has managed creative types agrees on is that they have to be left to their own devices more than other employees, even to the extent of insulating them from the normal bureaucratic rules and imperatives. The process begins with you, their manager. "One of the things we try to do," says Krogh of 3M, "is to keep our mouths shut." He adds that at times it's also necessary to keep your eyes half-closed. Bootleg projects — work done without formal authorization — may not end up making money for the company, but ruthlessly eradicating them may cost you plenty in terms of the curiosity and initiative you'll need from the troops to make authorized projects a success.

If you want to be sure that your creative cowboys and cowgirls don't get fenced in, you can set up a so-called skunkworks — a facility apart from the rest of the corporation where innovators are sent to come up with new ideas in peace. IBM watchers caught the telltale odor emanating from an installation in Boca Raton, Florida, where the computer giant developed the PC. For all its current popularity, such a facility may not be a good idea, though, for reasons that go to the heart of managing creative types in a company that's perhaps not all that creative. "If you have a skunkworks as your only form of innovation, then the skunkworks idea will be short-lived," says Gifford Pinchot III, consultant and author of *Intrapreneuring,* a book on how to be entrepreneurial inside a corporation. When people, ideas, or new products eventually leave the skunkworks and rejoin the rest of the company, the bureaucrats may attack them as white blood cells do bacteria invading the bloodstream.

Andrew S. Grove, author of *High Output Management* and C.E.O. of highly innovative Intel, frames the problem as even companies without a skunkworks encounter it: "You have to be careful that in your quest to cater to these people you don't create a new class system in place of the old one of executive dining rooms and reserved parking spaces." If yours is a relatively young company — an Interleaf or Apple Computer, say — you can partially avoid the problem by working to establish a culture that treats everyone like an innovator. If a mailroom clerk wants to park his bicycle in the office, so be it.

In companies that have had time to ossify, you may have to be downright sneaky to avoid getting folks riled up, at least according to some experts. Pinchot recommends that managers school their creative types in skills well suited to an agent operating behind enemy lines: discretion, concealment, and camouflage. "What you should tell a person," Pinchot says, "is that attracting attention to himself is bad, not good."

Nurturing innovators is not just training moles, however. For all the freedom afforded creative types, they do need to be managed. Much of what is critical to the process is just between you and them, and need not scare anyone else in the company.

One does not tell an innovator what to do. After discussing the matter with him, the two of you agree on a goal. Unless you both are working for Walt Disney Productions, the goal had better not be Mickey Mouse. "We only ask our programmers to work on projects that we as a company are firmly committed to," says Boucher of

Interleaf — no mucking around in the vice chairman's pet harebrained scheme. As another expression of your confidence in him, provide your creative subordinate with the resources he needs to reach the goal — enough money for him to do the job but not enough to get himself, you, or the company in serious trouble.

Joe Lee, an executive vice president of General Mills, who got there partly by building the company's Red Lobster restaurants into one of the most successful chains in the U.S., sums up in a word the relationship you're trying to create: "Trust." You trust him to work hard and try to do his innovative best. He trusts you to give him a long leash, to be interested and, if possible, helpful when he comes around for advice, and to stand behind him when his baby faces the world. "Once you've done the editing on your people's effort, you must back them totally," asserts Barry Day, vice chairman of the McCann-Erickson Worldwide ad agency. "On the day of the presentation, you must never move away from them and say, 'I agree with you, Client, I didn't like it, either.'"

Within this framework you may occasionally have to supply firm guidance, even discipline, but here tread carefully indeed. You will want to help your innovator navigate periodic passages of insecurity, mostly with support but also by keeping the goal before him. "You make sure that anything he can hide behind is slowly and surely taken away," suggests Day. "If he says, 'I wouldn't have used that director,' you say, 'Fine, you choose the director.'" Deadlines are also helpful in managing your creative flock. "They seem to work best if they are event-driven," notes Jay Elliot, vice president for human resources of Apple Computer, citing the introduction of Apple's Macintosh machine — everybody knew it was to be trotted out at the annual shareholders' meeting; nobody could expect extra time.

What you should not do by way of disciplining creative types is chew them out. Veteran managers report that this gets you nowhere, and may even set you back. "You never yell at people," says David A. Litwack, vice president for development at Cullinet Software. "You can lean on them if you feel they're doing something wrong, but they have to be treated as professionals."

This includes being rewarded like professionals. Money is necessary — you have to pay them as much as their peers in industry get—but not sufficient. By now you should have figured it out: what these folks want is to turn their ideas into realities and to have the world, and in particular their colleagues who understand the details, bear witness and smile. IBM, which knows a little something about managing people, has a program it calls the IBM Fellows. The Fellows, typically scientists and engineers who have put in fifteen to twenty years of consistently creative labor at the company, are given executive salaries, five years to work on what they want to, and resources to support their research. Why does IBM do it—in the hope of new, breakthrough products? No, says George S. Howie, director of technical personnel programs, it's "primarily for recognition of outstanding work."

Now, if somebody would just devise a program to recognize the real heroes of innovation—the people who manage the creative people. But then, maybe somebody already has. It's called a vice presidency.

※ 12 ※

Managing Expense Accounts

*What people get away with on their expense reports
tells a lot about them — and their employer.*

CALL IT a Jungian archetype, or simply the universal expense-account chestnut: a company functionary is sent on assignment to Alaska (or rainy London, or the jungle). He outfits himself with a fur parka (an umbrella, mosquito netting). After the trip, he turns in his expense account, including on it the amount spent on this item. The accounting department promptly bounces the report back to him with a notation that it's against company policy to pay for such furbelows. His next expense report, filed a month or so later, swarms with nickel-and-dime entries — $5 taxi fares, $2 tips — each well below the level that requires a receipt. To the report, he appends a short note. It says: Find the fur parka.

The first point of this pregnant tale, variants of which are repeated in a wide range of organizations: how an employee handles his expense account tells a lot about him and his attitude toward his employer. There's little suggestion here that the functionary originally intended to rip off the company — he duly recorded the expense. But when the bureaucracy responded bureaucratically, he got mad, or disgusted, and exploited the limitations of the system to get even. The second point: how the employer responds says a good deal about it, too. Is it merely bureaucratic? Suspicious? A patsy? Wise executives, both as auditors of others' expense accounts and as managers of their own, endeavor to understand where both sides are coming from, as they say in California.

In setting policy on expense accounts, most companies look initially to Internal Revenue Service guidelines: corporations may deduct as a business expense 80 percent of the cost of "ordinary and necessary" travel and entertainment; expenditures above $25 require supporting documentation. If this sounds a bit abstract, be apprised that if you work in a big company, even now there may be a semipermanent team of IRS auditors working at your headquarters reviewing the company's tax records, which presumably include the receipts turned in with expense reports. Expenditures currently receiving a lot of scrutiny include country club memberships and travel for spouses — do they really serve enough of a business purpose to warrant the company's paying for them?

It's what a company does in enforcing the IRS guidelines, and in setting further guidelines of its own, that separates the corporations serious about managing expense accounts — and perhaps about managing generally — from the loosey goosies. Ask about expense account policy at ServiceMaster Industries, the supplier of housekeeping help to institutions that has been among the profit leaders of the Fortune Service 500. You will be told of recommended limits on meal and out-of-pocket expenses, of requirements that employees get advance approval for group reservations, and that everyone in the company flies economy class, including the president and the chairman.

Ask American Home Products, the food-drug-and-packaged-goods powerhouse that ranks among the most profitable of the Fortune 500 industrials, and you'll hear that prior approval is required for expenditures above $500, that expense accounts are reviewed regularly and thoroughly, and that people are disciplined for violating the rules. Says American Home Products spokesman Jack Wood, speaking public-relations-ese, "Reportedly, a fairly high-level person at this company was dismissed because of a discrepancy."

At the nether extreme are companies that seem to invite the vigorous use of expense accounts, if not their actual abuse. At a none-too-successful forest products outfit, a newly hired manager was pointedly told the following story by his vice president: a company employee submitted an expense report whereon the only item was a request for reimbursement for a fifty-cent milkshake. His boss called him in, pulled two quarters from his executive pocket, and handed them to the subordinate, saying, "Don't spoil it for the rest of us."

At another company, when an employee asked for a raise, his boss replied, "We can't give it to you this year — you'll have to live on your expense account." Of this remark, John Lobuts, a professor of management science at George Washington University's graduate school of management, observes, "The boss told him to steal."

Sometimes the top dogs convey the message indirectly, by their example. Marshall Romney, a professor of accounting at Brigham Young University, reports that the place where he witnessed the most flagrant expense account abuse by underlings was an insurance company where everybody knew that higher-ups were actively engaged in cooking the books.

Provided a company stops well short of criminal behavior, why shouldn't it take a relatively liberal line on expense accounts? Doesn't a little benign neglect in this area, tantamount to throwing the troops a freebie now and then, just make for higher morale? Not necessarily. A company's failure to promulgate clear guidelines and to stand behind them can leave a conscientious employee in uncomfortably ambiguous territory: here I am, a wallflower at what everybody else takes to be a pretty wild party — what's the matter with me? Or, in the words of the country and Western song, I'm going to the dogs with a bunch of swinging cats.

Such a policy can also cost the corporation a bundle. Runzheimer International, which monitors corporate spending on travel and advises companies how to control it, reports that at many corporations travel alone — forget entertainment — has come to represent the third-biggest expense, after salaries and data processing. Airline deregulation hasn't helped: even companies minded to watch their travel dollars now confront a perplexing jumble of ticket prices, not to mention frequent-flier plans aimed at luring their employees onto the same carrier every time, whatever the cost.

Technology may offer a way out of the morass, perhaps even the next giant stride forward in the management of expense accounts. Executives at American Express and at Diners Club claim that their respective corporate credit card systems — the employee gets the plastic, the company gets a report on how it's used — can provide tons of enlightening, potentially money-saving, information. Want to know who keeps flying on Bribery Air even though lower-cost alternatives on other airlines abound? Interested in the possibility of someone being issued a full-fare transcontinental ticket and putting it down on his expense report when the ticket was never used and somebody got a refund? The computer will tell you.

Corporate card systems do have their critics. "When a guy is buying on his own credit card he feels a limit, whereas a company card looks like an unlimited license to buy everything," argues Stephen Zelencik, senior vice president for sales and marketing of Advanced Micro Devices. It's not that AMD is averse to plastic, mind you — the California chipmaker accepts only credit card receipts as proof of business meals taken. Somebody in Sunnyvale obviously knows just how quick waiters and bartenders are, after the real bill has been paid, to come up with a blank tab bearing the restaurant's name.

Whether aided by new technology or not, a manager should be looking mainly for one thing in reviewing a subordinate's expense report: anomalies. Hmmm — why does Barbara always spend twice as much as anybody else making a sales trip to Sheboygan? Gosh, on Otto's credit card receipt, the one where the carbon-copied figures were so faint that the poor guy had to trace over them, it says that the meal cost $200, but he only left a $15 tip. Was the service really that bad at the Casa de la Food, or is Otto out to make an extra hundred simoleons?

If you do turn up some puzzling discrepancy, before you speak with the alleged perpetrator, you will, of course, want to run through your Standard Issue Mark 1 Mod 4 Semiautomatic Managerial Checklist of questions. What do I know about this person? Has anything like this shown up on his expense reports before? Did we tell him the rules? Are there alternative explanations of what happened? How can I get more information? Once you've satisfied yourself on these points, or done as well as you can, talk it out with Otto, bearing in mind that for him, now, you are The Company.

Even if you don't detect an anomaly, you may discover a lot else of managerial interest. For starters: how does so-and-so approach the drudgery entailed in keeping good records? Is he prompt? Meticulous? Too meticulous — to the point of devoting inordinate time to making sure he gets reimbursed even for borderline expenses? Usually of greater import: has so-and-so been getting around as much as he should? Who has he been talking to? Why to them? Is there a deal cooking, one that you could help out with?

Since you, unlike the Big Manager Upstairs, are in all probability neither omniscient nor omnipresent, there will remain a few things you can't know. Only the author of the expense account can say whether he actually took that $20 cab ride to the airport, or the $5 bus ride instead. Was that man whose dinner she paid for really a buyer for an out-of-town chain, or just some luscious hunk left over from her carefree bachelorette days? As Ed Michl, the corporate expense-account expert at General Electric, wisely notes, "How in the hell could a company find out who you took to lunch without private detectives?" Nowadays, most of the trendy how-to-manage books advise that you have to trust your people. Here's a good place to begin.

13

Living with Human Resources

*Believe it or not, managers can profit by working
with what used to be called the personnel department.*

LOOKING FOR A SUREFIRE ICEBREAKER next time you're
with a bunch of line managers? Just raise the subject of working with
the human-resources department. Eyes roll heavenward, heads shake,
snorts and knowing laughter break out on all sides. After an initial
round of muttering about "idiots" and "bureaucrats," the game
quickly becomes Can You Top This Horror Story? "Listen, let me
tell you about the time I tried to fire this drunk we had working for
us . . ."

What line managers may not realize is that the folks in human
resources can match them horror story for horror story. And guess
who serves as the butt of these tales? "I've seen a C.E.O. issue his own
human-resources policy manual without consulting a professional in
the field," says J. Jennings Partin, senior vice president for executive
development at E. F. Hutton. "It was just an abomination." Partin
goes on: "I've heard about hiring decisions made without checking
references, about things said in termination interviews that were
absolutely libelous, about employment agreements that had to be done
over completely when the human-resources department finally got a
look at them."

There is clearly obloquy enough to go around. What is equally
clearly lacking is the kind of mutual understanding necessary for line
and staff to work together effectively. The best human-resources
specialists have always taken it on themselves to figure out what was
in the head of the manager they were trying to help. Line types
enlightened enough to return the favor may find themselves increasingly at a loss for horror stories, but well supplied with results, including financial results, that they can brag about.

As a modest first step toward enlightenment, consider some of the impressions of human-resources people commonly entertained by operating managers — and the rebuttals that human-resources people offer.

They are wimps, more concerned with keeping employees happy than with making a profit for the business. Somebody has to represent the organization to its employees, comes the reply, and Lord knows, line management doesn't win any prizes for communicating with them. Are you ready to play chaplain yourself, to listen to a subordinate who has problems? Maybe we do set ourselves up as the guardians of the company's reputation for fairness. Don't underestimate the value of that reputation in keeping good employees and attracting more of them.

They are a bunch of liberal activists, trying to saddle us with the poor, tired, huddled masses — obviously unqualified people — in order to meet some lunatic affirmative action quota. At a lot of companies, the first time top management ever paid any attention to the personnel department was to assign it the job of ensuring that the company didn't get sued for violating laws on hiring. When the brass found that the people then in the job were not up to the new assignment, they installed better people. Personnel became human resources. While the pressure from government may be less intense these days, sophisticated human-resources executives see reasons for continued attention to hiring the so-called disadvantaged: "It's the right thing to do economically," argues Hal Johnson, a senior V.P. at Travelers Cos. He goes on: "In 1990 more of the work force is going to be minorities — Hispanics, blacks — and women. The companies that started building bridges back in the 1970s will be all right. Those that didn't, won't."

They are pettifogging, obscurantist bureaucrats. Okay, replies the unwimpishly combative human-resources exec, at some companies top management sets personnel policy and leaves it up to us to enforce it. Suppose top management says, "No raises for the year." You come to me and say, "I gotta give a raise to Golden-haired So-and-So here. He's working way above his job level, and I already promised." If I say no, do you get mad at top management and tell everybody that it's to blame? Hardly. But if I say yes, in four nanoseconds in comes your counterpart in the next division bleating, "I gotta have raises for

So-and-So and So-and-So, I already promised, and besides, you let *him* get away with it." The moral: it's only fair, and also self-preserving, to avoid making exceptions.

They are spies for top management. Well, Mr. Line Manager, what would you do if the chief executive came to you and said, "I'm very interested in this or that aspect of our operations and I want you to check into it"—would you just shrug him off? Not likely. Or say we spot something truly egregious, a foreman making patently racist remarks, for example. We talk to the line manager responsible, and he replies, "What, me worry?" Are we supposed to stand idly by?

They're always coming around with some new program, which they can only describe in the most incomprehensible jargon. A hit, a palpable hit. Of course, the line often speaks in a language of its own too. For every human-resources staffer intoning, "You've got an OD problem"— meaning something's wrong with the design of the organization— there's a line stalwart talking about impacting throughput. If both sides worked together more closely and consistently, they might learn to speak each other's language, and to be less surprised by each other's initiatives. Indeed, they might even produce programs that please them both.

Real live managers of both the operating and the human-resources persuasions testify that serious cooperation is possible. In fact, they maintain, the chances for it have never been better. Helped along by the example of the Japanese and by best-sellers ranging from *In Search of Excellence* to *The One Minute Manager*, an increasing number of line types appear to be getting the message that people are important.

Even more promising, the folks from human resources are bringing more to the table. At many companies these days, the man or woman from you-know-where is likely to be not an embittered survivor of thirty years' annotating personnel records, but someone who combines professional credentials in the human-resources field with— ready for this?—an interest in his employer's making money. The best senior human-resources executives these days earn $300,000 or more a year, and have the ear of the chief executive. Hotshots starting out in the field often have a graduate degree, maybe even an M.B.A. If there's deadwood, you're likely to find it somewhere in the middle, between smart people at the top and bottom.

"The perception used to be that human resources thought about the happiness of employees, and line managers thought about costs," says Jean Coyle, director of human-resources planning at the Bank of America. "Now both realize that the overriding concern is the yield from employees." Others talk about employee efficiency or productivity, but they all mean much the same thing.

Morgan Burke, a veteran personnel specialist turned line manager at Inland Steel, tells how to get the full benefit of the new breed of staffers: "Get the human-resources people living with you. And get them involved early on." If it's a particular problem that needs addressing — say the competitive necessity for your workers to learn new skills — form one of those task forces with representatives from both line and staff, including human resources. At a minimum, seek the counsel of your friendly local human-resources staffer on issues of mutual concern: manpower planning, communication with employees, controlling the cost of benefits, even the compatibility of the people at an outfit your company might acquire.

"If you have put a human-resources person on your team," advises Coyle, "don't be afraid to ask for what you want." You can even ask for data, in the past not exactly a human-resources specialty. What would an early-retirement plan cost? How has morale changed, according to surveys of employees in the division? Don't expect dollars-and-cents valuations for every move you're contemplating, but usually you can get answers that go well beyond somebody's gut feel.

A human-resources specialist should also be able to serve you as a troubleshooter — for example, asking questions of people caught up in a dispute and providing you an unfiltered account of it. Getting out there to the front lines may also have the benefit of helping to rid Harry Heartfelt of any residual naiveté. If your staffer really gets into the role, he or she may even become a sort of resident oracle on the corporate culture.

To be sure, not all representatives of the human-resources department may be up to the new standard. For all the talk in advanced circles of the need to get human-resources people involved in making corporate strategy, there are still personnel folks who jealously guard their hermetic wisdom, or who simply may be unable to see a larger picture. Observes Noel M. Tichy, a professor at the University of

Michigan business school and one of the leading lights in the field, "For years, human-resources people have been standing outside a closed door, asking to get in on the important stuff. Now that they are in, some are finding that they don't know what to do, that they can't deliver."

And what should the well-intentioned line manager do if he finds himself confronted with an unreconstructed, uninterested, nay-saying bureaucrat? Simply bypass him, maintains one fast-track manager. Ask for somebody whom you can work with, suggests another. Perhaps the most trenchant counsel comes from Richard H. Bierly, recruited by C.E.O. Mike Blumenthal to head human resources at Burroughs Corp.: "Throw him out of your office."

14

How to Fire Someone

What you did months before counts more than how you finally deliver the blow. But don't screw that up either.

THE MANAGER WHO SUFFERS no self-doubt when he has to fire a subordinate is no manager at all. It isn't my fault, he tells himself, the company just has to slim down. And his conscience whispers back, "Who managed the enterprise into this sorry strait anyway?" The guy turned out to be a total bozo. "Who hired him? Trained him? Supervised his work? Nobody could do *anything* to help save him?" It's strictly business. "You're depriving someone of his livelihood."

If it's any consolation, know that firing people has become such a common, if still unpleasant, exercise in the executive manual of arms that a substantial body of wisdom has accumulated on the subject. The experts — veterans of the ordeal, business school professors, and consultants in what its practitioners call outplacement — agree that to successfully navigate this, the most unpleasant moment in workaday capitalism, you have to begin preparing for the possibility early. Like the day your organization hires the person. The key to relatively guilt-free firing is having behind you a performance appraisal system that let the individual know where he stood every step of the way in his career with the company.

Let's say that a while after being hired, but long before anyone thinks of firing him, he proves to be not up to the mark here, here, and here. Tell him so. Set goals for improved performance. Do what you can to help him get there. Poor soul, he still can't do the job. Repeat the drill, and this time make sure he understands where he ranks with respect to his colleagues: if there has to be a cutback, he'll be among the first to go. (Managerial hotshot that you are, you of course keep your people informed of any changes in the business that might affect their jobs.) He doesn't get any better. Red lights flash, warning bells sound. Give him a set period to measure up in certain clearly spelled-out respects. Let him know that if he doesn't improve, he'll be fired. No euphemisms, please. The ax may still come as a surprise, because people have a way of hearing only what they want to hear and not believing the worst.

All right, you've finally resolved to do the dreaded deed. Act like an executive: control the situation. First, gather information. Is there anything you should know that the busy folks in the human-resources department may have overlooked? The fact, for example, that his retirement benefits are scheduled to vest in only two more months; if you are going to play the unredeemed Scrooge, at least do it deliberately. What can you find out about his situation at home? You're not going to feel wonderful if, after firing him, you discover that his spouse has been in the hospital for the past six months. Also, check with the legal department. Could a jury construe your actions as discrimination or as a breach of contract?

If the auguries are propitious, proceed to set the stage. You owe him or her the common courtesy to deliver such overwhelming news personally; only cowards and corporate Neanderthals have the personnel department do the job. That doesn't mean that it has to be just the two of you closeted together, though. Indeed, the lawyers may recommend the presence of someone else from management, if only to witness what goes on. You might also want to have someone from human resources sit in. Dan R. Dalton, a professor of management at the Indiana University school of business, notes that the mere presence of a one- or two-person audience can help contain emotional outbursts.

Pick the day carefully: not his birthday, a Friday, or the day before a holiday. The aim is to arrange matters so that he'll have something to do the next day and won't suddenly be left with time on his hands to brood, or worse. The experts recommend that you choose a neutral location, perhaps a conference room. While this might seem like inviting someone into the gas chamber, they say it's better than your office. Summoning him to your inner sanctum might seem an attempt to intimidate, and you won't be able to walk out gracefully if an exit is called for. Certainly not his office — talk about an invasion of privacy. Not a bar or a restaurant, either. As the New York City outplacement firm Lee-Hecht & Associates notes crisply in its guide to the subject, "The termination is business, not social." Above all, decide in advance what you're going to say. You want him to escape with his dignity, but you also need to make sure that he comes away knowing he has been fired.

The experts recommend that you come to the point immediately. Deliver the bad news, and explain the business reasons for the decision. It may soften the blow if you can honestly say, "Your position is being eliminated" instead of, for example, "We have to get rid of you." But you still must put across the fact that now is the time to say sayonara, and that the decision is irrevocable. Emphasize that everyone else in authority agrees; there's no hope of appeal.

Try to be businesslike, but also sympathetic. Give him a chance to express his feelings. If he gets angry, avoid becoming hostile or defensive in response. Tell him that this isn't the occasion to hash out the conflicting claims in his case, and that you will be available to talk to him about the matter another time, after he has had a chance to think things over. If he dissolves in a rain of tears, be solicitous — assure him, for example, that it's all right to cry — but not so solicitous that he may think you will change your mind.

When the air clears a bit, go over the benefits he will receive on severance. Hand him a written description of the package. It's not just that he still may be so stunned that nothing said to him registers; the paper will help bring home the finality of your action. Discuss with him, too, how you propose to break the news to the rest of the organization. If you're going to issue a statement, have him look it over.

The session should last no longer than ten or fifteen minutes, the experts say. How you end it will depend on what help you've decided to provide him. You should at least consider bringing in an outplacement consultant. For a fee, paid by your company, of up to 20 percent of the fired person's annual salary, the consultant will help him deal with the turmoil of feelings he's likely to wrestle with. An outplacement firm will also help him search for a new job, counseling him on everything from how he comes across in interviews to places he might begin looking. Before you jump up onto the stump to deliver your standard damn-the-consultants tirade, think hard about whether your

company can really do this kind of work better than an outside specialist. Remember, too, that every smidge of assistance you give the
firee probably lessens the chance that he'll sue you or otherwise
besmirch the company's reputation.

If you do retain a specialist, the last step in your session with the
person being outplaced should be to require that he talk with the
consultant right away. You may even want to have the outplacement
counselor waiting in the next room. The sooner he sees the victim, the
sooner he can begin to stanch the bleeding. "You can help people get
back in control of their lives if you help them maintain their dignity
and get them moving immediately," observes Clifford Benfield, president of Hay Career Consultants, an arm of the Hay Group, a big
consulting firm headquartered in Philadelphia. "Get them to pick up a
pencil and they have already started to reconstruct their lives."

Whether you use a consultant or not, you will probably want to
convey the fired individual off the premises as quickly as is consistent
with maintaining his dignity. His loud complaints to co-workers
about his so-called superiors in the organization won't improve
morale — or his chances of getting a good reference from those superiors two weeks hence. On the other hand, almost nothing justifies
nonsense along the lines of "Clean out your desk and be out of here in
fifteen minutes," not even the worry that a disaffected someone might
take proprietary information with him. Give the person another office to use temporarily, preferably one at a face-saving remove from
his old colleagues.

In the days and weeks following the firing, be prepared to talk with
him again. The two of you will need to agree on what he can say to
prospective employers when he's asked why he left his job with your
company. Outplacement counselors, those masters of euphemism,
can help with this.

The bigger challenge will be managing the effects of the firing on
the people who remain in the organization. "Is this just the first of a
series of dismissals?" they may well wonder. "Am I next?" Be straight
with them, and if you can honestly tell them that this was an isolated
instance or that the bloodletting is over, do so emphatically, and often.
If they believe that the performance appraisal system worked in this
case and will continue to work, and if they see that the person fired

was treated with consideration right through to the last, the episode may actually strengthen their confidence in the perspicacity and fairness of their employer.

What attitude you want them to have in this regard is a matter of some debate at a time when each morning's newspaper seems to bring tidings of managers laid off at still another company. William Morin is chairman of the world's largest outplacement firm, Drake Beam Morin, with offices in thirty-seven cities. Having seen a host of people fired for just about every conceivable reason, he thinks employees should view employers with what he calls, using a slight touch of the oxymoronic, nondependent trust. People should rely on their own career skills instead of expecting the company to take care of them. But even if that gets to be the universal substitute for old-style corporate loyalty, it probably won't make the job any easier when you have to call Joe into the conference room for the toughest ten minutes in a manager's life. And maybe in Joe's life, too.

❈ 15 ❈

How to Manage Your Boss

*An artful subordinate, say the experts, can shape
the boss's behavior. A key tactic: straightforwardness.*

AMONG THE VARIOUS MARTIAL ARTS imported to our
peaceable country from the Orient, there is a discipline called aikido.
While to the untutored eye it may seem merely souped-up judo, some
rabid exponents claim considerably more for it. Indeed, they maintain
that when a master of aikido is really cooking — when, in the parlance, his ki is on — he can throw an opponent *without touching him*.
Picture such an encounter: the opponent tries a karate kick or a
roundhouse right, the master feints, and his adversary lurches through
the air, ending up a quivering pretzel on the ground. Properly done,
managing one's boss is much like aikido.

In recent years, a surprising amount has been written about managing the boss, mostly by psychologists, business school professors, and
consultants. Their advice typically begins with the arresting thought
that you the underling can manage, if not your boss, exactly, then at
least your relationship with him or her. The pundits use the word
relationship about as often as modern urban singles do. Managing
upward has all sorts of attractions. It can give you greater freedom to
do your own work, while ensuring that you both are toiling toward
the same goals.

Start working on the relationship, the experts say, by studying your
boss's style, a managerial euphemism for how he thinks and acts.
What tends to rattle him? How does he treat people? Then, the advice
goes on, consider your own style. In reviewing your psychology,
dwell especially on how you have got along with so-called authority
figures — no use repeating the mistakes you made with Dad and
Mom. This done, about all that's left is for you to adjust your behavior
so that the boss finds it easy to go along with what you want to do. Let

us call this approach to managing upward Theory Y, in that it slightly resembles Douglas M. McGregor's famous hypothesis about the proper way to motivate subordinates — by helping them satisfy needs for self-esteem and self-fulfillment.

There is, however, another approach to managing the boss. Call it Theory X, in that it more closely resembles McGregor's notion of how management has traditionally wrung work from employees — by cajoling, rewarding, punishing, and controlling. Theory X of boss management takes as its initial premise that you can in fact do something to shape not just your relationship with this exalted personage but the personage's behavior as well. You can't simply order him around, of course; he is the boss. But you can subtly direct his efforts, or at least so say some businessmen and -women who have wrestled with the challenge. The conclusion reached by a former Atari executive who worked for a martinet might be taken as the watchword of Theory X's proponents: "Bosses have problems with wimps." So don't be one.

In pursuing Theory X, the opposite of wimpery is not idiot machismo — full of bluster, overbearing — but rather an aggressive yet artful straightforwardness. After getting the requisite facts, and giving their presentation a bit of crafty thought, "be straight up in the boss's face," as one Silicon Valley manager puts it.

Robert C. Bleke, a management psychologist who seems more comfortable with Theory X than most of his professional brethren are, elaborates: "It is very important that a subordinate not try to play psychologist with his boss. Don't try to interpret, outguess, or read something into what he may say or do."

Academic experts and businessmen alike attest to the overriding importance of achieving agreement with the boss on what you should be trying to accomplish in your job. Take the advice of one who has helped pick up the pieces of many a failed boss-subordinate relationship — Stephen Morris, an outplacement counselor. Morris suggests easing by the boss's office door early in the week and saying something like "You know, over the weekend I gave a lot of thought to what I ought to be doing with the job. I made a brief list and I'd like to bounce it off you, now or whenever." You and the boss then proceed to play a friendly but meaningful game of intellectual medicine ball, and with your ball. "What you're doing is writing a contract," observes Morris.

A similar subtlety should inform any attempt to procure that most-precious-because-most-scarce object of desire among subordinates, an honest performance appraisal. An adept proponent of Theory X gets his appraisals by being observant when working on assignments with the boss. "In my thirty-five years of business, I've only had one decent formal performance review," says one savvy executive. "You get feedback in a task-oriented situation," the man concluded. "From the way your boss responds to things that you do, even from his body language." And don't forget that bosses need bolstering, too. If you think he did a job particularly well, tell him so.

Most bosses are interested in the progress made on assignments, not in what subordinates have done to achieve that progress — results, in short, not the hours you've put in. They are also interested, believe it or not, in problems, threats, and obstacles, but here be careful. As devotees of Theory X know better than anyone, if you simply present the little fellow with a problem, he's likely to get strange ideas — such as why don't we try this, or have you thought of that, or, worse yet, how did you let this happen to me? The lesson: never ever ever go see the boss about a problem without bringing along a proposed solution. Better yet, three solutions.

Where the champions of Theory X really show their stuff is in the management of problem bosses. These difficult characters typically fall into one or more of three categories. There is first the bully, or screamer. An executive who works for one of the toughest bosses in America sums up the correct tack to take: "It's like a parent handling a child — you just let him know that there are certain things you're not going to put up with. When he has a tantrum, you don't have a tantrum back — you shut things down until there's a time more conducive to a meeting."

The proper response to such a boss goes well beyond mere passive resistance. "This guy's primary tactic," the executive continues, "is probing for a weak spot; he will invariably cause a confrontation in a meeting. I deliberately pick the terrain where I want us to have this inevitable confrontation. I set up this area as the weak link so that he'll come charging through, thinking he's caught me, then I slam the door on him. This way he gets the need to have a confrontation out of his system." Talk about aikido.

The second type of problem boss is the incompetent. You probably can't manage him into effectiveness, and, cruelly, you can't fire him. About all you can do is to keep on doing the best job you can, whatever his response, while energetically attempting to establish good communication with others in the organization so that they'll be able to distinguish your abilities from his inabilities.

Finally, and most discomfiting, is the unethical boss. When he or she tells you to do something utterly nefarious, listen carefully, maybe even asking questions to make sure you heard what you can't believe you heard. Then forget about it. "I always say, 'Okay, Sam, I understand you perfectly,'" comments a manager who has confronted the problem more than once. "Then I do exactly what I intended to in the first place." Which is, of course, precisely the purpose of boss management.

16

The Boss Is Coming to Visit

When the Maximum Tamale from headquarters is about
to descend on you in the regional office, don't panic. Plan.

THE JAPANESE IDEOGRAM for "crisis," we are told by a steadily swelling number of allegedly inspirational speakers, is a compound of two ideograms, the first meaning "danger," the second signifying "opportunity." In Japanese or any other language, a visit by the boss to one of the company's regional offices is a crisis.

The feeling of panicky fear that besets people in the field is captured nicely in the sobriquet that folks in outposts of the General Electric empire have for that corporation's chief executive, Jack Welch. They call him "Neutron Jack." As one regional manager explains, "You've heard about the neutron bomb? Well, when Jack visits, he leaves the building standing, but the people are dead."

The opportunity at hand is less apparent to the untutored eye. Veterans of the corporate wars report, however, that if properly managed — which means managed mostly by the head of the local office, with some help from the deity descending upon the folks — visits can achieve the following wonders. The boss comes away invigorated, with a fresh sense of his own potency and a first-hand impression of the really solid job that the people in the field are doing (so unlike the backbiting and turf-battling of the staff at headquarters). The local manager establishes a sense of closeness with the Maximum Tamale analogous to that experienced by the guys back at the head office who rub shirt-sleeves with his corporate eminence every day. Underlings in the region are dazzled, inspired, and made to feel part of the corporate family. Moreover, as if all this wasn't richness enough, the company may actually make some money on the visit, immediately and directly. Visits from the boss can be an ideal occasion for cementing ties to existing customers, perhaps even developing ties to new ones.

For the regional manager who wants to make the most of such a potentially blessed event, the secret is managing expectations — first and foremost the boss's, then those of the individuals he'll encounter, and, finally but not insignificantly, the manager's own.

You can make the process of satisfying everyone much simpler by seeing to it beforehand that they all expect approximately the same thing.

This isn't easy. Few events this side of a French bedroom farce are as susceptible to comic misunderstandings — Person A thinks this is going to happen, Person B is sure that just the opposite will occur — particularly if the boss's visits to the field are infrequent. An executive tells of traveling as one of many outriders with his boss on a visit to the company's California offices. The contingent from East Coast headquarters was supposed to get to know the West Coasters in a gathering that would combine business and recreation. When the plane landed, it disgorged the headquarters crew dressed in their version of California casual — luau shirts, obscenely bright sportswear. They were greeted on the tarmac by a phalanx of nervous executives gussied up in what they thought was standard eastern business dress — blue suits, ties, and starch.

Too often, the boss will plan a sojourn believing that he's going to get the lowdown on operations in the field while at the same time achieving a just-one-of-the-folks rapport with the troops. On receiving the news that he's coming, people in the region will launch a flurry of phone calls to their friends in the home office to find out what the top guy is, as they put it, "really up to." They will then proceed to labor mightily to put the best possible face on things, usually an artificial face. As one astute observer of the corporate scene notes, the creation of such a Potemkin village is sometimes the only project that a factory manager and the local union can agree on.

The key to avoiding a Herculean waste of corporate effort is for the local manager to carefully plan the whole encounter, consulting and informing the boss, or at least his staff, at every stage. This kind of planning begins with good intelligence on what the boss is likely to want. If the process is handled correctly, the local man may be able to subtly shape those wants.

Among the bits of information to be gathered, there is first — let's get it over with right away — the seemingly silly stuff: the visitor's personal tastes in food, drink, lodging, and recreation. While the corporate grapevine can sometimes have you believe, wrongly, that catering to idiosyncrasies is the very essence of planning a visit, it is true that a decent, hostly regard for them may make everything else that happens more pleasant for all concerned.

Discussions with people inside companies and with others well situated to observe these occasions — hoteliers, managers of private clubs that cater to corporate trade — suggest that such wants are, in general, surprisingly innocuous. Strangely enough, the desires most often mentioned are for a particular variety of potable: Armand Hammer likes a supply of orange tea in his suite; Hugh Hefner of Playboy Enterprises requires Pepsi-Cola wherever he travels. Slaking the visitor's thirst can take a bit of doing. The head of a regional office in Tokyo, on learning that his soon-to-visit boss was a Diet 7-Up fanatic, discovered that the nearest available source was Hong Kong. He had a case of the stuff shipped in from there, of course.

Sometimes, too, the visitor will himself bring along the particular accouterments he requires. For the local man, this requires merely making sure that they get picked up along with their owner and delivered to the appropriate destination. A former General Foods executive tells of a high-ranking officer of that food-processing company who had a bad back and who always took his own special pillow with him on trips. Members of his entourage or minions from the office being visited would be charged with carrying it to the dignitary's suite.

If the boss visits the field a lot and is genuinely fussy about such small matters, word of his preferences will probably reach the local manager via the company's jungle telegraph long before the person himself arrives. Alternatively — and probably a good idea, anyway — the manager or his secretary can simply telephone the dignitary's secretary or someone else on his staff to get the requisite information. Proper phrasing of the inquiry is important. Not "Gosh, what does Mr. Big like?" but rather "We were planning a little get-together and wondered if he preferred French, Italian, or our local cuisine with the peppers that will lift the top of his head off. Is there any other way that we might make him more comfortable?"

With the little things that mean a lot attended to, the regional manager can turn his attention to more substantive issues. Principal among these is the purpose of the boss's visit. This may be cut-and-dried: he's coming as he does every year to review the region's operating results and plans for the future. Or, after a little discreet inquiry, it may turn out that his intentions are not that completely formulated: he just thought it would be a good idea to come see you. In either case, but particularly the latter, take what you find out as the basis for proposing a schedule to him.

List the meetings you would like him to have, with specifics on the subjects to be discussed, the participants, and the purpose of each gathering if that isn't apparent. In drawing up the list, think first about what he hopes to accomplish, but also reflect on what your people can get out of an encounter with him. Kay Wallace, a Saint Louis–based consultant and the author of *You're the Boss*, a treatise on how to get along with corporate higher-ups, makes the point that a visit is the ideal time to show off those good people you've been developing.

If there's time for it, you might plan to have selected individuals from all levels of the local hierarchy make brief, formal presentations on what they've been doing. If that seems too hokey, try to schedule as many of them as possible to sit in on the meetings you will be having, giving each a clear-cut assignment of what he or she should be prepared to talk about. Don't confine the homework to your subordinates, however. You may find that your boss actually welcomes a list of the locals' concerns that he might speak to.

If customer calls are on the agenda — and they should be, with all the current talk about the importance of top management staying close to you-know-who — make sure that Himself is thoroughly briefed on the status of the account, the key players, and any problems that have arisen selling your stuff to these folks. Later on, you can give him a brief reprise of the key points five minutes before your appointment begins. Consider, too, the suggestion of Robert H. Welsh, formerly a division manager for Boise Cascade and now an executive recruiter with Heidrick & Struggles: the boss should call not just on good customers but, perhaps more important, also on companies you wish you were selling to but aren't. In a sales-oriented organization, he presumably got to where he is in part because of his ability to, as they say, move product.

Three final points on scheduling: First, be flexible. Have meetings or other events planned that you can kill at the last minute if you run over in more important sessions. Also, have substitute activities arranged that you can plug the boss into if something else falls through. Second, be sure to arrange some time for you to be alone with the man. It's your opportunity to create or firm up a bond between the two of you — think carefully about what you want to discuss, and how you want to talk about it. Finally, try to build into the schedule something that the boss is good at and feels good doing. Former salesmen, for example, seem to love to address — or, more accurately, exhort — assemblies of salespeople.

Once you and the boss have settled on a final plan, rehearse your people, nail down arrangements, try to foresee, and if possible head off, what might go wrong. When the big day arrives at last, meet him at the airport, get an initial reading of his mood, and set the choreography in motion accordingly. Don't expect that everything will necessarily go like clockwork, though. If things don't, be consoled by the story they tell at one of the world's largest banks of a visit by a high executive to an overseas office. Scheduled almost down to the minute, he was proceeding precisely according to the agenda. As he left one appointment and headed down the street to the next, he was promptly mugged.

Besides flagging security as an important consideration in planning a visit, the banker's story reflects the fact that there are special situations that require an extra effort on the part of the local manager. These include the visit to overseas offices, the visiting boss with spouse in tow, and the unannounced, or announced-at-the-last-minute, visit of malevolent intent.

The visit to offices abroad is conducted according to its own distinctive set of guidelines. Typically, no events, social or otherwise, are arranged on the first evening — that's reserved for recovering from jet lag. More attention than usual is paid to ensuring that the boss gets the food and drink he prefers, particularly, it seems, if he's a foreigner visiting the U.S. Lastly, there's the mandatory cocktail or dinner party with leaders of the expatriate business community.

As described by Carl Menk, formerly head of Boyden Associates, a headhunting firm with offices in fourteen countries, the drill goes something like this: Local manager has boss visiting from headquarters in the U.S. Local man calls up his counterparts around the town, the station chiefs for other U.S. companies with offices thereabouts. Counterparts dutifully turn up and talk the boss's ear off about what a great job his company's local guy is doing. Boss leaves town impressed with his local manager's contacts. The station chiefs go through the exercise on a continuing, round-robin, quid-pro-quo basis for whoever among them has a boss winging in.

Much the same supportive ethic obtains among the spouses of folks at a regional office when the boss arrives bringing with him his better half. The local manager's spouse typically spearheads the effort to entertain, but others join in to help keep the visitor pleasantly occupied. The secret, as with the boss himself, is careful planning based on good intelligence. What does the visitor like to do — play tennis, look at gorgeous scenery, take photographs? Avoid the somewhat condescending assumption that the spouse's chief passion in life is necessarily shopping.

The last of the special situations is when the boss turns up unannounced or calls you at 5 P.M. to tell you that he will be there at 10 A.M. to see you. This is usually a very bad sign — it's not unlikely that he's coming to tell you that your operation is being spun off or closed down or, even more probably, that you're fired. Telltale signs beyond the unexpected nature of the visit may warn you that the last eventuality, the ax, is coming your way. Has your pattern of communications with headquarters deteriorated or changed noticeably in any way over the last few months? Does the boss ask to meet with you at a neutral location — at a restaurant perhaps, or in a conference room rather than in your office? Does he bring with him a mysterious stranger? The stranger just might be an outplacement counselor. The boss will deliver the terminal message and then, before you can ask any questions, hand you off to him.

And how do you prepare for this kind of visit? Principally by recognizing when you get the telephone call that this could be the end. Bert Upson of the Fuchs Cuthrell outplacement firm tells of one executive who got the message late one afternoon that he should meet his boss from headquarters the next morning in the coffee shop of a local motel. When the two met, even before the boss got very far into delivering the bad news, the local man presented a three-page typewritten statement of his contributions to the company over the years, together with his demands — a continued salary for so long, ditto for benefits, and the services of an outplacement firm to help him find his next job. The startled boss acceded to all the requests, as well he should have. He had just met a man who knew how to prepare for a visit from the boss.

17

Asking for a Raise

It's like the army on the subject of sex—first we'll tell you not to do it, then we'll explain how to do it.

AT MOST COMPANIES, short of acts of moral turpitude or sheer insanity, asking for a raise is just about the worst thing you can do. It may get you fired—it happens in the real world, biz sports fans, as well as in cartoons. Even if the gambit succeeds, it stands to render you a pariah in your boss's eyes, or a piranha, or both. Unfortunately, asking for a raise is also sometimes necessary. If you feel you must persist in this terrible and dangerous undertaking, at least be apprised of the correct way to go about it.

As a first step, realize that very few managers ever explicitly request more money from their employers. While the actual number is known only to the Big Compensation Specialist Up There, people here below whose wild guesses are worth listening to generally estimate that fewer than 5 percent of executives ask for a raise in any given year.

Indeed, some of the experts are prepared to be categorical: "Executives don't ask for raises," asserts Louis J. Brindisi, Jr., a well-known compensation specialist. Brindisi, who helps companies design executive compensation plans, believes that such plans, with their negotiated performance targets and scheduled reviews, pretty much take care of the problem. There still seem to be a few managers, though, who haven't got the word that the system will provide, no questions asked, please.

What this crew is up against is the belief, ubiquitous among employers, that asking for a raise is tantamount to disloyalty. The boss feels betrayed. To fully appreciate how and why, put yourself in his shoes—an important thing to do at every stage of the raise-seeking process. There he sits behind his big desk, content in his view of himself. In come you, his trusted subordinate, who tries to hold him up. However subtly the stand-and-deliver message is worded, he'll rapidly get the point: something is wrong. He has failed to notice the good job you've done; he has let the system get out of whack; he has screwed up as a manager.

And who is it, he goes on to ruminate, who has brought him the bad news? You—the person he relied on, brought along, taught, went on business trips with. He liked you, he thought you liked—and respected, and maybe even admired—him. But it all finally comes down to the ol' cash nexus, does it? Money must be pretty important to you, more important than the company or anything that the two of you have been trying to accomplish together.

What makes the raise-seeker's dilemma particularly excruciating is that the boss may indeed have been at fault—he may well have overlooked some aspect of your performance, or not kept up with what people in your field are making at other companies. The error he is most likely to have committed, the experts say, is to let the company's performance-appraisal and associated-salary-review system fall into desuetude.

As any right-thinking person would expect, companies generally tie their decisions on salary increases to the formal performance reviews that managers receive. A real problem arises when the boss simply fails to deliver the performance appraisal, or delivers it in such a way that the subordinate doesn't know he's being formally evaluated.

If you're going to ask for a raise, you have to know how you're doing—honestly, objectively, and based on facts that you and the boss can agree on. If you don't know, it may be the boss's fault. But then again, it may be yours. In the somewhat world-weary assessment of one astute observer of life within corporations, "Fully ninety percent of the people think they're in the top ten percent."

In working toward an undeluded assessment of your own performance—which will be the basis of the case you eventually present to the boss—begin by gathering hard data on what you've done for the company. Lists of sales consummated, reports generated, or projects completed represent usable ammunition; memories of when the chairman said a kind word to you do not.

As you sift through the adventures and misadventures of the past few months, continually pose one question to yourself: why am I asking for a raise? Are you really looking for more money to compensate you for an unnoticed job well done, or are you looking for something else — more recognition, say, or salve for some wrong the company has done you? If it turns out that you're chafing for more authority or angry because someone else was promoted but you weren't, you'll probably do better wrestling with those problems directly than converting them into a bid for higher pay.

In assembling the facts to be used in making your pitch, be aware of the kinds of information that the company will look at in evaluating it. At enlightened employers', salary decisions are based on the individual's performance, of course, but also on how the business he's working in is doing, along with consideration of what people in comparable positions elsewhere are getting. The company's information on the last item, based on industrywide surveys, is inevitably better than the anecdotal stuff you've got.

Some types of information that you might be thinking of proffering will not, in fact, be of interest to the boss. The experts all agree that talk about how much you need the extra money is simply irrelevant, particularly coming from managers. Your employer also need not concern himself with your impressive educational credentials if they have no bearing on what you do for him. Drawing comparisons between your salary and what others in your shop make will probably be of limited effectiveness. It will alert the boss that you think you're being treated unfairly, but usually won't set him to weeping guiltily, especially if — as is usually the case — the dope you've got on somebody else's pay is wrong.

Certain other cards are almost too dangerous to play in discussions of salary. Chief among these is the one bearing the legend "I have an offer from another company, and if you don't raise my pay to match it, I'll go there." Employers have a name for this type of overture — they call it blackmail. While their responses to it vary widely, none of these responses is particularly propitious for the perpetrator.

The boss may cave in, join the bidding, and end up giving you the raise. You'll probably be sorry anyway. "Nine out of ten people who get the raise and stay on end up regretting they stayed," observes

Robert C. Bleke, an Atlanta-based psychologist and consultant to corporations. "They're never treated the same way again."

Other bosses will try to talk you out of it—"This is a fine company, you have a great future here"—but, that failing, they will send you on your way with best wishes. As one honcho who has been through the drill puts it, with an almost sincere smile on her face, "Sometimes, in good conscience, you just have to advise them to take the other offer." Still other bosses may, after a bit of deliberation, fire you. The standard line goes something like this: "Gosh, I realize now that it hasn't been working out between us. Why don't you take the other offer, and if for some reason it falls through, we can arrange for outplacement." Is this a rare riposte? Hardly. "God, it happens a lot," reports William J. Morin, chairman of Drake Beam Morin, the outplacement firm.

Besides knowing which cards to play, you need to know when to play them. The best times to ask for a raise, to the extent that there are any good times, are, in decreasing order of attractiveness, when you're promoted, when you're given significant new responsibilities but no promotion, and just after you've pulled off a major coup.

The standard raise for managers when they're promoted runs around 20 percent to 25 percent, compensation experts say, about what you should expect if you jump ship to take a job elsewhere. If your company wants to give the newly promoted you more money but not that much, and you call them on it, then in a sense you're not asking for a raise—you're just dickering over the amount.

Okay, you've gathered your evidence, calculated the timing, and you're determined to go through with this horrible mistake, you reckless devil you. What precisely do you do next? You send a memo to the boss. The last thing you want to do is surprise him; he'll be defensive enough anyway. You, in contrast, have to be what corporate types call positive—upbeat, solicitous, reassuring.

In preparing the memo, follow the formula of Molly Lukenheimer, the head of the career-counseling practice of Hay Associates, probably the nation's best-known consultants on compensation. Your missive should consist of four parts. In the first, express your loyalty and commitment to the company briefly but warmly. In the second, list the goals that were set for you and your operation, together with your accomplishments in meeting those goals. In the third part, with all the tact that you can muster, request that you be considered for a salary increase and ask for an appointment to disucss the matter. In the fourth part — as by now you should have guessed — reiterate your loyalty to the company. It may help if you offer to sacrifice your firstborn child as a demonstration of your fealty.

When you have your meeting, at the start assure your boss that you don't expect any resolution of the matter right then — you just want him to think about it. Then present your case. Remember, remember, remember: never seem to be complaining, never whine, never ever threaten. What may be most important is that your boss and you agree on a set of expectations about your future performance and how you're to be compensated for it. If you can't get even that out of the session, all the experts say, you probably should look for a job somewhere else.

Just don't say we didn't warn you, though, you ingrate.

CAREER CHOKEPOINTS

☒ 18 ☒

The Neglected Art of Career Planning

Where will you be in twenty years?
Even more problematic: how are you going to get there?

WE WORRY about it endlessly: how am I doing? They sure are moving Al ahead quickly — why, he'll be a vice president next year at what, age thirty-three? Here I am, hopelessly stuck, thirty-five, and a bare ruined choir where late the sweet birds sang. We fatigue our loved ones with whining on the subject: I just know the boss doesn't like me — he barely had three civil words for me today, the churl. We dream: when I become regional sales manager, that'll really set their heads bobbing. What we don't do about our careers, astonishingly enough, is to plan them.

It is the almost universal impression among people in a position to know — executive recruiters, career counselors, professional advisers to the recently fired — that the only time most businesspersons do any systematic career planning is when they're just starting out ("What do I do with my M.B.A.?"), when they've been let go, or when they're so unhappy with their jobs that they'll clutch at any alternative. Gerald Simmons, president of the Handy Associates headhunting firm, expresses the common perception: "The executives I've seen are good at the tactics of career planning, thinking about the next job and how to get there, but they don't give sufficient thought to strategic planning for fifteen or twenty years hence."

The rule that almost no one plans his career, and then only at the wrong time, seems to be changing, however. Already there are interesting exceptions. According to published reports, Mary Cunningham, of sainted memory, in her first months at Bendix prepared a two-hundred-page career plan. In her twenties, she was going to develop her "instrument" (whatever that means); in her thirties, maximize her financial independence and credentials; in her forties, position herself for real power.

Ms. Cunningham may be a harbinger of a trend. Business schools at Harvard and Dartmouth now offer formal courses in self-assessment, designed explicitly to be the basis for career planning. Self-help books on making job changes proliferate — the best-known example, Richard N. Bolles's *What Color Is Your Parachute?*, has sold two million copies. Even computer technology is being called into play. With programs such as the Educational Testing Service's SIGI, short for System of Interactive Guidance and Information, an undergraduate can sit at a computer keyboard and define personal values, find compatible occupations, look at employment prospects in those occupations, and then plan a course of study leading into the right field.

Another information-society example of good technology being used to cast fake pearls before an ever-widening audience of real swine? The basic question is whether you can indeed plan a career. Can a computer, or your own assiduous calculations, ensure that in thirty years you'll be head wookie of a Fortune Interplanetary 500 corporation? Of course not, no more than a business's strategic plan can guarantee a certain market share five years hence. But a career plan, laying out as it should a few goals, almost certainly improves your chances of attaining those goals. It also brings with it a bit of serenity, which just may even out your stroke as you swim through the riptide-swept waters of corporate life.

The essence of good career planning, you see — or you will see, as the scales drop from your dream-clouded peepers — is casting a clinical eye over careers in general, over the setting in which you pursue yours, and, finally and hardest of all, over yourself.

On careers in general, you should begin by making explicit which concept of a career you've been employing, and then think about whether that truly suits you. Ah, you didn't realize that you were using a concept? Sure, you have been. To the extent that you've been running on such questionable assumptions as "If I work hard, I'll keep being promoted to higher and higher levels of responsibility," you've implicitly adopted a concept.

The point is to broaden the repertoire available to you. In this regard, consider the work of Michael J. Driver, a professor of management and organizational behavior at the University of Southern California. Driver posits four different career concepts, identifies the kinds of organizations you're likely to find each in, and outlines the challenges and rewards particular to each concept.

The steady-state concept, for example, centers on a lifelong commitment to a particular profession or craft — law, say, or medicine, or carpentry. People are drawn to steady-state careers, the research suggests, either out of a desire for security — the tenure that professors win, for instance — or by the prospect of steadily increasing their competence in a discipline. They have to make their choice early in life, and thereafter must zealously guard against falling behind technological changes in their area. Anybody opting for a steady-state career these days ought to make some provision in their plans for retraining along the way.

The linear-career concept, by comparison, takes as its crucial assumption continued upward movement through a hierarchy. Much beloved of corporations, this concept is likely to flourish in organizations whose structures resemble a tall, narrow pyramid. Beckoning as rewards are the power and status of the top jobs and, at least for some climbers, the recognition and sense of achievement that go along with attaining each new level. The attendant danger? Becoming what in certain quarters of the AT&T empire used to be referred to as a "po-po"—someone pissed on and passed over.

Devotees of Driver's transitory-career concept typically aren't in one place long enough to have this happen to them. Their bag — or hobo's bundle — is erratic movement from job to job, employer to employer. Among the transitory types, you may find semiskilled workers, corporate-turnaround artists, members of the underclass, and your twenty-eight-year-old son who's having a little trouble deciding what he's going to do. They all seem to enjoy the variety that their career concept affords them, and the time off.

Last, and least clear, is Driver's spiral-career concept. Someone with the spiral concept makes at least one major career change after investing years in something else. The concept accounts for all those manufacturing executives who, in the course of their midlife crises, decide to become psychologists. Spiral types seek personal growth and, in some cases, the chance to be nurturant.

Just knowing which concept fits you best isn't enough by itself — as Driver points out, you also have to take into account how favored that concept is in an organization you might work for and, indeed, in society at large. Steady-state types, for example, may encounter a bit of turbulence if they go to work for a neo-Darwinian, linear-loving enterprise where every self-respecting manager is expected to be red in tooth and claw. Driver worries, too, about the baby-boom generation: after flirting with spiral values in the late 1960s, they seem increasingly to be turning toward objectives associated with the linear. While the latter concept is still the most common in our society, that won't ensure top-of-the-pyramid jobs for the hordes of boomers who seek them.

Armed with alternative career concepts — whether Driver's or someone else's — you can proceed to the second imperative in career planning: know thyself, or, more specifically, thy wants, skills, and style. Wants might seem at first blush the easiest to divine, but often, O treacherous human heart, they prove to be the toughest. This seems especially true for individuals who have been riding the lemming express at every stage of their lives: do well in secondary school so you can get into a good college; do well in college to get into a good professional school; go there immediately upon leaving college and do well so that you can get the job all your peers want. Suddenly you find yourself an investment banker with nary a clue to your true inclinations.

Career counselors tend to get at wants by exploring values and interests. To do this, they may simply talk with you, or they may have you take a test, such as the ubiquitous Strong-Campbell Interest Inventory. If psychological tests have a place anywhere, it's here — they're being done at the testee's behest, not for his employer; the test taker has every reason to be honest.

Still, results must be interpreted with caution born of a thorough understanding of the test's limitations. Moreover, in deciding whether to take a particular job, test findings have to be applied with intelligence bordering on cunning. The late Roderic Hodgins, formerly the director of placement and counseling at Harvard Business School and later a psychologist with a private career-counseling practice, used to offer an instructive hypothetical example. Two men take the same test. It shows that the first is interested in the big picture and not inclined at all to think about details, while the second man is just the opposite. On the strength of the test, the first man takes a job as executive assistant to someone who thinks megacepts as he does. The boss, it turns out, is looking for an assistant, not to share his oceanic speculations, but to pick up his plane tickets and handle other details. The second man probably would have been a lot happier in the job.

On the matter of skills, you might think that after ten years in the work force, you have a pretty good idea of just what your aptitudes are. You just might be wrong, though, you cocky so-and-so — here too a bit of systematic digging can be enlightening. Outplacement expert Stephen Morris tells of counseling an accountant of twenty years' standing who had recently been fired. Morris administered a standard battery of aptitude tests and was surprised to find that the accountant scored in the lowest 10 percent in terms of quantitative abilities. Confronted with this somewhat incongruous finding, the test-taker's response was, "Gee, maybe this explains why I've been unhappy for twenty years." A counselor at school had told him that accounting was a good field to get into; he's now a salesman.

An assessment of personal style — the euphemism that, along with "chemistry," is used by businesspersons afraid to breathe a whisper of "psychology"— should be attempted, too, particularly by managers who have encountered problems dealing with folks on their current job. The object is to figure out your own style, and to compare it with the norm in any organization or field you're thinking of joining. The outplacement firm of Drake Beam & Morin, for example, helps job-seekers see themselves as predominantly one of four different stylistic types: the misleadingly labeled sensors (get-it-out-the-door, do-it-now types), feelers (interested in people, and how they're getting along), thinkers (analytic engines, they love to crunch numbers), and intuiters (long-range thinkers, always casting their minds five years out).

Pop psychology? Plumbing the Freudian depths it ain't, but it can be a boon to nonintrospective types who have gone around stepping on people's toes, or being stepped on. Drake Beam's experts say that many an executive, once he has become familiar with the categories, achieves a better understanding not only of what he should do, but also of why he was fired: he was a feeler, say, his former boss a Neanderthal sensor.

If you want to be utterly complete about the self-analytical side of career planning — and even few professional counselors go this far — you'll have to take into account the ways you'll change as you grow older. This will lead you into a field called adult development, which holds that just as there are phases a child goes through — the terrible twos, for instance — so are there also phases in adult life, each with its own developmental challenges to be overcome, each likely to be encountered at a particular age. Erik Erikson, the Harvard psychologist, and Daniel Levinson, the Yale professor whose research provided the basis for the book *The Seasons of a Man's Life,* have done scholarly work on the subject; Gail Sheehy popularized it in her best-seller *Passages.*

The implication for career planning is that you should seek some fit between what you'll be doing at work and the developmental tasks you'll be wrestling with at each stage of life. Levinson's research indicates, for example, that in their late thirties, most males go through a phase he calls "becoming one's own man" — the characteristic challenges include becoming "a senior member in one's world," speaking out in one's own voice, and attaining a greater measure of authority. If you've adopted a steady-state career concept and find yourself at thirty-seven working exclusively with professional peers, you may have to seek channels for your developmental energies outside work.

Once your career-concept and self-assessment ducks are lined up and quacking euphonically, the choice of a particular field of endeavor may be surprisingly easy. Most of the standard sources of career-counseling information offer reams on what people in particular jobs do, and a surprising number can provide you something approaching psychological profiles of persons happily pursuing this or that vocation. Your best information, of course, will come from chatting with such folks. Don't ask, "How do you like your work?" Do ask, "What precisely do you do — day by day, hour by hour, even minute by minute?" A number of M.B.A.'s who thought that by getting into strategy consulting they'd soon be whispering policy in the chairman's ear have found themselves doing lots of glorified cost accounting instead.

In all this it may help to have an outside counselor assisting you —

indeed, when you do the self-assessment part, the cold bath of objectivity he offers may be impossible to achieve on your own. While the industry of professional career counselors is still small, it seems to be growing. The human-resources department at your company may be able to refer you to one; if asking there would be impolitic, try the placement office at the college or professional school you attended. One caution: investigate thoroughly before using any firm that advertises itself in the newspapers as offering executive placement and associated career counseling, particularly if it asks you to pay up front.

Finally, leave room in your calculations for the inevitable effects of old-fashioned luck, whether good or bad. Career planning, properly done, won't necessarily deliver the breaks, but it will ready you to take full advantage if any should come your way. There you are, strapping yourself in for a long, boring transcontinental airplane ride when who should sit down beside you but the vice chairman of your company. Somewhere over the Rockies, after the second or third martini, he idly asks you, "Bob, where do you see yourself in five or ten years?" You'll have an answer. Boy, will you have an answer.

19

Just Promoted

*Oddly enough, the experience of being elevated
can bring with it some low-down disquietude.*

CONGRATULATIONS, boyo or girlo — you've just been promoted. And the fantasies begin. It's *Chariots of Fire*, and you're crossing the finish line before everyone else: your face in a rictus of exertion and elation, dewy-eyed fans gasping with delight, background music hitting the heights of fortissimo. Or something out of *Patton* perhaps, maybe the final scene where old Blood and Guts recalls the details of a Roman triumph: your garlanded, laughing subordinates astride the horses that draw your chariot, your enemies — those guys in the finance department who said your project would never work — dragging themselves along in chains before you, a slave standing beside you holding above your head the crown of top management.

Hold, as they say, your horses. The slave, you will recollect, has another function — to whisper repeatedly in the victor's ear that he is not a god. In your case he should also be murmuring that the transition to come is trickier than it looks, and that your ties to others in the company may be strained considerably. If he's a distinctly savvy corporate apparatchik, he will confide too that there are a few rules for successfully negotiating this particular career passage.

The process should begin with a ferret-eyed assessment of precisely why you were promoted. First disabuse yourself of the illusion, surprisingly widespread even if usually secret, that it's because the company loves you. Corporations don't love people, at least not the way Mommy and Daddy do. On the other hand, neither should you assume that they're so blindly bureaucratic that they've promoted you just because you've served time and paid your dues.

The big boys apparently saw in you the qualities they deem necessary for getting results in your new job. No cause for a swelled head there. The requisite qualities may not be all that healthy — your maso-chistic tendency to work inhuman hours, say, or your Mack-the-Knife ability to fire people, which promises eventually to send your spouse to divorce court and your kids to reform school. You may be merely a right-body-in-the-right-place-at-the-right-time historical accident — the only Urdu-speaking petroleum engineer on call when the company decides to build a refinery in Pakistan. Moreover, the big guys may be wrong or, worse yet, caught up in their own fantasies. "It's pernicious if the boss has a habit of making and breaking golden boys and girls," says Abraham Zaleznik, a Harvard Business School professor and a psychoanalyst. "Such bosses run through people like paper clips. They have to have an idealized subordinate, and no one can possibly measure up."

To bore through the confusion and get a sense of what the bosses are looking for, at the outset seek a definition of exactly what your new responsibilities will be. Not "I'm the new West Coast sales manager (wow!)," but rather "Hmmm, here's what I'm expected to do on a day-by-day, even hour-by-hour basis." You may find yourself a bit overwhelmed, particularly if you haven't worked closely before with the person whose shoes you're expected to fill.

For help in sorting out your new responsibilities, go to the author-ities. If you're replacing someone, and he's leaving the job amicably, debrief him as thoroughly as possible, particularly on reporting rela-tionships, hidden agendas, and the political lay of the land. If the company puts great faith in written job descriptions, do a close textual examination of yours — you may want to negotiate changes. Robert H. Thomas of Peter Rogen & Associates, a consulting firm that helps companies help their employees through the thickets of "transition management," says the result can be an "empowering document."

Most important, talk to your new boss. Talk seriously — take notes if it doesn't cause him to freeze over, ask questions, listen, listen, listen. Get the meat and potatoes — his version of what the guy in your job is supposed to do — but also be alert for the sauces and seasonings — what he thinks of your subordinates, how the last in-cumbent screwed up, what he likes and dislikes in his own work. Whatever else you do, though, get straight precisely what he expects of you.

Look to his example, too, in matters of style, both managerial and social. Academic research seems to confirm the common perception that the higher one looks in a company, the more one finds that business is accomplished by means of personal relationships, the exchange of information, and yes—pardon the expression—networking. To play this game you may have to learn, or even adopt, some of the folkways of the natives. The obvious dilemma: how much is merely taking on the patina of top management and how much is surrendering your individuality? If your new peers are, for example, a bunch of Ivy League milksops, do you think twice about mentioning your bowling scores? If they're all burr-headed ex-Marine commandos, do you go easy on the big words and the Nuit du Wimp cologne?

Here it also helps enormously to have a mentor. No chortling about psychobabble, please. Perhaps because the idea has grown so fashionable that we now see the helpful creatures where we didn't before, perhaps because of the way people get ahead these days—whatever the reason, one recently promoted manager after another reports that he has such a figure boosting him, and that the mentor's advice is particularly valuable in learning the new job.

He may be the only soul you can confide in—promotions can chill relations both with your former peers and, more surprisingly, your new peers, who used to be your superiors. "It was rough," a twenty-eight-year-old promotee in a biomedical manufacturing company says of his dealings with past equals. "Rather than go out with me for a beer after work, they'd find something else to do or not invite me." Others noted a lot of testing questions from former peers, often in the guise of joshing: "Well, how's the air up there?"

To reassure the folks, talk to them more than usual, maybe even sharing some of what you've learned after your elevation. In the trickiest cases—former peers who are now working for you and subordinates who were jockeying for the job you won—make a point of having serious conversations. After a little banter on themes like the luck of the draw and the mysterious ways of corporations, you should discuss what each of you hopes to get out of your work together.

Dealing with your new peers may be even more unsettling. "I felt like the new kid on the block," recalls a soft-drink company executive of his last promotion. *Kid* is the right word—people commonly feel somewhat infantilized by the change, even as the process forces them to grow up and see the once-looming parental figures, their former superiors, as regular old flawed adults. The rule of behavior to be observed here is just opposite from the one for dealing with former peers—talk less, listen, and watch.

At the same time—and this is the most important precept for the newly anointed—act like what you've been promoted to become. If you've got the boss's job, play the boss. You'll undoubtedly have to acquire new skills, particularly if it's your first managerial post. "It's a big challenge when you move from running yourself to running other people," as one junior executive put it. "I had to throw out a lot of personal habits"—commonly in such areas as managing time and delegating work. But while you're learning the ropes, everyone will be watching, so you should appear to know what you're doing.

There will be temptations to do otherwise, many brought on by what may prove surprisingly sharp self-doubts. "A certain amount of anxiety is perfectly normal," observes Sandra Kirmeyer, a professor of industrial relations at Cornell, who echoes the view of most experts. Many argue that women have it worse in this respect—that they tend to question themselves more or fear that increased authority entails a loss of femininity.

For men and women alike, the true test is what you do with the anxiety. One bad idea: becoming too dependent on subordinates for advice—a natural enough response, according to the psychologists, but something you may rue when you get your feet on the ground. One good idea: making a plan. It need not be a five-year strategy for your new unit. A step-by-step program to acquire necessary technical skills or a systematic scheme to meet your new staff will serve equally well to steady you and provide some sense of accomplishment.

You should also build into your thinking the possibility that the new job simply won't work out. The Peter Principle—that one is promoted until he reaches the level where he's incompetent—still has a place in American corporate life. Your only consolation may be that you'll probably know before anyone else, sometimes after only three or four months in your new position. After thinking it through, go to your boss and confess, but carefully. Not "I can't handle this," but rather "It seems a bad fit." In an enlightened company, he may take your approach as a cry for help, or the two of you may agree that some other job suits you better.

Such considerations point up a frequently overlooked opportunity inherent in being promoted: elevation provides a wonderful occasion to meditate profitably on your ties to the corporation. When the company smiles brightest on you, what better time to think about how important those smiles have become in your life? You might use as your text the tag line from a movie you probably didn't see, a box-office failure called *One Trick Pony*. It's the bittersweet tale of a rock musician fallen on hard times, a character who has discovered that he has turned into the limited-repertory animal of the title, no big draw with audiences. While the music industry may not be a precise analogue for the ball-bearing business in which you serve, the movie's message may have a certain resonance in describing the solicitude of some employers: rock 'n' roll will give you a few laughs, but it won't do you any favors.

20

Passed Over

Sure, it's a blow to your ego, but maybe not to your career—at least not the first time it happens to you.

OH, MAMA, it hurts. You wanted the promotion. You worked hard for it. In the secret, smug recesses of your heart, you even expected it. Then the company ups and gives the job to someone else. In the eyes of the brass, you're not as good as he is. And now everybody knows it.

Steady, boy, or girl. While being passed over does rank high up there among job-related affronts, experts on the subject say there is life afterward—maybe better life. True, it typically takes a while to recover from the blow, and even years later few executives want to talk about the matter. But according to people they confide in—executive recruiters, career counselors, and business school professors—many have found the experience a real eye-opener.

Ideally, your boss should call you in privately to give you the word before it reaches the rest of the organization. Unless you saw the blow coming and are prepared to discuss it coolly, just tell him that you are disappointed and want a little time to think through your situation. Before leaving his office, make an appointment to talk the matter over two or three weeks thence.

Once you have a grip on yourself, go congratulate the promotee. In your words to the winner, dwell not on the horse race or its conclusion, but on the future. You may end up working for the lucky devil, so you might as well get the new relationship between you two off on the right foot. In the late 1970s, Stanley Gault was one of six or so General Electric executives in the running to succeed Reginald Jones as chief executive of the company. When he didn't make the cut to vice chairman, he telephoned each of the three finalists. "I congratulated them and wished them the very best," he recalls. "I had become a big shareholder at GE and I told them to put their noses to the grindstone to protect my interests." Class-act Gault quickly went on to success elsewhere, as C.E.O. of Rubbermaid Inc.

The public decencies attended to, you can go back to your office, close the door, and brood. Don't be surprised if you find yourself on an emotional roller coaster, suffering periodic breathtaking swoops of anger and occasional descents into something like depression. It may help to take a fairly clinical perspective toward what you are going through. Professor Larry Cummings of Northwestern's Kellogg Graduate School of Management says that his work has uncovered some key variables that largely determine the severity of anyone's reaction to being passed over. Among them:

Did you expect it or not? If you did, it probably won't hurt as much. If you didn't, you should ask yourself why. Did the organization do a bad job of telling you where you stood, or were you oblivious to realities you should have picked up on?

Where are you in your career, and in your life? The point is not how old you are, but how many alternatives you have. Being passed over at thirty-five can be just as painful as it is at fifty-five. If you have prospects, though, whether of transferring to another division or taking early retirement and starting another career, you probably won't feel as bummed out.

What do you think caused you to be passed over — was it you, or the proverbial circumstances beyond your control? You obviously are going to feel worse if you think you lost out because you didn't work hard — or well — enough.

How supportive are your family and friends? If you can't talk the pain over with your spouse or someone else, you're probably in trouble.

Your aim in mulling all this over is to quiet your emotions sufficiently to let you think straight. Joseph A. Alutto, dean of the school of management at SUNY/Buffalo, summarizes what you have to figure out: "Your failure to win promotion may be a blow to your ego. But how damaging is it to your career?"

Wise managers understand the difference. Hicks Waldron, chairman of Avon, recounts his experience of being passed over: "When I was at GE, I was interviewed for the job of general manager of the radio department. Becoming a general manager at GE is like going to heaven without the inconvenience of dying. I wanted the job so bad I could taste it. I lost out to a friend of mine. I decided there were plenty of general manager jobs at GE. If I just kept my nose clean, logic told me I would be a candidate again. Three months later the job as general manager of the phonograph department opened up. I got it."

In assessing the effect on your career, you need to find out as much as you can about why they chose someone else instead of you. Begin preparing for your interview with the boss. Review your last few performance appraisals. Was there some theme your superiors kept sounding but you never quite heard? Try to get your friends in the organization to talk to you frankly about how you come across, and don't limit the discussion to issues of job performance. Consider the unpleasant possibility that you lost out not because of your work, but because the boss gets along better with the other guy.

From the outset of your conversation with the boss, frame what you say in terms of the benefit to the company. Your tune should be "I'm just trying to do my best for The Old Corp. How can I improve?" Proudly display whatever shreds of enthusiasm he may have left you. In asking questions, a bit of indirectness may help at first: What does that job require by way of expertise? Who exactly makes the selection? The real decision-maker may turn out to be not your boss, but his, or somebody even higher up. Gradually circle in on the big question: Why did he get the job rather than me?

The experts differ on whether you can expect straight answers to such inquiries. Particularly if the reasons for the choice smack of chemistry, the boss may simply find some way to rationalize the choice, blowing up this or that kind of experience — which the winner has but you don't — as a prerequisite for the job. You may have to force the discussion a little by raising possible problems that the boss may have with you but can't bring himself to mention. "Am I too easy on my subordinates? Too demanding? What do I do that rubs you the wrong way?" You are looking for a response along the lines of "Well, now that you mention it, you could do a bit better at . . ." In all the probing, don't forget to ask the cleanup question: What are my chances of being promoted in the future?

With the answers you receive, begin to do some remedial career planning. Remind yourself of your long-term goals. Does what happened to you represent an insuperable obstacle to reaching them at this company, or merely a slight setback? One special caution to include in your calculations: if this is the second time you have been passed over at this company, you should begin to seriously consider the possibility that you may have plateaued, as they say. William J. Morin, chairman of the Drake Beam Morin outplacement firm, offers some blunt advice: "Prepare to leave if you get passed over once. Leave if you get passed over twice."

Well, maybe. You probably do have more options than you realize. Consider, based on what you have learned about the reasons for your failure, whether this organization is the right one for you. Have you been treated fairly? Do you respect the person who was promoted? Nothing reveals more about the values that currently prevail within a company than the people management chooses to promote. Do you really want to do all that you now understand may be required to win the next promotion?

The ultimate question, of course, is whether you want to continue to define success as movement ever upward through the hierarchy. Is it just possible that you could find happiness, whether in your present job or elsewhere, without ever being promoted again? Don't think it will be easy. Judith Bardwick, author of *The Plateauing Trap*, describes what's required: "You have to develop an understanding that there are other forms of success. This means understanding how deeply the motivation to win out in the competition for upward mobility has been drilled into you." That's why being passed over hurts so much. But should it?

21

When a Manager Stumbles

Even good managers suffer reverses. What separates the winners from the also-rans is how they bounce back.

WILLIAM R. LAIDIG had it happen to him. He describes it: "As a young manager, I tried to put in a maintenance system at a paper mill that had been doing things the same way for a thousand years. I never could get to first base. In the three years I was responsible for that operation, I tried my damnedest. It never did get done." How did he explain the failure to his superiors? "With my hat in my hands," he says. "I told them that instead of making headway, I had solidified resistance to the system enough that we should go off and do something more profitable. My boss looked at me and said, 'I knew this was happening six months ago. Next time don't be so stupid for so long.'"

That was more than ten years ago, but the lesson stayed with Laidig. "I probably learned more from being unsuccessful at that one than I did from many successes," he recently told an interviewer. "I learned that if I couldn't get the crew that I wanted to apply an idea to appreciate and understand it, then it was a lousy idea whether I thought so or not." Of such insights is managerial acumen made. In October 1984, Laidig, fifty-seven, was named chief executive of Great Northern Nekoosa, No. 222 of the Fortune 500 industrial corporations and one of the better-performing forest products companies.

A curious discontinuity clouds the way most executives think about managerial reverses. In describing the careers of others whom they believe successful, they tend to sketch a pattern of uninterrupted movement upward. "I'd bet anything that the highly successful executives didn't have a real bust or failure," opines the vice president for human resources of a large computer company, who ought to know better. On the other hand, in reflecting on their own histories, even high achievers admit major stumbles. Researchers from the Center for Creative Leadership, a nonprofit outfit in Greensboro, North Carolina, that delves into these matters, interviewed eighty-six successful Fortune 500 executives about their careers. One finding: "Sixty-six percent of the executives reported either missing promotions, being exiled to poor jobs, being caught in a major conflict with the boss, contributing to a business failure, or simply being overwhelmed by the enormousness of the job."

In another CCL study, researchers compared the careers of twenty successful executives with those of twenty so-called derailed executives from the same companies. Both types had made mistakes. But where the also-rans typically tried to deny or conceal their errors, or blame them on others, the managerial winners stepped up to them — forewarning colleagues, trying to solve the problems caused, and then, when the dust had settled and the lessons had been learned, moving on to think about something else.

An executive's response to any particular reverse will obviously depend in part on the circumstances. Does it occur early or late in his career? How quickly do new opportunities present themselves? And, of great import, how bad are the effects on others? Ann M. Morrison, a member of the research team at the Center for Creative Leadership, tells of interviewing one executive who had had a subordinate die in his arms, the victim of an accident that might have been prevented if better safety procedures had been in place. Years later the executive still carried around with him thoughts of what he might possibly have done to avert the tragedy.

How an executive responds to a setback will depend finally on what psychologists call his ego resilience. How strong, and realistic, is his sense of self-worth? Is his conscience energetic enough to spur him to take remedial action — to acknowledge his error, say, and try to understand how he went wrong — but not so insatiably punitive that it never gives him a moment's peace thereafter?

The answers to questions like these tend to divide managers into four types in terms of their response to setbacks.

The Bulletproof. These managers may have swelled heads, but their egos are so hard and unbending that mistakes just bounce off uselessly. The stumble didn't happen, or if it did, was somebody else's fault. Such executives fail and fail again, but almost never learn from their experience. Their tendency to play it close to the vest, and to cover up if necessary, makes them prime candidates for derailment.

The Rebounders. They score the highest on ego resilience. Besides learning from their setbacks, these executives use the experience to reassure themselves about their ability to cope with adversity. "They have huge successes and huge failures at times," notes Roderick Gilkey, a psychologist and professor of management at Atlanta's Emory University, "but they don't experience themselves as losers, and therefore they don't come across as losers."

Charles Spector, vice chairman of Apollo Computer, admits that while he was a young executive at Digital Equipment Corp., he managed a few products that "didn't fly at all." In bouncing back, he displayed an attitude characteristic of rebounders: "I don't get emotionally tied to an idea, issue, or business consideration," he says. "I'm always willing to change my mind based on new data."

The Changers. These managers' egos are less flexible than the rebounders', and a bit weaker. Reverses almost always present an opportunity for self-examination, to put it mildly. Changers avail themselves of the opportunity, and come away transformed: they gain a more realistic sense of their own strengths and weaknesses and of their career potential — which can be a gut-wrenching experience. Yet experts report that executives who survive such a passage frequently become better managers of people — having blown it once themselves, they're more tolerant of others' shortcomings, more patient, more helpful.

The Broken. Brittle, eggshell egos. These managers just don't make it back, in the sense that they're never again as effective as they were before trouble struck. If they're ambulatory at all, they're likely to overcontrol others and to run from risks.

Within the limits of your own ego resilience, there are steps you can take to come out of a reverse more like a rebounder. First, don't be panicked by the welter of emotions that hits you initially, including the predictable fear, depression, and anger.

Second, take control of any aspect of the setback that you can — even if all you can get a hold on is your own response. Begin by acknowledging that you have a problem and trying to figure out just how you were responsible. You may then be able to control some of the fallout by warning others.

Finally, talk to other people about what you should learn from the reverse, especially what you should learn about yourself. Opening such conversations isn't easy, but the payoff may be more enduring than the crisis itself. You may, for example, finally be able to get straight talk from your superiors on how you're doing.

Take to heart the experience of a young manager at Intel whose group missed a fundamental turn in the market. He was afraid to tell his wife. "Her initial reaction turned out to be, 'Gee, that's too bad. What can we do about it? I want to help any way I can,'" he reports. He then mustered the courage to talk the matter over with friends. "Some of them said, 'It's about time you opened up and let us help you.' That probably cemented some friendships I still have ten years later." Even the company was supportive, heaping him with loads of advice and encouragement.

It's almost enough to make you want to go out and take a stumble.

❈ 22 ❈

When the Boss Is in Trouble

He needs a cool head and a clinical eye somewhere about him.
The best candidate just may be, gulp, you.

QUIETLY AT FIRST, the jungle drums begin the threnody. Who would have thought they'd ever turn down one of his projects? The division's sales are going nowhere, and with all that inventory he built up . . . Man, I've never seen a presentation of his received so poorly. Soon, just about everyone has the word: the boss is in trouble.

Step by reluctant step, he's dragged closer to the precipice, and with every step the natives hunker down a bit farther. The top floor cut his budget by 40 percent. Gee, have you noticed how everybody's door is shut all the time these days? The chairman avoids him like the plague. Hmmm, maybe it's a good time to take a vacation.

Finally, to a crescendo of mutterings and cries, he's thrown off the cliff — sacked, fired, axed, a sacrifice to whatever Baal presides over the fortunes of executives.

Short of being given the old heave-ho oneself, few passages in the managerial life offer as much opportunity for sheer, gut-wrenching disquietude as watching one's boss go down in flames. "It scares the hell out of you," confesses an executive who went through the experience twice, each time registering "an honest-to-God fear reaction." Professor Neal Thornberry of Babson College, who teaches a course dealing in part with office politics, compares the emotional hardship worked upon subordinates to the loss of a loved one in private life, "whether you liked the loved one or not."

Still, for the executive one or two rungs below the marked man, there are ways to cope. Be prepared to ask yourself a few simple questions — how good am I at what I do, really? how loyal? to whom or what? — and perhaps to be a bit thicker-skinned than before. You may well emerge a better manager.

The first point to absorb is that it *can* happen to you. Bosses are an increasingly endangered species. Accurate statistics probably can't be compiled — how many resigned-to-pursue-other-interests situations are actually jump-or-be-pushed? — but imprecise indicators point to an upswing in executive firings. Under the banner of restructuring, one company after another has trimmed its managerial staff. Outplacement counseling firms report that business is terrific.

In part this reflects the lessons learned in the recession of the early eighties; in part it's a result of the wave of takeovers. Observes one worldly-wise headhunter, "Whenever an executive friend at a recently acquired company calls to tell me about the assurances that the new parent has given him, I just tell him, 'Don't believe them.' " But a more fundamental, long-term trend may also be at work: in the face of strong foreign competition and an increasingly skeptical stock market, newly active boards of directors are growing restive with less-than-immediately-successful executive performance.

The plight of a subordinate who thinks his boss may be drowning in the new currents divides into two distinct questions — first, what to do before the blow falls, if it ever does, and second, what to do after he's fired, particularly if the event took the subordinate by surprise.

With respect to the first, the common wisdom among the organizational-behavior boys holds that underlings usually are the first to sense trouble, sometimes six months before the leader knows, or admits to himself, that anything is wrong. Executives who have been through the drill question this, however. "The nature of people who get into trouble," concludes one veteran, "is such that more often than not their direct subordinates are the last to figure it out." The same psychology that keeps someone from going to his superiors with a problem — or a chief executive from constantly informing his board, soliciting their views, and generally dragging them into the whole sordid mess — also prevents him from leveling with the troops.

Indeed, a won't-delegate-anything honcho often seeks to monopolize the communications that his subordinates receive, whether from the boss's boss or from elsewhere in the organization. "He kept saying, 'Don't pay any attention to what's going on,' " recalls a corporate P.R. man who used to report directly to a now-deposed chairman.

Somewhat ruefully, another executive describes his enmeshment with a president who was subsequently shot out from over him: "We were so focused on the problems, and working so hard, that I let my contacts go."

Don't. What you, and just maybe the boss, need most in this perilous strait is information — objective, unfiligreed, and from outside the bunker. The available sources might be a well-connected peer in another division, a friend at a competing company, or that old guy in the controller's office who knew and liked you when you were an M.B.A. in knee pants. In chatting them up, you will not, of course, speak ill of your boss, or in any wise play Chicken Little. It's just that, oh hell, we over in industrial fasteners get so insular at times . . . If you can manage it tactfully, you might also inquire how, or if, your own performance is perceived.

While gathering intelligence is tricky, the hard ethical question comes when you've accumulated enough to confirm that your side is in serious trouble. Do you tell the boss? Outsiders — headhunters, counselors to management — tend to say you should not. Robert Lamalie of the executive-search firm of Lamalie Associates raises the possibility that your information may be incorrect: "If it is, then the boss will think that you've been a party to spreading rumors. He'll wonder what your motives are, and whether you're trying to undermine him."

On the other hand, real live executives — bless their hearts of oak — seem generally in favor of speaking up. "The last thing the boss needs at that point is a lot of baloney," maintains a company president who suffered through the ouster of his chairman. If the man (or woman) has trusted you and been relatively open, and if the information might do him some good, give him the facts as you've come to know them. In arguing for the hang-out route, executives mention "integrity" a lot.

You probably need not worry that the boss will unburden himself to you on his own initiative. While free and frank communications up and down remain just about everyone's ideal, just about everyone also observes that the downward variety are extraordinarily uncommon in this situation. Typically, too, the higher an executive rises, the less likely he becomes to confide in subordinates.

If your boss turns out to be one of the rare characters who want to share their concerns, listen sympathetically, perhaps employing the parrotlike interrogative technique so beloved of journalists and disciples of psychologist Carl Rogers. ("Mmmm, so you really feel that they're sending you contradictory signals on the new marketing plan?") Do not take up the cudgels of argument, though, or the hot knife of vendetta.

Indeed, one of the few points that outside experts and battle-scarred veterans alike agree upon is the necessity for subordinates to preserve a certain emotional detachment. This isn't easy, but it isn't disloyal either. Now, more than ever, your boss needs a cool head and a clinical eye somewhere about him. His best interests manifestly will not be served by hysterical partisans leading the charge of the light brigade against whatever salient first presents itself in the political mist.

For a subordinate, two uncertainties hang over a boss who may be fired. First, he may indeed get the ax. Second, and sometimes almost as unpleasant, he may survive and go on to manage you another day — it happens. Bear the second possibility in mind before launching yourself on too audacious an independent political course. Even sympathetic behavior, if carried too far, may provoke later trouble. If he has cried on your shoulder every afternoon for a month, for example, he may, after recovering his footing, resent the former reversal of roles. Awkward, awkward.

Once the kibosh has been delivered, a host of new uncertainties takes the place of the old. Your first clues that something has happened may come a while after the body has been whisked off the premises. The purpose of this seclusion is to prevent the fallen leader from "ventilating"— an outplacement term — to co-workers or superiors. Ventilate he must — if he doesn't blow off steam, he won't be able to take the search for a new job seriously — but not to the people who fired him. They may be most important to him in locating another position.

Once he's cooled out, go talk to him. It's like visiting someone with a terminal illness, psychologists suggest: your presence matters more than what you say. If you can do so honestly, tell him you're sorry he was fired and thank him for helping you, citing specific instances.

Ideally, this will lead to a discussion of your prospects, one in which he can be quite candid: You know I've always admired your work, George, but I've never been able to persuade the senior vice president . . .

Don't get so busy trading valedictions, however, that you neglect your subordinates. The boss's firing sends powerful signals down through the ranks. Sadly for morale, these signals are usually ambiguous, because the goals of the organization, the benchmarks against which the boss's performance is evaluated, have not been spelled out. If companies posted production, return-on-investment, and market-share figures — target and actual-to-date — as conspicuously as they post days since a major industrial accident, the troops would know when the boss was sinking. (Indeed, they probably would welcome a failure's departure.)

In the absence of such information, employees will quite rightly conclude that the boss got it because top management wanted things done differently. But "differently" how — with different workers or different procedures? In the best managed of all possible corporate worlds the company would send the executive who did the firing to explain to subordinates why it was necessary. If Pangloss doesn't arrive, though, it may be up to you, the surviving leader. Stress facts, avoid criticism or praise, and play for all they're worth whatever vestiges of continuity remain.

Meanwhile, prepare for change, including, just possibly, a change of jobs. In the estimate of some outplacement counselors, the most common harbinger of churn in the executive ranks, leaving aside the effects of business combinations, is the arrival of a new boss.

When that happens, keep a weather eye on how the organizational seas are running, looking in particular for the first signs of chop. You might do well to heed the not-entirely-facetious advice of one executive who had been heavily identified with his recently axed boss: "Hide — out of sight, out of mind." Warns psychologist Harry Levinson, "Sometimes the new man they put in thinks he's supposed to demonstrate how gutsy he is by getting rid of people."

James Gallagher, an outplacement specialist in New York, posits an eighteen-month scenario: "In the first six months, the new boss focuses on the problem and decides on the people to help him solve it. In the next six, he attacks it. At the end of a year, he looks around and asks, 'Who are those people sitting next to the wall?' If you're one of them, he spends the next six months building a case to fire you."

There are ways to improve your chances of being included on the team. One is to work terrifically hard all through the period of uncertainty, though not perhaps on bold new initiatives that the boss may loathe. It helps if you can become an easily raided trove of information on the organization, the product, whatever the new man may need to know. In short, make yourself indispensable.

At the same time, it clearly is a good idea to update the résumé you probably neglected during the long months when you were laboring frantically to help the old boss avert disaster. If you've brushed up against friendly headhunters in the past, call to remind them of your continued existence.

The executive recruiters will tell you that if you're the old boss's loyal second-in-command, you're the most precariously situated individual of all. Understand that if the corporation wants to promote you to the vacated spot or even is determined to keep you around, you probably will be the first person the boss's boss talks to after delivering the coup de grâce. To prepare for this contingency, you should be up to date on all the division's operations, on time with your current projects, and bubbling with responses to the unlooked-for question: Well, Frank, how do we get the business out of this sorry pass?

Quite often, however, your senior's corporate demise will leave both the company and you wondering what to do. You probably should wait for the dust to settle — scouting career possibilities in the meantime, calming the troops, and working hard at any new tasks that befall you. Beware being named acting boss, though, and left twisting in the wind for months with neither you nor your superiors and subordinates knowing exactly what the appointment presages. According to the psychologists, the uncertainty inherent therein can, over time, devastate your self-confidence.

The experts also observe that if you haven't as No. 2 created a reputation of your own, by the time your boss is fired it's almost certainly too late to do so. Indeed, this insight, writ large, represents the final wisdom to be derived from having a boss in trouble.

Having an accurate, confident sense of your own abilities — a sense communicated to others both inside and outside the company — is probably the single most important card you can bring to this tricky game. Couple it with a modicum of career planning, enough to tell you where you're going and that you're not going to be thrown off by occasional detours, and you have a winning hand, called independence. Polonius was a fool, and a pretty bad No. 2, but his advice — "To thine own self . . ." and the rest — rings rather true in the executive suite.

🐝 23 🐝

A New Boss, from Outside

If you're the newly arrived superior, be careful.
If you're a subordinate, be even more careful.

PARACHUTING IN, that's what they call it.

The old boss is gone — retired early, transferred laterally to oblivion, maybe even, gulp, fired. A new boss is coming, but not up from the ranks or from somewhere else in the outfit. No, he's parachuting in from outside. And in the drop zone the troops wait and wonder: Will what comes down be John Wayne, Omar Bradley, or Vlad the Impaler?

The troops have other worries too. We've got to be in trouble. There isn't anybody here who could run this operation? The big boys must be plenty unhappy with the way we've done things. Why, they may even be unhappy with the way I've done things. Aieeee . . .

Up there in the blue, the new guy has some questions of his own. What's it like down there? Do I go in with a smile on my face or a knife in my teeth? Is this contraption going to work?

There are some answers for everyone. Parachuting in has grown so common, along with executive turnover, that a good bit of collective wisdom has developed on the subject among executive recruiters, students of organizational behavior, and veterans of the jump.

For an executive being furiously wooed to take a parachuting assignment, wisdom begins well before accepting the job. Avoid being borne along passively on the wave of attention being paid you — gee, I must have answered their questions correctly; gosh, they think I'm the best candidate; wow, they're going to pay me that much. Ask a few questions of your own — headhunters are surprised that more heads don't — and think hard about the answers.

The single most important query: Why is this job being filled from outside? This should elicit some good stuff on the business plight of the organization, the plans and hopes of whoever's doing the hiring, and the depth of talent within. Then try bouncing what you've been told off others. Before coming in to take the president's job at sagging Munsingwear in Minneapolis, Raymond Good touched down at the Minneapolis Club, the main corporate hangout in town, to squeeze a little intelligence out of the grapevine. He also talked at length with Munsingwear's directors, customers, and suppliers. He even checked with consultants to the industry.

Also wonderfully instructive can be the reaction to your simple statement "I'd like to talk to the guy I'd be replacing." "Uhh, well, we haven't told him"— how up front will they be with you? "He's just so bitter"— diddled him, did they? Even if you can't chat with him before the ax comes down, try to afterward. Robert Hazard did so as part of moving from the Best Western chain to become president of Quality Inns International. His predecessor, he says, was "particularly accurate in his appraisal of the people."

Politics bear attending to explicitly. Indeed, by sufficiently lining up your ducks on this little matter before you take the job, you'll spare yourself the necessity of chasing them later, or being chased. After you've decided you have the skills to make a measurable change in the organization within the life of man, after you've thought through where the company and the industry will be in five years — presumably the vision coincides with that of your bosses-to-be — then nail down precisely how much authority you'll have to shake things up.

"It should be made crystal clear," says a chief executive who made sure it was, "precisely which decisions you can make on your own, which ones the board wants to be consulted about, and which ones they want veto power on." You want to be certain, for instance, that you can replace Exec V.P.'s Wynken, Blynken, and Nod, who have been so close to the board, if you can't get along with them. In making this demand, it may be fortifying to bear in mind the First Law of Holding a Corporate Job, as posited by John Johnson, a headhunter with Lamalie Associates: "If the system wants to get you, it can." Can, that is, unless you get hold of it first— importing new people if necessary, ushering out some old ones.

The proper assurances given, you take the job. In describing your situation now — the issues you face, the constraints on your choice of tactics — the experts almost universally converge on the same comparison: it's like a physician being brought in suddenly to treat someone he's never encountered before. If the patient is hemorrhaging — as it was when Lee Iacocca arrived at Chrysler, or Lou Menk at International Harvester — you're going to have to apply radical measures quickly on the basis of limited information. You won't be able to give much thought to long-term consequences, or to the feelings of the interns hovering around the intensive-care unit. If, on the other hand, the patient simply needs a good physical, a diet, and a few pills, you can proceed more deliberately.

When you do have the luxury of time, you can choose from essentially three strategies, observes Fred Luthans, a professor of organizational behavior at the University of Nebraska. You can go for "compliance" — telling people what to do and making damn sure they do it. You can hope to foster "identification" by subordinates with what you represent — from the outset leading by bold example. Or you can seek "internalization" by the organization of the way you want to do things — you get to know them, they you; over time they become persuaded that your changes are their changes. Obviously, an executive's style will, and should, influence his choice.

Exacting compliance may be the easiest, in the short run. No messy ambiguity about what's to be done, no softheaded anthropological study of the corporate culture, just nice, firm Parris Island straightforwardness. The only problem is that the behavior you hope to engineer will probably last only as long as you can maintain direct, drill-instructor-like surveillance of the troops. Moreover, you may incite them to rise up and smite you. Edward Jordan attempted to import the dictatorial style he had used at Conrail to his new job as dean of Cornell's business school. He lasted less than a month.

Pursuing identification holds out special appeal to the recently arrived executive because it's a technique that works well when you're a fresh face. In the jargon of social scientists, a newcomer is salient. Everything about you, from the tie you wear to the way you talk, will be scrutinized minutely, gossiped about, made legend throughout the organization. William Francis, an industrial psychologist on the faculty of Lawrence University, says organization members will reinforce your salience by exaggerating any differences they detect between you and your predecessor. When Barry Sullivan took over from Robert Abboud at First Chicago Corp., employees happily glommed on to the fact that their new boss addressed them not from behind a lectern as the imperial Abboud did, but from a casual perch on the edge of the stage of the company auditorium.

Such psychodynamics suggest to Francis that the new boss should step off briskly, making decisions right away, courting victories, doing whatever it takes to get himself labeled a winner. Subordinates will then start acting the same way, supposedly. Other experts aren't so sure. The difficulty, they say, is that identification based on salience endures only as long as the salience does — two to three months among the people who see you every day, six months to a year in the more distant reaches of the organization. According to the studies they look at, the only way to work lasting behavioral change is through the more gradual, cooperative process of internalization.

Real live executives, at least the ones who've been through the drill, tend to favor the internalization strategy (without calling it that). Their consensus is that you start by getting an organization chart and identifying the key people or groups. Then you go out and talk with them, gradually getting to the lowest echelons.

In private conversations in particular, your best tool will be the open-ended question: What do you do; what can I do to help you? For a more hard-edged approach — the "you gotta get their attention" school — there's the formulation of Archie McGill, the former IBM executive whom AT&T brought in to head its new marketing push: Why shouldn't your job be abolished? What you're trying to find out, of course, is not only whether Old Joe knows what he's doing, but how much sense of the organization's mission he has, and how well he serves it.

You can also put out a bit of your own vision. You may not know enough yet to set goals with numbers attached, but you can talk about how you see the competition, the industry's future, the better days ahead. Above all, try to make your conversations less than threatening. The experts suggest that you avoid taking notes. Scribbling away will cause the other guy to choke up. It's important, too, that you not confine your question-and-answer sessions to headquarters. If the folks at the Chula Vista plant never lay eyes on the real you, they'll make up a version out of rumor, gossip, and innuendo.

Once you've discovered where the bodies are buried — and which ones are occupying corner offices — you can proceed to, as they say, implement change. The toughest decision will be whether to implement a number of veterans out the door. You'll be particularly tempted to replace them, or at least augment them, with people you know, most likely trusted lieutenants from your last outpost.

Rare is the parachutist who doesn't, but there are a couple of cautions. First, each outsider you summon will go through the same passage that you're embarked upon. Each also begets the same initial response — a little shock, a lot of uncertainty, a bit of paralysis. Observes Robert Hazard, who brought fourteen executives with him from Best Western, "We all had to learn to be good listeners." Second, if you're going to perpetrate a bloodbath, do it with one volley. Then tell the survivors loudly and explicitly that it's over.

Any new boss should be prepared for surprises. "I don't think the board lied to me," reports an executive who parachuted into the top job at a troubled company. "They just didn't know how bad it was." The biggest surprise of all may be how difficult it is to change a culture that has been in place for a long time. As the experts, both academic and real-world, have come to recognize, it usually takes years to do it. "Change is just so hard," says McGill, who ended up leaving AT&T. "I knew that, but I didn't really know it."

About all one can do is, in the language of the novelist, to endeavor to persevere. "There are two problems that I've found to be the toughest," reports George L. Ball, who left the presidency of E. F. Hutton to become chief executive of Prudential's Bache Group. "One is managing my time effectively — beyond the normal pressures of keeping things running, there's the extra burden of being seen, listening, absorbing. The other is appreciating that I can't master the nuances as completely as if I'd grown up in the place. You do it in building blocks."

Parachuting has compensations, even beyond the monetary ones. Observers note that most new bosses from outside experience an initial period of euphoria, euphoria that the wise ones try to share with their subordinates. "It's just such a kick," said Ball, not long after taking his new job. "I can't believe they're paying me to do this."

The folks being parachuted in on may not be quite so blissed out. What do you do if you get a new boss from outside?

Just what a Boy Scout would — play it straight. Jerry Simmons, the head of the Handy Associates executive-search firm, prescribes a course of conduct that tallies neatly with the advice offered by other veterans of the game.

First, try to determine what if any changes are going to be made in the long-term strategy, the direction of the business. Next, do your best, most objective assessment of what headhunters call the "personal chemistry" between you and the new guy. Work hard to understand his priorities, and support them if you can. The old chief was crazy for market share; the new one is nuts for product quality. Throw yourself into the current enthusiasm.

Look for ways to demonstrate, without showboating, the past contributions and future potential of your department. At the same time, be candid and, if possible, constructive in your dealings with Mr. Wonderful. Don't, don't, don't play politics, meaning don't curry favor or say things like "Well, nobody else will tell you this but . . ."

Finally, be prepared for the worst, which consists in part of thinking seriously about just what the worst would be. You know more about making railroad ties than any living being; he intends to take the company high tech. You're the soul of participatory management; he makes Captain Bligh look like a softy. The crucial point, say the experts, is that you figure it out before he does. You can then begin setting up an orderly career transition, dignity intact, not freighted with bitterness. Who knows, you might even want to try a little parachuting in yourself.

24

The Managerial Midlife Crisis

Look back. Look ahead. Look inward. Try not to get too depressed.
It's just a phase you're going through.

THE PROMISES END HERE. Or at least here's where you stop believing them. "Work hard, kid, give us your best, and you'll get one of the top jobs." Sure. "Marry, start a family, make the money to keep them happy, and they will love you and be unfailingly grateful." Right. "Things are going to get better; just you wait and see." Uh-huh. Welcome, old clear eyes, to the rock 'em, sock 'em midlife transition.

Damnable uncertainty plagues the entire experience. It may, for example, be impossible for you to tell when you are launched on this particular passage, if you ever are. You're suddenly convinced that you're no longer on the fast track, or that the track leads nowhere, or that no one appreciates you, or that you're losing your marbles. But unlike at puberty, there are no bodily changes dramatic enough to signal that your mind is being taken over temporarily by forces beyond your control.

You aren't the only one who's confused. Even behavioral scientists cannot agree on the nature, timing, and extent of the phenomenon. In particular, they cannot agree on whether the typical fortyish executive goes through anything as disruptive as a psychological crisis. Perhaps the best-known authority on the subject is Yale psychology professor Daniel J. Levinson — he was the chief author of the best-seller *The Seasons of a Man's Life;* his research was the basis for the even bigger best-seller *Passages.* Levinson and his colleagues found that of the forty men they studied, including ten executives, more than thirty experienced "tumultuous struggles within the self and with the external world," beginning in their late thirties or early forties. Nor are executive women excepted from the turmoil. Levinson — who has lately been studying women's development in adult life, his sample including a number of businesswomen—concludes that females often go through an even tougher psychological transition than males do, and at the same age. He attributes much of it to the changing definition of their roles in society.

On the other hand, consider the findings of professors Michael P. Farrell and Stanley D. Rosenberg of the State University of New York at Buffalo and the Dartmouth Medical School, respectively, who examined the experience of three hundred men aged thirty-eight to forty-eight, representing all income groups. One finding: Subjects who had made it into the managerial class tended to weather the transition into midlife better than lower-status males, often without any psychological disruption at all. That could, however, merely mean that the crisis is yet to come. Rosenberg reports that follow-up interviews with these managers indicate they've had a surprisingly rough time in the decade since the original study was conducted. This comports with what seems a common impression among business types: that the crisis really hits in the late forties.

If you begin to do the midlife beguine — or the beguine begins to do you—know that you're likely to proceed through fairly predictable stages, at least according to some of the experts. William Yabroff, a professor of psychology at Santa Clara University who helps Silicon Valley companies counsel employees on the passage, offers about the most clear-cut formulation: "The transition begins with an ending— disenchantment with what one has achieved. It goes to a midpoint, where there's a real sense of loss. Then there's a new beginning."

You probably have lots to be disenchanted about. On the personal side, the list typically includes waning energy—particularly, in men, waning sexual energy. The prospect of taking care of your aging parents also weighs on your mind, along with the impossibility of getting along with your adolescent children.

Work, too, offers plenty of opportunities for dissatisfaction. At this point in even a fast-track career, promotions come more slowly, if they come at all. Instead of the unbounded horizon of job possibilities that seem to await you in your twenties, you face years of just rolling on in the same old rut. If you keep your job, that is—an increasingly nagging question in this era of continuing managerial layoffs. Counselors say that executives at midlife often express deepening worry about the obsolescence of their technical skills, especially compared with those of younger people at the company. These execs forget that by this time they are being paid for their managerial abilities.

Even success won't insulate an executive from the growing feeling that nothing means as much as it used to. Notes Atlanta psychologist Roderick Gilkey of his midlife patients, "I seem to get a lot of executives just after they've been promoted." A common executive plaint, according to therapists: "Damn it, I ought to be happy. Why aren't I?"

California psychologist Yabroff says that a manager's response to mounting midlife feelings of disenchantment typically takes one of three forms. He may suddenly get busier — working harder or plunging into community activities. He may try to escape into drink, drugs, erotic adventure, or some giddy combination of the three. Or he may go in a more spiritual direction, sometimes seeking meaning in religion. "My midlife transition was something I went through in terms of finding a new value system," reports a fifty-one-year-old man who at forty-five gave up a job as an executive with a Fortune 500 company. "My value system had been a material one — a big saltbox colonial house, expensive vacations, Mercedes. I wanted to start over." He got a divorce, earned a degree in counseling, and now works as an adviser to executives whose careers are in trouble.

As a manager becomes disenchanted, co-workers may notice a withdrawal from the usual hearty give-and-take, or bouts of irritability sometimes igniting into rage. The crisis sufferer may be undergoing what psychoanalysts call the return of the repressed: impelled by weird energies, he rehearses again all those conflicts with parents or other menacing authority figures that he thought he had settled long ago. He also begins to wrestle with the Ultimate Bummer: the realization that he is going to die, realio, trulio.

With the descent to the midpoint of the crisis, disenchantment can become depression. James A. Wilson, a psychologist at the University of Pittsburgh who counsels executives in his private practice, notes, "For some of these high achievers, it's the first depression they've ever experienced, and it's all the more frightening for that." The afflicted manager may also suffer a decreased ability to concentrate and deficiencies in memory that sometimes border on disorientation. One psychologist tells of an executive in the throes of a midlife crisis who was charged with introducing an up-and-coming subordinate to a large company audience. He forgot to. He was then asked to introduce the rising star at a board meeting. He began his introduction, and then forgot the man's name. Another practitioner tells of executive patients who, sitting in business meetings, forgot their own names.

At this juncture, the company stands to lose the executive if it isn't careful. He has to be convinced that he is not losing his mind, that it happens to others too, and — probably harder to put across — that it's not a result of his situation at work. This may be a good time for a sabbatical, if the company is enlightened enough to offer them. The individual has to back off, to retreat, and to grieve for what might have been.

While it may last for a few months, people do get through this dark night of the soul. What lies on the other side, ideally, is a process psychologists call integration — the putting together of aspects of the self heretofore in conflict or neglected — and the exploration of new opportunities. Executives may, for example, discover a hitherto unexplored capacity for nurturance. Helping to bring younger people along, sharing what they know, they become better managers. Says the chief executive of a metalworking company who at forty-eight went into a severe depression, "I took six months off and then bounced back. As a result of my midlife crisis, I have more sympathy for people and can understand why they don't do well in their jobs. I also looked at my values — I now rate family and self higher than business success."

Those who successfully negotiate the crisis learn a measure of acceptance, both of what has happened and what will happen. True, the dreams of youth are gone, along with some of the possibilities of youth. But in their place, hard won from the summer of life, resides some understanding, which just may be the beginning of wisdom for the autumn and winter.

25

Starting Over

Racked by fantasies of opening a restaurant or running a vineyard?
Here's what to expect of a second career.

WE TEND TO ADMIRE the people who do it. "He just chucked it all," we think, "told the boss where to get off, quit, and headed out West. By now he's probably got that little lemming ranch he dreamed of, somewhere in the Rockies. I bet he's just floating." What audacity. What independence.

What a lot of trouble. As just about anyone who has tried to launch a second career will tell you, the process isn't carefree. The move usually springs not from insouciance but from unhappiness. Often it results in more unhappiness. With a little calculation, though, you can significantly improve your chances of making it work.

First, let's be clear about what a second career is. The term implies a first career, work the individual devoted himself to seriously for an appreciable period. For this reason, the job selling auto parts that your hitherto shiftless brother-in-law finally finds fulfillment in, after casting about in twelve other fields in as many years, doesn't qualify as a second career. Nor does a new job that entails mostly a change of employers. You were an accountant in a Big Eight firm; you became controller of a medium-size company or retired and set up your own practice. Enterprising of you, but no second career.

The number of managerial types seeking more radical departures from what they've been doing appears on the increase. The closest thing to experts on the subject—individuals and firms that counsel people on career change—report that their business is brisk. They attribute the heightened interest in second careers to several causes: erosion of the individual's loyalty to the company; erosion of the company's loyalty to the individual—they may fire you any time, why not beat them to it—even the spread of the I've-got-to-be-me ethic from the you-know-what generation to just about everybody.

People who have attempted second careers confirm much of this sociology but go on to etch it more sharply with the acid of unhappiness. From a computer salesman who, at age forty, left IBM and soon got into the restaurant business: "I was a small cog in a large organization. I looked at the people who were working for retirement and realized they had no vitality. I didn't want to be like them." From a thirty-five-year-old engineer who's getting ready to make the change: "I'm bored and I'm under continuous stress. When you've been doing something for eight to ten years it becomes repetitive. I'm not using my real abilities." Nearly all say they want to make more decisions on their own.

Psychologists who treat people wrestling with the possibility of a second career see such remarks as fitting into a pattern. The therapists confirm the common perception that most of the folks who want to make the leap are men around forty.

"A large issue is the imminence of death," explains Professor James A. Wilson of the University of Pittsburgh, who at thirty-five left a thriving insurance business to take up psychology. "People see that they don't have that many years left and they'd better do what they want to do. They realize that they've chosen a career to please someone else."

Father always wanted you to be a lawyer; you knew your business school classmates would drop dead from envy if you landed that management consulting job. A look at where second-careerists come from does suggest that the careers most likely to be left behind are those in high-pressure, high-status industries — investment banking, consulting, almost anything on Wall Street. Observes Roderick Gilkey of Emory University, "Those are the jobs that it's easiest to get into for the wrong reasons."

The businesses that people choose for their second careers, or at least that they fantasize about most, are just about as predictable. If America were transformed in accordance with the dreams of its second-career wishers, the continent would shake and rend into a vast archipelago — this to accommodate all the marinas. On every island, several charming restaurants would beckon, and maybe a cozy inn or two. The rest of the land would be given over to vineyards.

Career changers, it turns out, are driven not only by the desire to be more independent, but also by what counselors call life-style considerations. Immured in the concrete canyons of the financial district, they begin to dream of the rolling hills of Vermont. Many second careers also grow out of avocations — sailing; cooking; collecting antiques; if not making wine, then at least drinking it. "I always had a desire to do something with my long-standing hobby, designing and making furniture," recalls Dietrich Baeu, formerly the president of a company that sold electro-optical devices. In 1980, at age forty-one, he left the corporate life and set up a custom-furniture business in New Jersey.

Most folks who embark on second careers quickly find that the dissatisfaction with the old career gives way to anxiety over new uncertainties. Indeed, psychologists say that it usually takes at least a year for most people to adjust and feel comfortable with the change. Brian Froelich, who in his mid-thirties left a vice president's job at a big insurance company to start a travel agency catering to corporations, recounts what the first week on his own was like: "I'd lock the door and lie down on the floor — I thought I was going to have a heart attack. I was literally trembling as I reflected on what I had done."

False starts contribute to the misery. Many career changers report that before they found a second career that stuck, they tried one or two other kinds of work — real estate development being the most commonly cited misadventure. Others brought their old psychological devils to their new life. Psychologist Gilkey tells of a New York City investment banker who in his early forties decamped for Vermont to launch a little maple syrup business. "He developed a maple syrup empire," Gilkey reports, "and soon found himself burdened by the same pressures he had tried to escape. By the time he came in to see me, he was suffering from agrarian burnout."

The second-careerist's biggest problem might seem to be maintaining his or her accustomed standard of living. Incomes from second careers tend to be low — often no more than one-third the annual compensation of the first career. "We did cut out a lot of things," says a man who deserted consulting for his original love, architecture. But few career-changers seem to mind much; they treat the change as a return to their student days, as pioneering in the wilds, or even as a plunge into the life Bohemian. It is also universally conceded that having a spouse who brings in a paycheck helps enormously.

For all the difficulty that attends them, second careers can be made to work. Experts estimate that something like 70 percent to 80 percent of the people who attempt the change succeed — in the sense that they stick with the new career they settle on after all the transitional messiness. The trick is to make the move with the least possible heartache.

When the second-career bug gnaws at you, begin, the experts say, by figuring out what you really want — as if you could. One way to get at this elusive subject is to try to write your ideal obituary: Killed last night, at age 119, when his (or her) sports car plummeted off a cliff, Mr. (or Ms.) So-and-So was well known as . . . what? A retired former chief financial officer of Limbruck Sheet & Tubing? The crusty but beloved proprietor of the Inn-We-Go Tavern, a favorite local watering hole? The operator of the best damn marina in New-port Beach? If you consistently draw a blank, consider a visit to your friendly local psychological testing firm. It might be able, by virtue of a few inoffensive exercises, to help you uncover your true interests.

Once you have some sense of what you want to be when you finally grow up, work backward. What position will you need to reach to be within striking distance of your ultimate goal? What position to reach that position? And so on, back to a step you can take from your present miserable position.

Think, and act, incrementally — that is, with the smallest possible change that will get you where you want to go. Maybe you don't need to buy a marina. Some less drastic choices, while they might disqualify you from what purists consider a second career, may be better. You may find it simpler to take your investment banking skills and parlay them into ten hours a week of consulting, which would bring in enough to keep both you and your yawl barnacle-free.

If you contemplate a move into a completely new field, accumulate work experience in that area, preferably before you sever all your ties to your old career. Gary Smyth was trading corporate bonds on Wall Street when, at age thirty-eight, he was smitten by the urge to oper-ate a restaurant. When the deal he was cooking up to start one in New York fell through, he took a job as a bartender at an East Side

steakhouse instead. Within a few weeks, he became maître d', responsible for closing the place up at night. After a sufficient number of
fifteen-hour days, he began to understand why so many restaurants
are run by first-generation immigrants. "After I got over the initial
fantasy fulfillment," Smyth recalls, "I wasn't really happy doing the
work." Now forty-three, he is back trading bonds. The difference?
He's contented.

26

Lifelong Retirement Planning

The hardest part of the managerial life may be the leaving of it.
Begin preparing when you're about twenty-five.

IMAGINE A TEST that would reveal how far you are likely to get in your career, how enduring your accomplishments will be, what you and your spouse really feel for each other, whether you have any unexploited talents, and how large your position figures in what others think of you and you think of yourself. You probably will take such a test. It's called retirement.

Many — perhaps most — flunk, a fact that barely registers on the rest of the population. Retired people certainly don't want to talk about it. "The first thing retirees learn is to lie with a straight face about how they're doing," says one human-resources type who counsels such folks. Retirement, the experts say, seems to bring an increase in the incidence of suicide, alcoholism, and divorce.

The experts also say that if you want to pass the test, you had better begin preparing early. Your employer may even be willing to help — these days more and more companies, including the likes of Ford, GE, and ITT, are offering so-called preretirement counseling. A typical program might consist of two days of sessions, covering not just finances and company benefits but also attitudinal adjustments, health, and housing; employees over fifty-five are invited, and usually their spouses as well. While a company's motives for providing such counseling are not always simon-pure — sometimes employees are right in thinking that a program represents subtle encouragement to retire — for participants the exercise usually proves an enlightening first step in facing up to what may seem an approaching black hole.

At least two problems, however, weaken most preretirement programs. First, they are not offered early enough in an employee's career. Pay attention, all you baby-boom hotshots: there you are, getting ready to ditch Plod Co., your employer of several years, to take one of those high-visibility, hands-on-responsibility positions at another company. Do you know when your retirement benefits from Plod vest? If the answer is "After ten years of continuous employment," and you have nine years and eleven months on the books, you might want to delay your departure slightly — this is called retirement planning.

Many conventional preretirement programs also fail to address the most important issues. Observes Joseph Perkins, corporate retirement manager at Polaroid, "The whole world thinks that the biggest problem for people facing retirement is money"— which corporate programs typically do cover —"but if you have enough to cover the necessities, money is the least of the problems." Executive types in particular have few worries on this score; other demons await them.

The toughest question that managerial types face in retirement — and one that it's especially useful to get an early start answering — is "What am I apart from my work?" Philip H. Dreyer, a professor of education and psychology at the Claremont Graduate Schools in California and an authority on retirement, elaborates on why successful executives have a particularly rough time with the issue: "These individuals have an enormous amount invested in their work. It's not work for them: they have been rewarded for it; the power they have, which they enjoy using, comes from it. The higher they go in the organization, the more they devote themselves to the well-being of the institution. It becomes their real self, maybe their only self."

After retirement you can't kid yourself any longer about how you're doing in the competition to get ahead, or console yourself with the thought that tomorrow is another day. As your gaze turns from the future to the past, you may not like what you see: new people running your old operation in new ways, your accomplishments becoming more evanescent as they become more distant.

Preparation against such epiphanies takes many forms. The most obvious is simply refusing to retire. Under federal law, a company can't force you to retire, however old you get. An exception is made for executives in so-called high policy-making positions who will receive at least $44,000 a year in benefits — the company can set the mandatory retirement age for them as low as sixty-five — but the

courts have defined the exception rather narrowly. A former employee recently won an age-discrimination suit against Union Carbide when the court ruled that his job as chief labor relations counsel
was not elevated enough to qualify. If they want to, though, companies can make it awfully hard not to retire — offering packages that
get less attractive over time, or gradually reassigning one's work to
others.

Hence an increasingly common alternative — retiring from the old
job and then, after a sobering glimpse of the void, taking on a new one.
A recent survey of retired presidents and chief executives of the
largest U.S. companies conducted by Russell Reynolds Associates, an
executive search firm, found that 61 percent of the respondents had
returned to work, the majority within six months of stepping down
from the catbird seat. A third of these people worked full time. From a
planning point of view, the lesson is as follows: You will probably
want to launch a second career. Better to lay the groundwork early,
and perhaps even start on that career, before you suffer a demoralizing
brush with retirement.

If, in taking the long view ahead, you decide that you really, truly
will want to retire, then take the advice of Davis W. Gregg, president
emeritus of American College in Bryn Mawr, Pennsylvania: "Start
early to disengage from work culture, which represents a great support system for most people. Look for substitutes." Think of it as
putting together a postretirement answer to that most American of
queries, "What do you do?" If you hope to reply, "I am the world's
foremost expert on sang-de-boeuf-glaze porcelains of the T'ang dy-
nasty," immerse yourself in the subject while you still have another
career. Recipe for despair: All your working life tell yourself, "Deep
down, I'm really a novelist — I just work as a lawyer to put bread on
the table." After taking early retirement, put in three agonizing
months at the typewriter before finally figuring out that you have
neither the talent nor the persistence.

Two further cautions are in order. First, do not confuse your
present leisure pursuits with what you want to give your life to in
retirement. Perhaps only the retired fully understand that the most
satisfying round of golf is the round stolen from the press of business.
This insight comes quickly. When recently asked how long it took

him after retirement to realize that he didn't want to spend the rest of his life on the links, a former insurance company vice president replied laconically, "About two days." Second, don't rely on volunteer work, however charitable, to fill the whole void. Managerial types, accustomed to having the value of their labor measured in dollars, find the wages irritating.

You will almost certainly need some sort of activity outside the home to avoid domestic strife. What retirees often find out about the state of their marriage is summed up in a quip that drops from the lips of every retirement counselor: for better or for worse, but not for lunch. Women retirees may encounter less of a readjustment in this respect — throughout their lives, they've been needed in the home — but then, they suffer other pangs: those who have returned to the work force late in life sometimes have their careers just up and running when the retirement bell rings.

The planning prescription? Get your house in order long before you and your spouse are sitting in it, facing each other over a lunch that seems like something out of an Ingmar Bergman movie. Find out what your spouse and children hope and fear, not just about your retirement but about their own lives as well. Listen, and don't treat what they say just as something to be managed as you manage the problems that creep up at the office.

Keep the not-so-old bod ready for the adventures to come. Probably the best way to forestall the health worries of retirement is to start living healthfully now. Give up smoking. Stand up straight. Start exercising. As you jog into the future, or swim that umpteenth lap toward glory, you can meditate on the summary imperative of lifelong retirement planning: When you retire, think and act as if you were still working; when you're still working, think and act a bit as if you were already retired.

❧ Part III ❧

LARGER ISSUES

27

Wanted: Corporate Leaders

Must have vision and ability to build corporate culture.
Mere managers need not apply.

IT'S IN THE AIR, trend spotters, just about ready to precipitate in the swirling clouds of economic change and rain down on us in a thousand articles and speeches. It's behind much of the business community's fascination with Lee Iacocca. It has something to do with why *In Search of Excellence*, a study of what authors Thomas J. Peters and Robert H. Waterman, Jr., describe as America's best-run companies, sold over five million copies and became a No. 1 bestseller nationwide. It's there just below the surface of all the talk about fostering entrepreneurialism inside the large corporation.

This very hot subject is leadership.

At the mere mention of the word, your eyes might reasonably glaze over, iced with recollection of too many politicians promising a new tomorrow, too many unread books with the big L in the title, too many after-dinner exhortations by football coaches who should never have been permitted to doff their windbreakers and eschew their gum. Wake up. This time there may actually be something there.

Item: In an interview a young associate professor at one of those ultraprestigious business schools announces that when he completes his latest tome on corporate strategy — a bandwagon he's been riding for five years — he proposes to devote himself full-time to the study of leadership. And where will he begin his research? "The military academies," he replies.

Item: Executive recruiters, asked what qualities their client companies are seeking in a candidate for a top job, report that they're hearing our old friend "charisma" a great deal more than they used to. "Vision" also seems in increasing demand; while the headhunters aren't sure precisely what the term means, they sense that it has to do with new and much-sought-after skills in motivating people.

Item: In 1981 Matsushita Electric Industrial Co. endowed a chair in leadership at the Harvard Business School — the first professorship devoted to the subject to be established at any major business school. In preparing students to deal with the flesh-and-blood variable in the business equation, these institutions have traditionally taught organizational design, human behavior in different organizational contexts, maybe a bit of labor relations — the skills, in short, that would be called on in planning and administering a bureaucracy.

Finally, after casting about hither and yon for an expert on leadership, Harvard awarded the Matsushita professorship to Abraham Zaleznik, already the holder of another endowed chair at HBS and one of the faculty members who had helped raise the money from the Japanese company. Zaleznik, a lay psychoanalyst with a private practice he conducts from beside a couch in his campus office, is the author of an award-winning 1977 article arguing that the psychology of leaders differs dramatically from that of managers. The article raised the hackles of many of Zaleznik's colleagues at the institution formally named the Harvard Graduate School of Business Administration.

Most of the interesting thinking about leadership these days — and the punch such thinking has, way beyond the usual pep-rally bromides — has its roots in this notion that, psychologically, managers and leaders are very different cups of tea indeed. Zaleznik claims no monopoly on the idea. He sees it reflected, for example, in the distinction James MacGregor Burns makes in his book *Leadership* between transformative leaders, who change the course of events, and transactional ones, who without much emotional involvement get things done through contractual relationships within some sort of organizational structure. Other academics trace the idea back to sociologist Max Weber, who argued that charismatic leaders launch enterprises, only to give way to bureaucrats, who take over the running of them.

The experts who of late seem to make the most sense of the leader-manager distinction are (hold onto your hats and your prejudices) Freudians — men like Zaleznik and Harry Levinson, the Menninger Foundation–trained psychologist whose Levinson Institute seminars are perhaps the only forum that routinely brings together businessmen and clinicians. The title of Levinson's seminar for corporate officers is, and has been for nearly twenty years, "On Leadership."

Just more psychohumbug? It may seem to the casual observer that the Freudians are on the run, pilloried in everything from trendy books such as *Psychoanalysis: The Impossible Profession* to movies. Ach, the followers of Sigmund rejoin, you have to distinguish between our underlying theory and our therapeutic techniques. Did any other theory survive the new-therapies-and-psychobabble explosion of the 1960s and 1970s with as much of its explanatory and predictive power intact?

Much of Freudian doctrine, you may recall from the psychology course you took in college to buck up your average, revolves around a sort of tripartite division of the psyche — into id, ego, and superego. According to the Freudians, it is the particular and characteristic way that these three act and interact within the leader that sets him apart from others, including the manager. Recognizing how these psychodynamics work and consciously trying to ape some of the resultant behavior may even make your own bureaucratic style more inspiring.

In just about everyone, the theory goes, the id is a bubbling, seething stew of instinctual energies, often energies of the randiest or most aggressive sort, all of which in a civilized person are usually kept unconscious. The superego, by contrast, incorporates what our parents and society have taught us about being good; it rewards us psychically for a job well done and also bestows that attribute essential to middle-class life, a sense of guilt. Finally, there's the ego, largely conscious and always caught up in mediating between the other two parts and outside reality. Thus, in Freudian theory, "Man is basically a battlefield," in the felicitous words of the British psychologist Donald Bannister, "a dark cellar in which a well-bred spinster lady and a sex-crazed monkey are forever engaged in mortal combat, the struggle being refereed by a rather nervous bank clerk."

For the leader, though, the internal struggle seems in some ways less bitter, less divisive. In him, the psychologists speculate, that harsh, nagging component of the superego that we commonly call the conscience isn't quite as punitive as it is in other folks. This lets him more readily admit into consciousness the impressions, energies, and associations that bubble up from the id. Asked for his definition of vision, Zaleznik replies, "It's the capacity to see connections, to draw inferences that aren't obvious, that are unprecedented." Some businessmen call it the ability to see around corners as the leader peers into his company's future. It's a talent that has come to seem all the more valuable as the pace of technological and economic change quickens.

This isn't the only element in the leader's vision, however. Perhaps because he has less energy invested in the conscience, he channels more into another component of the superego, the ego ideal. The ego ideal is the image of what he wants himself, and by extension his organization, to be. This vision, which he strives constantly to achieve, is perhaps the most powerful motivational tool in the leader's kit. It gives him a consistent sense of who he is and what he's after, a sense that he can, by words and example, invite others to share in.

As Harry Levinson parses the psychodynamics at work, the leader's pursuit of an ego ideal enables him to frame a transcendent purpose for his organization. (Zaleznik prefers the slightly less highfalutin' formulation "enduring goal.") This purpose usually includes within it the perpetuation of the organization, and hence necessarily entails taking a long-term view. Since merely staying alive isn't by itself all that beckoning an ideal, the transcendent purpose will commonly be cast in more inspiring terms — making the best computers in the world, say, or the best cars.

While your typical manager-bureaucrat tries to get people to do things for money or out of fear, the leader invites his co-workers to identify their pursuit of an ego ideal with his own, and with the transcendent purpose of the organization. If the purpose is sufficiently lofty, this identification infuses their work with meaning, meaning beyond just making a living. Hitting your profit targets each quarter probably isn't much of a transcendent purpose.

Without a transcendent purpose understood and enunciated from on high, the company's direction is at the mercy of the winds of corporate fad and fancy. Shall we become a conglomerate tomorrow?

If all this seems a bit mystical for your taste, try thinking of it in terms of that concept much in vogue nowadays, corporate culture. What, at bottom, is a corporate culture but a set of shared values, values that get reflected in behavior and, in the best cases, further everyone's pursuit of a common end? Each of the well-managed companies listed in *In Search of Excellence*, it should be noted, has a strong culture.

In interviews, authors Peters and Waterman observe that in most cases the culture seemed to be the creation of a strong leader who hammered away at a message to his organization for years. He might be someone who started the company, or who was present almost from the beginning — Tom Watson at IBM — or, considerably less often, someone who rose through the ranks to get the top job, from which bully pulpit he instilled the gospel in a previously less than excellent company — Rene McPherson at Dana. It's enough to make you slightly suspicious of those consultants who offer to help you build a strong corporate culture around your current wimpy management.

The leader's strong ego ideal, coupled with an active but not hypercritical conscience, has other effects on how he gets along with peers and subordinates. Because his aggressive energies are channeled into the pursuit of a goal larger than himself, when Joe the plant manager lashes out against him in a rage, he won't retaliate in kind. Indeed, if he's the McCoy, he'll probably find some way to help Joe direct his megatonnage against the common task.

The Freudian's typical manager, by comparison, has a conscience that's always keeping score and just maybe poisoning the wellsprings of self-confidence with guilt. All het up with nowhere to go — no very bright ideal to pursue — his aggressive energies will be sluiced into attacks on himself and those around him: he'll distrust his own competence and theirs. The result is corporate politics at its least productive: turf battles, a boss rivalrous toward subordinates and unwilling to help them along, demoralization in all its senses. While the leader devotes himself to getting the job done, the manager worries about "how am *I* doing?"— he is a careerist.

The Freudians, as you may imagine, tend to think that the way that we get along with our boss has much to do with how we fared with Mama and Dada. We bring to our dealings with the guy in the corner office feelings of dependency and a need for affection. You scoff: *Affection and dependency? We don't allow those at my company.* No, in the corporate world it's known as seeking recognition, feedback, support. Members of the baby-boom generation, perhaps because they've had to compete to be singled out from their too-numerous peers for so long, are becoming famous for demanding this warm stuff quite explicitly.

The leader — secure, serene in his commitment to task, and looking for people to help him accomplish it — does a better job handling
these demands than your average manager. Which, with the accession
of baby-boomers to more and more managerial jobs these days, may in
part account for why companies seem suddenly to be seeking leader
types to yoke the boomers' energies to a corporate purpose. He
doesn't just tolerate, he actively encourages all those would-be entrepreneurs in the company skunkworks.

Not that this fabled leader is any kind of cupcake. Because of his
overriding commitment to the common goal, and because he's less
hung up about his own aggressiveness and others', he can be utterly
forthright in telling people when they're not performing up to the
mark. If all else has been tried, he can even fire them with a clearer
conscience than is common among bureaucrats. Such forthrightness
does, however, present special problems for women who would be
leaders. Because subordinates expect deep down that the woman who
happens to be their boss will be, if anything, more supportive and
affectionate than a male — more like Mom — and because women
build some of these same expectations into what they demand of
themselves, it may be two generations before many women can act as
freely, as unconstrainedly, in a leadership role as a man might, at least
in Harry Levinson's view.

There are, of course, other problems with this model of a leader,
beginning with the question whether any of these paragons actually
exist out there in the world. The Freudians are distinctly reluctant to
cite examples on the current corporate scene — who knows what his
early childhood was like, and whether he really fits the model? Moreover, can the typical large company, with its entrenched bureaucracy,
accommodate such a wild man? Probably only if the pain — the pressure from foreign competitors, the inability to overcome economic
stagnation — is great enough.

Even if a company were positively hungry for one of these men on
horseback, it isn't clear where it would find him. Can leaders be
trained, can some latent potential for acting in accordance with the
leader's particular psychological makeup be brought out in, say, the
average M.B.A. candidate? "We don't know," confesses Harold J.
Leavitt, a professor of organizational behavior at Stanford. "We

never can tell until we try." Harvard's Zaleznik warns that any attempt to identify potential leaders early in their education and give them special training will have to withstand charges of that most un-American of sins, elitism.

But then, we may not have that much choice if we're going to compete globally with societies that seem to do a better job of fostering and giving rein to leaders. If the prospect gives you pause — and it should — you might want to dwell on the thought that the first endowed chair of leadership in this country bears the name of one Konosuke Matsushita, a peasant's son who in his lifetime managed to build the fifteenth-largest industrial corporation in the world.

28

Managing a Downsized Operation

Companies that set out to get lean and mean
too often end up depressed and lethargic instead.

WE'VE GOTTEN FAT—the chief executive intones to his intimates—too damn fat. Layers and layers of people clogging up the corporate arteries, occluding us with bureaucracy. The Japanese are crawling all over our customers, we can't make any money, and the security analysts are screaming about our overhead. We've got to cut back, men, trim down, eliminate some people. Just the fat, mind you, no muscle. We'll make ourselves just like one of those excellent companies—close to the customer, zilch corporate staff, lean, baby, and mean.

Such avowals have become so common in the past five years that Corporatespeak now offers alternative euphemisms for the process: it's called *demanning, delayering,* or—borrowing from Detroit's classic small-is-beautiful attempt to put the best face forward—*downsizing.* You may also know it as the squeeze on middle managers, the new decentralization—push that authority down the ranks, you managerial martinet—or the executive recession. Companies that have tried one variant or another on the process include General Electric, Du Pont, Eastman Kodak, H. J. Heinz, Lever Brothers, U.S. Steel, Polaroid, and Apple Computer. The basic notion has a lot of appeal. Who, after all, wants to stand up and be counted on the side of waste?

The problem is, companies that have been through the exercise report that in the real world, the results often seem awfully disturbing. One begins to get a sense of this from the initial response to questions about the experience: most corporations don't want to talk about it, at least not for attribution. Instead of testimonials to productivity achieved or entrepreneurship unleashed, one hears responses like the following from a company public relations man in Chicago: "Nobody here wants to talk about how he fired three hundred people and is working the hell out of those who remain."

If only managing a downsized operation were that simple. The biggest challenge, say those in charge of recently trimmed organizations, is helping survivors get over the multiple traumas that any large-scale cutback brings on. These aftershocks can last two or three years, or longer. William F. Joyce, now an associate professor of strategy and organization theory at Dartmouth's Amos Tuck School of Business Administration, provides a terse — if somewhat jargon-laden — overview of what can happen, based on his earlier experience as an engineer who survived a two-thousand-person downsizing at a manufacturing company: "Increases in stress, conflict, and ambiguity about each individual's role; decreases in job involvement; decreases in work satisfaction; dissatisfaction with leadership and co-workers. Decreases in the quality of coordination within the organization. All of which had negative impacts on the overall performance of the organization."

Tim Thorsteinson, director of human relations at National Semiconductor, which recently cut its work force by 5 percent in a single year, puts it more simply: "After this happens, an organization, psychologically, is in a depressed state, like a depressed person. When you're depressed, there's a general tendency to be very lethargic." You may see a brief flurry of activity right after the ax comes down. "There is an initial upsurge of doing what must be done, or what can easily be watched, or what can be counted," reports Robert Dewar, chairman of the department of organizational behavior at Northwestern's Kellogg Graduate School of Management, who lends consulting help to downsizing companies. Pretty soon, though, most survivors settle into what seems the universal human condition among such folks: sitting there numbly, wondering, "Am I next?"

The only effective managerial antidote to this paralysis is communication — talking to the remaining troops endlessly, answering their questions, standing by to hold their hands. This is particularly important — and particularly hard to make believable — if the company didn't let the employees in on the thinking that led to downsizing, which most don't. Having been kept in the dark before, the troops are all the more ready to believe that the company's leadership doesn't know what it's doing, that the boss won't be straight with them, and that more cuts are coming.

In describing the message that should be delivered to survivors, veterans of the experience use the word *focus* a lot. You must convey the idea, all the while praying it's true, that management has given up chasing after this or that extraneous possibility, and instead decided to concentrate on a few key aspects of the business — making a profit, for example. Stress the business opportunities implicit in this new focus, and help each individual identify the one or two most important things he or she can do to make the game plan a success.

Pay particular attention to your best people, taking them aside for private pep talks and an extra measure of reassurance. What companies that set out to downsize often don't realize is that in the process they stand to lose some top performers. It's precisely these folks who have the best chance of getting a good job elsewhere. When that oh-so-nice headhunter calls, or a rich early retirement package available to everyone their age beckons, why should they opt to stay aboard a sinking ship and work their tails off? Some suggested answers to whisper in their restless little ears: Because your sterling efforts will be more visible under the new regime. Because you'll have a bigger piece of the action, now that there are fewer people to share it with. And — probably best of all, if you can make good on it right then — because we'll pay you more.

The ultimate objective of all the solace is, of course, to quiet everyone's fears sufficiently to start getting work done again. From the outset recognize that the assignments you make — what is to be accomplished, and who is to do it — should be different from before; that was, you may need reminding, partly the purpose of the exercise. It's not so much that you should expect these recently depressed folks to do more. Rather, you should help them see that by attacking the work in new ways, the slimmed-down organization can actually get the job done. This may require teaching people new skills, which can be good for them. Unfortunately, it may also entail what Professor Joyce with a straight face calls negative job enrichment — going from working as an engineer, say, to operating a Xerox machine, as he did in his own real-world experience with downsizing.

Remember what you've been telling your people about the importance of being focused. Unless the troops were obscenely underworked before the cutback, don't try to have the remaining organization do everything it used to do. Look for tasks to eliminate. One good candidate: preparing all those reports. "We found a lot of things that had grown up over the years that were not that important," says a vice president of a much reduced chemical operation. "We had reports being written just so the people writing them could stay busy."

As you survey what needs to get done, you may, on the other hand, find that the original downsizing didn't quite get the cuts in the right places. Students of the phenomenon note that companies tend to get rid of a disproportionate number of production workers and sales reps, leaving deadwood in the managerial ranks untouched. Or they'll wipe out the obvious targets on the corporate staff—the P.R. people and the strategic planners—but retain lots of managerial cellulite in the comptroller's office.

Don't worry—the organization has its own perverse ways of telling you that critical functions are not being performed. "It's like squeezing a balloon," says Fred B. Fishman, a group president at ARA Services, a diversified service giant that has done some downsizing. "You eliminate a personnel job at the group level, then find that one pops up down in the division. Or you come in and ask who the three strangers are sitting out in the reception area, and it turns out that they're human-resources consultants that have been retained." Another veteran notes that because only one person is left who can do each job, if something happens to a key player, the whole operation quickly grinds to a halt. Asked how you can tell if you've cut too deep, Thorsteinson of National Semiconductor replies, "That's a question the customer answers for you—either your service goes in the tank or you start missing deliveries." Let such indications guide you if you decide you're going to have to start adding people again.

Is there nothing good to be said for downsizing? A few things. A human-resources V.P. who saw his division shrink from six thousand to four thousand offers the following encomium: "We find it a lot more fun, and get a little more satisfaction. You're involved in a lot more, have more of a sense of ownership." And the company just may survive.

But at what cost? It's a tad ironic that the same experts who preach the primacy of attending to your people — care about them and they will care about what your company does — also hold up the lean and mean as exemplary. At the very least, the pundits should footnote the fact that it's one thing for a company to be created spare and efficient and remain that way, and something else for the average corporation to try to achieve this ideal by letting people go. Consider, for example, the not so small matter of trust. Ask the same V.P. who's having more fun whether his people will ever trust the company as much as before. Somewhat ruefully he replies, "I don't know that we'll ever get that back."

29

Resurrecting Corporate Loyalty

Fido-like fealty is pretty much extinct.
Wary self-regard is trendy. But closer bonds are possible.

IT TOOK A WHILE for management to catch the tune. Birds in the secretarial pool knew it, bees on the shop floor knew it, even monkeys in the lower branches of managerial trees — supervisors, foremen — knew it. Their bosses didn't know it — that you might as well give up on being do-or-die loyal to the company. After all, goes the refrain, the company won't be loyal to you.

Survey data suggest that managers are learning fast. The opinion research firm of Yankelovich Skelly & White finds, for example, that according to its commitment index — a measure of the bond between an employee and his company — managerial commitment has dropped markedly in the last few years. The firm attributes the drop to corporate downsizing, new pressures to operate lean and mean, and a concomitant feeling among managers that they now have fewer opportunities to advance.

The people at the very top of the corporation still typically say they're true blue to it. The trouble is, as more corporate honchos have strapped on golden parachutes or enriched themselves with leveraged buyout deals, a gap has opened between them and the managers beneath them that threatens to become a yawning chasm. For fifteen years Opinion Research Corp., a subsidiary of the Arthur D. Little consulting outfit, has been asking employees, "How would you rate your company on the ability of top management?" From 1970 through 1974, 69 percent of the thousands of managers surveyed checked off "Good" or "Very Good." From 1980 through 1985, the percentage dwindled to 47 percent. Managers' rating of the brass has always been more favorable than ratings awarded by lower echelons — supervisors, professionals, clerical types, and hourly workers —

but nowadays managers and their subordinates are closer in their evaluations.

What gives this a certain poignancy is the impression, common among those who've looked into the trend, that many managers still want to be loyal — indeed, they pine for an employer worth their loyalty. George E. Breen, former director of marketing research for the Stanley Works, a toolmaker in New Britain, Connecticut, conducted a study of middle management in the 1980s for the American Management Association. From his survey data and discussions with 250 managers, Breen concludes that while corporate loyalty has declined considerably among them, they still wish "almost for a bonding with upper management." Breen says of the participants in his study, "They want to belong to something they can believe in."

What is it that we have lost? The classical notion of corporate loyalty went something like this: a company gave a would-be manager a job, for which he should feel grateful. He might have to put up with a good bit — tyrannical bosses, frequent relocation, lots of time apart from his family — but as long as he did, he had a place. The company, in turn, could expect him to stand by it, forsaking other opportunities — at least unless they were clearly better than he was going to get at Tried & True Corp.

Even in this stripped-down form, the classical notion had appeal — job security mostly, a big consideration for people with memories of the Depression. For companies it meant a relatively compliant managerial work force. But there was also a lot that was bad about old-style loyalty.

It wasn't just that companies got away with behavior toward employees that today seems unreasonable or unfair. Perhaps more perniciously, old-style loyalty sometimes bred a kind of my-company-right-or-wrong insularity, a mind-set that didn't do much to prepare managers for reacting to what are euphemistically known as changes in the corporate environment — increasingly critical customers, breathtaking leaps in technology, foreign devils invading the company's markets. Donald C. King, associate dean of Purdue's Krannert Graduate School of Management, cites a study he worked on that compared engineers and technicians who identified principally with their field of specialization to similarly trained individuals who identified more with their company. Employers judged the first type to be on average the better employees, more up-to-date in their fields and more productive.

What finally kiboshed old-style loyalty was a combination of changing managerial expectations and a new perception by top management of what companies could afford to offer. Baby-boomers on the managerial ladder wanted stimulation, advancement, and a voice — and if they didn't get it at this company, they would at another. They did not, on the other hand, want to relocate their dual-career families. Their skepticism about loyalty was confirmed by the spectacle of top managers taking the money and deserting the team when confronted with a takeover threat or the possibility of a buyout.

Companies, for their part, decided they could no longer carry as many managers, certainly not the ones who weren't pulling their weight. Possible reasons: competition was tougher, computers could replace some managerial data gatherers, and, just perhaps, company leaders had come to view managers as "corporate assets, not as people," in the words of Alexander B. Horniman, director of the Center for the Study of Applied Ethics at the University of Virginia's Darden School of Business. *Voilà*, downsizing. Even employers fabled for corporate stability, such as General Electric, ended up deleting the words *lifetime employment* from their personnel manuals and recruiting literature.

Does all this mean that we have to do without corporate loyalty? Not necessarily. Psychologist and consultant Harry Levinson, for example, suggests employer and employee may be able to come to a new type of understanding whereby "each can trust the other, recognizing that each side has appropriate self-interest." According to Levinson, the manager in effect says, "I will give the organization intensity of effort, providing the organization in return is fair to me — in particular, that it doesn't con me about opportunity when there no longer is opportunity." Two subtleties here: Such an understanding makes the manager more dependent on his immediate boss. He will rely on his boss to tell him, for example, what the company's intentions are for the business he is in. Second, to make such an understanding work, the company's performance-appraisal system has to work, honestly telling the individual how he's doing.

Fat chance, the wizened corporate veteran might reply. Recent Opinion Research Corp. surveys support skepticism. Asked how effective their last review had been in letting them know where they stood in the company, only 28 percent of managers replied, "Very Effective," the rest opting for "Somewhat Effective" or worse. Furthermore, despite all the recent exhortations urging top management to get in better touch with employees — go out there, wander around — communication from on high seems to be getting poorer, not better. The percentage of managers who said that their companies were doing a good job letting them know what was going on has declined since the early 1970s; it's now down to about 40 percent.

Even if a company inundates its managers with info, it probably still won't elicit the kind of loyalty that goes beyond careerist self-regard. To get loyalty that serves a greater collective good, Levinson allows, the company has to hold out something higher to managers — namely, values. These values must transcend marketplace imperatives like "Make a buck," must be given considerably more than lip service, particularly by top management, and probably should say something about how employees will be treated. Perhaps the best example is the well-known set Thomas Watson, Sr., laid down for IBM, a company that hasn't had much trouble maintaining corporate loyalty: The individual must be respected. The customer must be given the best possible service. Excellence and superior performance must be pursued in every IBM activity.

Unfortunately, as Horniman of Virginia's Darden School notes, "Lots of folks leading organizations today wouldn't know a value system if it hit them in the face." His simple test: Ask employees what principles they will be fired for violating. If they can't think of any beyond "Thou shalt not steal," don't expect much by way of values. If, on the other hand, they can cite a few that command your respect, then you just may have found a company worth being loyal to.

❈ 30 ❈

No Word from on High

For all the talk about getting in touch with employees,
executives seem to be communicating less, not more.

MANAGE BY WANDERING AROUND. Share your vision of the company's future. Act more like the Japanese—keep workers informed, encourage them to speak up, listen to what they have to say. Get out there and be a leader, not just a manager.

Splendid advice. The only problem: it isn't happening, at least not in the practice of most executives. For all the rhetoric in books like *In Search of Excellence* or *Reinventing the Corporation,* employee surveys indicate that the troops think management is doing a poorer job communicating with them than it did five years ago. From a report based on surveys of forty-eight thousand employees by Opinion Research Corp.: "Downward communication, measured by employees' ratings of their companies on letting them know what is going on, is rated favorably by fewer than half of employees in all groups."

If the brass don't wake up soon, they stand to get their sleepy little heads handed to them by the competition. Virtually everyone who has studied the problem—executives, consultants, business school professors—agrees that you have to share lots of information with employees if you hope to elicit their commitment. Commitment, an emerging buzzword, means high productivity, low turnover, and a better chance of avoiding corporate death at the hands of the Japanese.

Top executives at Tandem Computers, a California-based computer manufacturer, work at communications. In 1985 the company staged some six hundred hours of meetings in which honchos from the different disciplines—marketing, finance, manufacturing— explained the corporation's strategy to employees. The chief executive or another heavyweight presides over televised monthly confabs beamed to all the company's U.S. facilities, with telephone hookups to take questions. There are also junkets for high performers from the ranks that combine taking in some exotic scenery with still more briefing from executives on the company's plans. Tandem has, it claims, one of the lowest turnover rates in Silicon Valley, as well as high productivity.

Dialogue also works at GM's Packard Electric plant in Brookhaven, Mississippi. Besides providing a hefty dose of conventional communications — a monthly newspaper, frequent meetings of employee teams, an electronic news display in the cafeteria — management at the unionized facility puts on a quarterly meeting for all employees. Says plant manager J. Edward Zuga, "We share with our people all the pertinent information — financial performance, future plans, quality performance . . . anything of significance to them and the company." An open discussion follows the presentation. According to Zuga, the openness has helped keep turnover low and productivity high. Eugene Edwards, president of the union local at the plant, agrees: "There's more communication between management and labor here than I've seen in any other plant. It's a good atmosphere. No one wants to quit his job."

So why don't more executives get off the mute, inglorious dime? Partly because they haven't wanted to be the bearers of bad news — the global competition is killing us, we're being taken over, you've just lost in the downsizing lottery. Even in Silicon Valley, where entrepreneurs used to pride themselves on availability to the troops, the rolling barrage hitting high-tech industries has apparently caused some charismatoids to take cover. This comes at just the wrong time: when the folks in the trenches feel the most apprehension, they most need straight talk from the top. Roger D'Aprix, a consultant with Towers Perrin Forster & Crosby, assesses the damage done by clamming up while downsizing: "At the end, you have management looking to the future, ready to get on with it, at the head of a bunch of surviving employees who don't give a damn about the organization."

Good times or bad, workers these days expect more information on what's happening to the company and how it will affect them. Managers are too ready to believe that they have responded to these heightened expectations. Typically, top management commissions surveys of the so-called climate among employees — consultants say their survey business is booming — starts a new in-house publication, maybe even gives everybody a statement of the corporate mission. The trouble, as D'Aprix points out, is that effective communication isn't a program that the brass just launches; the troops quickly see through the latest one of those. It is, instead, a process that managers must commit themselves to — an evolving, give-and-take process that has to be worked at every day.

Most executives dislike this idea. For one thing, most are unaccustomed to communicating candidly even with fellow executives. Robert Lefton, president of Psychological Associates Inc., a St. Louis consulting firm, notes that in working with top management groups at twenty-six companies, twenty of them Fortune 500 corporations, he found that the executives consistently rate communications among themselves as their principal area of difficulty, ahead of such challenges as handling conflict, holding better meetings, or making decisions.

They're not concerned about formal, memo-through-the-chain-of-command communications, Lefton says, but rather about how tough it is to have probing, problem-solving conversations. Opinion Research Corp. consultant William A. Schiemann seconds the point, based on his work with top executives: "If you look at the tier immediately below the president, in 80 percent of the cases we find most of the group afraid to share their feelings about problems in the organization." No wonder the troops get confused about the direction of march.

Consultants tend to tiptoe a bit around the issue of managerial insecurity as a barrier to communications, but most finally come around to admitting its importance. They speak of executive defensiveness. They talk about executive isolation on mahogany row, about the need to maintain a wall of infallibility or the appearance of omniscience. What the consultants don't talk about is cowardice.

If the top dogs are going to be paid so much, can't the rest of the kennel reasonably expect a little more of them by way of guts? Guts enough, for starters, to go out and talk to their people face-to-face, if that's what it takes to make the company work. While even gutsy communicators cannot expect to achieve perfect amity — that's for the angels — they can expect, through better communications, to improve the lot of the employees, the shareholders, and themselves.

Becoming a charismatic communicator, the kind that builds commitment, seems not beyond the ability of the typical managerial mortal. Consider the research findings of Charles O'Reilly, a professor at the University of California's graduate school of business at Berkeley. Expert after expert has noted the importance of a strong corporate culture if a company is to be a winner. O'Reilly studied how workers at Silicon Valley companies with strong cultures perceived their corporate leaders. A credible leader, he found, had three principal attributes. He or she was perceived to be trustworthy — from seeing him in action, workers judged that he had their interests at heart as well as his own. He was thought to be an expert. And he was seen to be dynamic and attractive, by which workers meant not much more than that they could see him in motion — walking around, talking about the company, working on projects with them.

If you still feel you have to structure your downward communications, the experts say, build in some way for the underlings to talk back. Face-to-face sessions are by far the best. If you're talking with a small group, try to see that they're all from about the same level, and that nobody's immediate boss is sitting there glowering. You're going to have to convince the troops that you're interested in what they have to say, and that you actually want them to speak up — which means nobody gets zapped for asking a tough question or challenging a managerial judgment.

If your organization is so big that you think you have to use the magic of video, bear in mind the criticism of W. Charles Redding, professor emeritus of communications at Purdue: "Television is just so one-way." In a corporate setting it can all too easily come to seem like the exhortations of Big Brother. Provide telephone hookups for questions, or televise an appearance before a live audience capable of asking questions.

What should you talk about? That's easy: the corporate strategy — where the company is, where it's going. As James M. Kouzes, director of the Executive Development Center at Santa Clara University, observes, "I've never talked to anybody lower down in an organization who says he's had enough of that." Surveys confirm that this is the numero uno request among employees. When you do talk about strategy, be specific and detailed — the experts say that you're kidding yourself if you think that by keeping the strategy from the people who have to carry it out, you can keep it from the competition. As Roger D'Aprix advises, talk in terms of the forces driving the business, not just about a recent event or a particular problem.

After all the talking, show that what you heard makes a difference. Open your thinking, not just your ears. Act on what the people in the ranks have told you. Then keep walking, talking, and looking for that competitive edge for your company. Lions prowl; the Sphinx merely sits there, the dead sand of history blowing over its silence.

31

Beyond Sexist Management

Trying to be a nonsexist executive isn't easy.
But it can pay off big in how you handle both men and women.

WHAT IS A RIGHT-THINKING MALE MANAGER to do? He has expunged all sexist terms from his workday vocabulary — there are no more references to "girls" or even "gals," no more "honey," "sweetie," "gorgeous," or "lamb chop." He wouldn't think of telling an off-color story. He hires and promotes women. But it doesn't seem enough. He still hears the women in his organization grumbling the old grumble: you're discriminating against us.

Now wait a minute, sister — or so he would like to say — *discrimination* is a hard word. I don't hate women, and I certainly don't go around setting police dogs on them or spraying them with fire hoses.

You're discriminating against us without even realizing it, comes the response, which only makes the problem more intractable. You discriminate by not treating us exactly the same as the men you work with.

You've got to be kidding. You really want me to treat you exactly the same way, and if I don't, it's discrimination?

Yes.

Hmmmm.

What is a right-thinking male manager to do? He can throw up his hands, of course, and become a sort of grouchy neo-sexist. This is not recommended, however: too much revanchism, particularly in hiring and promotion policies, could bring on a lawsuit.

Alternatively, the right-thinking male manager can press on, trying to understand what women are criticizing him for, seeing if he should, or can, do anything about it. It's a long slog: you won't put the criticism to rest in a day, or with just what you learn from a chapter in a book. The wise businessman doesn't take this path in order to be a good guy. He takes it because he wants to be a good manager, getting maximum results from everyone who works for him. The curious thing is that along the way he may learn to be a better manager of men as well as women.

At the outset, be aware of the scope of the undertaking. You are trying to remove impediments to clear and productive communications with women co-workers. In the process you need not embrace the Equal Rights Amendment, give up your stand against job quotas for women and minorities, or solve the Problem of Sexism for society — or even for your company. Kate Kirkham, associate director of the M.B.A. program at Brigham Young University, recommends to corporate managers the following structure for thinking about sexism in their organizations. Level one — do I do anything myself that may be perceived as discriminatory? Level two — in this organization, what happens to people because of their sex? How, for example, are the three women in a department with forty men treated by their male co-workers? Level three — do management policies here affect people differently because of their sex? You will do much better on levels two and three if you first get your act together on level one. For now, stick to that.

Probably the best way to start is by tackling the unwitting discrimination you're supposedly guilty of. What do businesswomen mean when they say they're not being treated exactly like men? The experts — academics, consultants, and businesswomen themselves — say that the complaint subsumes three more specific complaints. First, women often think that their bosses won't criticize them when they deserve, and indeed need, criticism. This is commonly attributed to the boss's abject fear that if he really lowers the boom, she'll burst into tears.

Second, women believe that they are excluded from certain assignments, informal deliberations, and ad hoc social gatherings. He has to send somebody parachuting into Baluchistan to settle a little distribution problem — caravan delays or something. Does he bother to even offer the assignment to Wonder Woman, his female subordinate? He should at least ask if she wants the job.

Finally, there's the almost ineffable matter of tone. Some women hear their bosses talking one way to males, another to females, even though the words are the same. It isn't necessarily that he oozes condescension, or, next worst, that he loses no opportunity to call attention to the fact that there are ladies present. Quite often it is instead a sort of guarded quality to what he says, or a lack of the customary heartiness.

Okay, the right-thinking male manager may reply, it's clear now what I have to do. I have to say the same thing to both men and women — whether it's a bawling out, a posting to Namibia, or an invitation to an after-hours drink — and in precisely the same way. I shall become, to use the jargon of the enlightened, gender-blind.

The trouble is, you probably can't. Barbara Gutek, an associate professor of psychology at Claremont Graduate School in California, puts into social science language what you knew all along: "Gender is the most salient difference between people. Someone comes into your office for a moment. Afterward you may not remember whether that person had blue or brown eyes, but you won't forget the person's gender."

No, some experts counsel, what you have to do is recognize the differences in the ways men and women behave in business situations. There are differences, at least according to the research of certain academics and the observations of consultants. Here's a short list of their admittedly controversial conclusions:

Politics: Men tend to be better at office politics than women, in the sense that they seem to understand they have to get themselves and their work noticed. Men are also better at working with people they dislike, if that's what it takes to get the job done. Women are inclined to believe that if you do your job well, the organization will treat you fairly.

Reaction to Criticism: The boss says, "Glutz, you really messed up on that one." If Glutz is a man, he will immediately begin pointing to the circumstances that made it impossible to do the job right. He won't, as they say, take it personally. If Glutz is a woman, she will allow as how she thought this or that, and then proceed to flagellate herself mentally because it was all her fault.

Short-Form Communications: Men can exchange significant information with one another in seemingly casual fifteen-second conversa-

tions; women, witnessing the back-and-forth, won't notice that any-thing much has been communicated. It's as if men speak a different language from women. If a male subordinate begins to make a mistake, the boss can, with a quick zap, call him back into line; a woman won't hear the criticism.

Explanation: The boss says, "What about this situation?" A male subordinate will respond, "The problem is A, the solution is Z." A female subordinate will say, "The problem is A, and I went through B, C, and D to come up with solution Z." A male boss may think, "She's wasting time."

Decision-Making: This is the big difference, in that it sums up or explains several other differences. Women are painstaking, seeking everyone's opinion and trying to build consensus; they want their own views listened to carefully in any deliberation. Because women dwell so on all the disastrous consequences that may ensue from a decision, they are less willing to take risks. Male behavior in making decisions can be summed up in a phrase: go for it. In the parlance of behavioral science, men are interested in outcome, women in process.

All right, now that you have all that straight, what use do you make of it when next in a meeting with men and women? This is tricky. What you do not do is expect Ms. Larue necessarily to be laborious in her description of the matter before you. Nor do you rely on young Mr. Furp, just because of his sex, to catch the meaning of your cautionary three-nanosecond verbal sally.

Leonard Chusmir, a professor of management at the University of Colorado at Denver, has studied behavioral differences between the sexes for five years. He sums up the problem in applying his and others' findings: "You can't draw conclusions about how an individual will behave from research on how the average member of a group will behave." Anyone who has been around the corporate breed for a while knows that individual animals, whether male or female, differ greatly in their grasp of office politics, say, or their sensitivity to criticism. Moreover, any generalizations based on sex may quickly be out of date — twenty-five-year-old female M.B.A.'s don't necessarily behave like career women now in their fifties.

What you should do with the information is use it in a nonsexist way to inform, and enlarge, your understanding of how individuals behave, whatever their sex. Who knows? You just might discover that your macho chief executive is quite process-oriented, which may explain why your here's-the-problem, we'll-do-this presentations have been such bombs.

Fine, you reply, but I still don't know what to do if Ms. Larue starts crying. Here take the advice of the late Kaleel Jamison, a consultant wise in the ways of the heart: treat it just as you would a display of anger from a man — they're both outpourings of intense feeling. Tell the woman it's okay to cry, let her weep it out, and then go to work together on what's bothering her. You may not have to face the problem, though, at least not in the form you expect. James Crain, the vice president of finance for New England Telephone and a longtime student of the treatment of women in the phone company, reports that in the last two years he hasn't had one woman cry in his office. But a man did.

32

Bunch and Crunch on the Fast Track

*Many baby-boomers aren't getting ahead as fast
as they expected to. Herewith a few strategies for coping.*

IN THE CAREERIST REVERIE of the baby-boom elite, it was all supposed to be so simple — arduous, but simple. Bust your hump in college to get good grades, then parlay those into admission to a business school, the bigger the name, the better. Upon graduation, take a high-prestige job in management consulting or with some corporate colossus and use it for two or three years to hone your skills, promote your visibility, and generally "develop your instrument," in Mary Cunningham's curious phrase.

After the first job, a brisk hopscotch onward: change positions, change companies, touch down in a given square long enough to leave an imprint but not to get stuck. Pretty soon, you break into the category labeled "general management." From there on in your ascent to the top, it's a matter of steadily increasing responsibility, concomitant perks and status, and enough money to do what you want. Not that the bucks are the most important thing, of course — along the way there have to be challenges, accomplishments, satisfactions. After all, a career is a lot more than just a succession of jobs.

It was supposed to be so simple, but it isn't turning out that way.

In the careers of the best-situated members of the baby-boom generation, the next few years promise to be critical. In 1986, the children born in 1946, the first fruits of the boom, celebrated their fortieth birthdays. Conventional wisdom holds that if you haven't reached the ranks of management by age forty — in charge of a profit-making operation, with two or three tiers of subordinates — your chances thereafter are much diminished. Even members of the cohort of 1957, one of the largest, have cause to be concerned. While they have just turned thirty, they'll be competing with the swollen cohorts that immediately preceded them. "It may make everyone like a balle-rina," suggests a veteran career counselor. "If a company doesn't take her in her early twenties, it never will."

For most baby-boomers, the ones without the glittering creden-tials, merely having a place on the road to the executive suite would seem success enough — forget about the pace of traffic. These are the hundreds of thousands who have already had to adjust their expecta-tions downward, finding, for example, that a college degree doesn't guarantee you an interesting job.

Until recently the bad news hadn't caught up with the folks on the fast track — the graduates of good schools who have or expect to have good jobs with good companies. Observes Arthur Shapiro, head of an organization that samples public opinion, "They're the last ones to keep the expectations from the late 1960s"— expectations redolent of the greening of America: personal fulfillment, wide-ranging free-dom, and continuing material advancement.

Just as many fast-track careers enter the make-it-or-break-it pas-sage, a few discouraging cautionary flags have begun to wave. Some of the biggest employers of M.B.A.'s and career-minded B.A.'s — huge manufacturing companies, package-goods giants, the largest banks — report that incumbents are remaining longer in entry-level jobs and at the second and third levels thereafter. Salaries for protomanagers three or four years out of school are not increasing as fast as starting salaries. There seem to be more complaints, too, about the managerial style of the baby-boomers, complaints that go beyond the cliché of the M.B.A. as arrogant whippersnapper to stab at precisely why this generation can't, or won't, exercise authority.

The message of trouble ahead may even be percolating into the consciousness of those most directly concerned. At its crudest, the collective reaction takes the form of clinging to the main chance. One survey from the early 1980s found that while a large preponderance of M.B.A. students at twenty top schools still rated "fulfillment" as their chief career goal, a majority of the graduates of those same institutions who had been in the work force five years assigned the highest place to "money."

Subtler changes, in the form of new rationalizations and ambiva-lence, have also begun to creep into the attitudes of many fast-track hopefuls, particularly ones who have been on the job for three or four years. It can be argued that much of what their seniors found objectionable in the ideology of this generation — their loyalty to the managerial profession rather than to a particular company, their emphasis on having a life apart from work — was only an adaptation to a corporate sphere beset by unprecedented mutability and insecurity. (Unprecedented, the graybeards ask? Yes, reply the young and the restless; when before have we seen such oil shocks, inflation and then disinflation, or so many interest-rate gyrations?)

The current trimming to the wind suggests, if anything, a new resignation: if I can't get the brass ring, maybe what I am going to get will be better for me, anyway. A hotshot graduate of the University of Chicago Graduate School of Business was recently asked, after she had talked at great length about how a series of essentially lateral job changes had provided her with broad experience, if she had any fears with respect to her career. "Only that I might be put into a position for which I'm not qualified," she replied. Let's hear it for the take-charge generation.

What went wrong on the path to glory? Human-resources types at the corporations that have slowed down their fast tracks generally cite three or four causes. There's the current stratospheric level of M.B.A. starting salaries, of course, which makes it harder to just hire such folks, much less shoot them up into the managerial ozone. Some personnel types have given up on the effort entirely.

Solemnly, solemnly they intone that this is not the go-go era of growth and diversification — O happy lost time of too much money and too few managers, the bright vision of which may permanently haunt baby-boom dreams! No, this is a season for restructuring and the redeployment of assets — sell off the businesses you finally admit you don't understand, park the money or buy back your stock, take cover.

Among the assets being redeployed, in some cases right out the door, are managers. Company after company has quietly put out the word that it intends to function with a "leaner management structure" in the 1990s — fewer rungs on the ladder, fewer footholds on each rung. Those already holding on to the remaining positions for dear life, often forty- or forty-five-year-olds who originally came aboard in the heyday of expansion, probably can't be expected to give up their spots to satisfy some bright young thing's career-planning objectives. Not without first trying a few brisk kicks downward, anyway.

Farther down the managerial ladder, three or four rungs from the bottom, kicking of another kind is already going on. Even corporations whose continued growth has enabled them to move folks up at the old rate report concern over "salary compression." Pay increases granted to three- and four-year veterans simply haven't kept up with the rise in starting salaries, particularly the starting salaries paid to masters of you-know-what from highly regarded schools.

Despite what peevish recruiters say, the explanation of this problem is not limited to the money-grubbin' of them blankety-blank M.B.A.'s. Adjusted for inflation, the median starting salary for graduates of the Harvard Business School did not increase at all from 1970 to 1980. It's just that the pay hikes extended to most junior managers — including the M.B.A.'s of yesteryear — didn't come anywhere near keeping even with inflation. As a result, the difference between what you make after a few years of loyal service and what the newest kid on the corridor receives has steadily shrunk.

The salaries commanded by graduating M.B.A.'s are set by the market. (Could that be why the top ten or so schools have not increased their enrollment in the past few years?) By contrast, in making decisions on pay raises, many companies have been relatively insulated from the markets for managers farther along in their careers. What's Joe Lending Officer in Seattle to make of the salaries his peers in Boston or Chicago pull down, even if he knows?

A lesson — an unsettling one — appears to be emerging from all this. According to a director of career development at one top-flight business school, "We may be getting to where the British already are — if an individual wants to realize his full financial value after years with an employer, he has to put himself on the market" — that is, shop for a new job at another company. But what if that market is contracting?

The resistance that fast-track types increasingly encounter isn't just a function of impersonal economic forces, however. Noting the baby-boomers' universally acknowledged and seemingly insatiable desire for more feedback from above — how'm I doing? — University of Texas Professor Carl Weick observes, "People faced with uncertainty have to check on themselves more frequently. This group senses that their bosses have very ambivalent feelings about them."

As with most fallings-out between executives, this souring may largely be a conflict over "managerial style," defined as "how you treat the people over and under you." Weick hears a swelling chorus of complaints that managers formed in the Age of Aquarius — peace, love, and understanding: oh, wow — lack certain basic skills in dealing with others. "They don't seem able to graduate their responses — they come on way too strong, or don't come on strong enough."

On the not-strong-enough theme, others wonder whether the baby-boom elite, for all their endless talk about seeking to assume responsibility, really want to *boss* anyone. In a study comparing young would-be managers in the Bell System with their counterparts tested twenty years ago, AT&T's principal analysts of the company's human resources, Ann Howard and Douglas Bray, found the current crew scoring significantly higher on measures labeled "nurturance" and "succorance"—they apparently want to both give and get warmth. On a measure of "dominance," however — roughly an indication of a readiness to kick ass — the more recent group scored only half as high as the good gray Organization Men.

Even if companies can't arrange for mass transplants of old-fashioned spine — and how useful would such vestigial skeletage be at quality-circle meetings anyway?— there are steps that a manager of baby-boomchiks can take to ease the pain of deceleration for those on the now not-so-fast track. Most of these actions boil down to lavishing attention upon the lost-in-space generation as individuals. Reassure each that he or she is not fading into the crowd. In other words, if you can't give them promotions or whopping pay increases, at least try to talk the worry out of them — supportively, nurturantly, never-endingly.

Planning, as many companies are, an increased number of lateral transfers? Don't stress that this is in lieu of vertical movement. Tell the lucky devils what may in fact be true: that the company hopes to grow executives with a broader base of experience, thereby avoiding what the human-resources people at B. F. Goodrich term "the tall, thin manager."

Thinking of providing that bright young woman in the marketing department a modest step up the ladder, but one that requires relocating to Sasquatch Junction? Make neither the old mistake of calling Friday to tell her to be there Monday nor the new one of assuming that because her husband is V.P. of a local bank, she won't move. Take the risk of seeming to shop the job around and offer it to her, but don't be surprised if she doesn't take it. Baby-boomers turn down transfer promotions all the time, but everyone's better off if she understands that it's her decision.

For the managerial baby-boomer him- or herself, probably the best advice is to substitute new dreams for the old ones. Are there means of obtaining in other spheres of your life the same satisfactions that you expected from a position high in management? If you can't run your company's board of directors at age thirty-four, for example, maybe you can get at least some of the same political kicks wrestling with the problems of a professional association or a local charity.

For a generation still often labeled antiauthoritarian and anticorporate, the ideal of independence represented by having your own business also holds out considerable appeal. Indeed, business schools across the country report an upsurge of student interest in entrepreneurship. Whether this will turn out to be anything more than a widely held dream remains to be seen — the hours required in a start-up situation unappealing — but it's a lovely dream.

Or you might think about preparing yourself for some very different line of work. Enlightened companies such as IBM are already paying to reeducate employees for new jobs somewhere else in the corporation. But why not try something completely novel in a fresh setting — after fifteen years in corporate finance, for example, why not segue into university administration? Says Winn Price, until recently director of career development at the Harvard Business School and himself a product of the baby boom, "I expect that many members of my generation will have two or even three careers in their lifetimes."

Remember, too, that the brass ring is, after all, only brass.

✖ Part IV ✖

CURIOUS CUSTOMS OF
THE NATIVES

33

Business Gift-Giving

Perhaps fifty million business gifts changed hands last year.
They can be a problem for both giver and getter.

ON THE NORTHWEST COAST of the continent, among the forested inlets above Vancouver, British Columbia, there lives a tribe of Native Americans called the Kwakiutl. While nowadays much reduced in number and in circumstance, the Kwakiutl of yore achieved lasting fame among anthropologists with a practice called the potlatch. In a potlatch ceremony, a Kwakiutl personage would confirm his status within the tribe, or strike for higher status, by inundating his fellows with gifts. We're not talking abalone shells here, either. In the great Village Island potlatch of 1921, for example, party-thrower Daniel Cranmer of the Nimpkish clan handed out five gasoline-powered boats, twenty-four canoes, two pool tables, three hundred oak chests, four hundred Hudson's Bay blankets, a thousand sacks of flour, sewing machines, gramophones, bedsteads, bureaus, and some cash. For recipients of the gifts, there was a catch, of course: the only way to keep up with the Cranmers, status-wise, would have been to throw another potlatch where still more stuff was given away. No one ever did.

On the northeast coast of the continent, on the banks of the Charles River in Boston, there occasionally exists another band with its own curious folkways. These are the students of the Advanced Management Program (AMP) of the Harvard Business School, typically men and women sent by their companies for a last academic fill-up before being propelled into top management. By long-standing custom, toward the end of the thirteen-week program each student gives every one of his 160 or so classmates a small "token"—as a Harvard spokesman terms the gifts, stressing that they're never more expensive than, say, a $20 Cross pen with the logo of the donor's corporation. Dormitory suites become crowded with glassware, boxes of golf balls, cases of beer, and ugly ten-pound ashtrays. A paper company with students in the program sometimes provides boxes to ship the swag home in. If managers from the U.S. Postal Service are attending, they may arrange to have a couple of hearties from the local post office come over to help out with the packing.

While there are clearly differences between Kwakiutl and AMP gift-giving — the AMP's isn't really a competition for status; Kwakiutl donors pay for their gifts with their own money — note the similarities, for they characterize most business gift-giving. Any matching of the gift to the actual wants and needs of the recipient is, at best, approximate. During the period when potlatching Kwakiutl were giving away thousands of blankets, the tribe dwindled to a little over a thousand souls, living, as always, in a fairly temperate climate. Professor Jay Lorsch, who teaches in the AMP and receives the same gifts as the students, reports that he has so many so-called gimme caps — farmer walks into local John Deere distributor, sees billed cap with Deere logo affixed, says, "Gimme one of them caps"— that he could wear a different one every day.

Neither Kwakiutl nor AMP giving is an act of spontaneous largess. Both are calculated to cement a relationship between donor and donee: among the Kwakiutl, social superior and subordinate; among the AMPs, classmate, acquaintance, or maybe just — O utilitarian world of commerce — contact.

In that world, the giving of gifts is big business. *Incentive Marketing* magazine, basing its conclusions on a survey of its readers who buy business gifts, estimates that some fifty million were purchased in 1983 in the U.S. at a total cost of just over $1 billion. Add in "specialties"— those little logo-bearing knickknacks, defined in the trade as items selling for $4 or less — and the cost of the goods handed out probably amounts to over $3 billion, according to Specialty Advertising Association International, a trade association. The munificence is not confined to corner dry-cleaning establishments handing out ballpoint pens. Ira Neaman, head of Vantage Custom Classics in Linden, New Jersey, which makes golf shirts and sweaters with logos embroidered on them, says that his company has done work for 380 of the Fortune 500 industrial corporations.

Some of these goodies are given to the donor's employees, no doubt; gift manufacturers won't hazard a guess as to how many. But a survey of 262 companies by the Bureau of National Affairs, a private research organization, found that only about 25 percent planned to give their employees year-end gifts, while another 15 percent intended to hand out cash bonuses. This would seem to leave lots of seats at the corporate potlatch for customers, suppliers, clients, and others "with whom we maintain a business relationship," as the phrase goes.

Purveyors of some of the more popular items for executives to give — expensive chocolates, boxes of fruit, liquor — say that their best corporate customers are typically Wall Street investment banking and brokerage houses, advertising agencies, law firms, and banks. These are precisely the businesses that must worry most about keeping a few big clients happy. As Jennifer Woodward, manager of corporate sales for Godiva chocolates, points out, they are also the outfits that don't make a product they can use as a gift, though one wonders how much goodwill an auto-parts maker might engender by sending out cartons of fan belts.

Items given range from the sublime to the ridiculous. According to *Incentive Marketing*'s survey, the top choices were, in declining order of popularity, pens or pen sets, clocks, liquor, calendars, diaries, watches, knives, fruit, glassware, jackets, and desk sets. Richard Ebel, a vice president of the Specialty Advertising Association, explains the preference for desktop items: "You want it to be right there where the purchasing decision is made." More imaginative gifts include a day of beauty treatments at an Elizabeth Arden salon, given by one company to the wife of each board member; a weekend in the corporate condominium in Florida; and — ever popular — a membership in Harry & David's Fruit-of-the-Month Club, these days run not by Harry and David but by RJR Industries, which bought it from them.

The chief force making for sanity in business gift-giving is the tax code. By law, gifts given to people outside the company are deductible business expenses only if they cost no more than $25. While some companies and executives choose to exceed this limit, most do not — excess generosity can always be channeled into business entertaining, where the limits are not so well defined. For companies that lay down a policy on the giving and receiving of gifts, the $25 limit provides a handy benchmark. There are, however, corporations — Sears notable among them — that hold up a more Draconian standard: no gifts at all to or from outsiders. These companies have the right idea.

Consider the reasons most executives offer for giving business gifts. According to a Specialty Advertising Association study, most say it's either to thank customers or to develop business. An anthropologist, Associate Professor Sylvia Forman of the University of Massachusetts at Amherst, amplifies: "In a business setting, a gift is a symbol that there is something else between the two of you besides a strict business relationship. It leaves you the opportunity to make the relationship more complex."

Which is precisely the problem. Yours is supposed to be a business relationship: limpid, functional, on both sides based on calculations of what is best for the company. A gift muddies the waters. Even the universally proffered defense of small gifts —"Nobody was ever bought with a (fill in the blank)"— implicitly suggests that perhaps the donor hasn't paid enough to buy the recipient outright, but for a lesser amount he presumably gets something. A kind thought? A willingness to have lunch and listen to his pitch?

Or maybe he just wards off potential displeasure. Marilyn Moats Kennedy, who heads a consulting firm named Career Strategies, observes that most companies give gifts "not because they like you, but because they are afraid of what would happen if they didn't." Many managerial givers, when promised anonymity, concur. They also say that the logistics can be a colossal pain. Concludes the president of one of the largest advertising agencies, rather wearily, "It's easier not to get them, or to give them."

But he does both. If you feel compelled to, then at least do it right. The point is to make your gift memorable but not embarrassing. Within the confines of the $25 limit, attempt to fit the gift to the recipient's tastes, while also conveying something distinctive about the donor. For example, Guest Quarters, a chain of apartment hotels headquartered in Washington, D.C., gives out about 1,500 decorative English tins made specially for the chain — a bit like those containers commemorating the wedding of Prince Charles and Lady Di, or the National Horse Show — which its local hotels have filled with foodstuffs appropriate to their region. "We hope the people we give them to see the same attention to detail, and sense of fun, in the gifts as in the hotels themselves," says Michael Dickens, the president of Guest Quarters.

If possible, convey the gifts in person, accompanying them with a brief handwritten note — otherwise, it's just another business delivery. If you want your present to be truly distinctive, give it at some time other than the holiday season, when the corporate potlatch is at its most frenzied.

Come next December, that will leave you more time to think about the very best gifts. For Christians, this presumably includes a little reflection at Christmas on the astonishing gift of transmutative love delivered in Bethlehem. And for every manager, or at least every one with friends, lovers, or family, it should embrace consideration of certain frequently neglected gift possibilities, namely your time, energy, and imagination, in amounts sufficient to communicate love.

34

Out to Lunch

A little white wine and fish won't kill you.
In fact, they may do your career some good.

DOESN'T ANYBODY want to have a nice business lunch anymore? From a salesman in Chicago: "It's getting harder to get customers to go out for lunch." From a management consultant in San Francisco: "I just don't do lunch — I use the time to go to the gym and run."

The business lunch isn't dying — most big-time business lunch spots across the country report their trade unhurt by either the fitness boom or corporate cutbacks. But interviews with restaurateurs and private-club managers from Atlanta to Seattle confirm an impression widespread in the managerial community: the quotidian business lunch is becoming lighter in fare, less boozy, often shorter, and generally more purposive. As if to corroborate the shift toward flat-tummied asceticism, business breakfasts are dramatically on the increase.

A look at the customs and uses of lunch makes it clear that we may be eschewing more than calories. What's going out of lunch is not merely the double-loin-lambchops-and-a-couple-of-silver-bullets joy, but also the gossip, the backslapping — or, to be modern, the "bonding" — the rumination, and the flights of fancy. Individuals blessed with what the trendy call "interpersonal skills" know that the traditional form has its own special uses, ones not to be dismissed lightly.

In certain outward respects, lunches are much the same wherever you go in corporate America; regional differences are steadily diminishing. If you find yourself in a strange burg and are asked to appoint a time to eat, pick 12:30. Fashionable types in New York City may deem this a shade early, businessmen in the Midwest or on the West Coast, perhaps fifteen minutes later than they're used to. It's not a gaffe anywhere, as it would be to suggest, say, 2 o'clock to a potential lunchmate in Kansas City. (The waiters will have gone home.)

Expect the proceedings to take from an hour to an hour and fifteen minutes, except in San Francisco, where the lotus-eaters linger longer. At that city's Commercial Club, in fact, bank presidents and similarly elevated executives play dominoes with one another all through the meal, which customarily goes on until 2 or so. Just about everywhere else the push seems toward shorter rather than longer business lunches, with forty-five-minute bolt-downs becoming not uncommon.

All bets on duration are off, of course, if you're lunching with a denizen of Wall Street or with a trader at an exchange in some other city. Caught on a random day, an executive at E. F. Hutton's Battery Park headquarters in New York proffered dismally typical plans: "I'm going to midtown to have lunch with a client who's also a friend. We're eating at the Yale Club because it's right across the street from the subway at Grand Central. I've allotted thirty-five minutes for the meal itself."

Time limits may be stretched if something besides the food is really cooking. Charles Negohosian, the general manager of the Fox and Hounds restaurant in Bloomfield Hills, Michigan, recalls witnessing in his bistro what may have been the longest business lunch in history. It extended from noon until 1 A.M., with an exhausted participant saying as he left, "If it had taken me another twelve hours to land this sale, it would have killed me."

Even if the action is heavy, however, almost universally the food has become lighter. The co-owner of New York's Four Seasons, Thomas Margittai, sums up with one word the trend in what business-men are having for lunch: "Fish." Scrod, shrimp, snapper, whitefish, sand dab, or aquatic whatever — executives from sea to shining sea are putting the stuff away like crazy. In certain purlieus that cater to a business clientele — not just fish joints, mind you — seafood often constitutes 75 percent of the entrées sold.

The mania for taking care of the old bod has also meant a decline in desserts, both in the number consumed and in their heft. Fresh fruit is in, cherry-topped cheesecake out. Happily, there are exceptions — one Houston club that still purveys a lot of steak and potatoes to oilmen reports that its most popular dessert is hot raspberry cobbler served over vanilla ice cream in a champagne glass.

To wash down their sole meunière and green salad, working stiffs are increasingly turning to — what else — white wine, iced tea, or to nothing at all in the form of Perrier. The last bastion of the martini with lunch appears to be the smokestack belt stretching from Pittsburgh to just short of Chicago. Where these heaven-and-hell delectables continue to be downed, they're typically ordered with vodka rather than gin, which makes easier — never mix, never worry — the Detroit custom of sneaking up on a martini by having a Bloody Mary first.

With a forty-five-minute lunch of lettuce, cod, and Chablis to look forward to, you had better have something for breakfast. But then, if you have to eat — the new earnestness whispers — why not do a little business as well?

While the business breakfast, like the poor, has always been with us — particularly in the Midwest — today a steadily growing army leap from warm beds, and from the embraces of wives, husbands, or inamoratas, to rush off to a 7:30 or 8 A.M. chinfest with similar freshly showered, beamingly virtuous go-getters. "Our business-breakfast trade has increased fifty percent over the last three years," estimates Phillip Hughes, the managing director of New York's Plaza Hotel.

The rising and dining has gone so far that certain breakfast spots have become positively fashionable in the business community, if you can imagine fashion by the dawn's early light. In New York City, the limousines of lawyers and real-estate tycoons stand three-deep outside the Regency Hotel, throttling the morning traffic on Park Avenue. In Omaha, the more modest conveyances of local accountants and merchants chase the crowing cock from CoCo's parking lot.

Aficionados of the business breakfast say they like it because everyone gets down to brass tacks quickly. Says one fan: "There's none of the ceremony you can get at lunch." Also — asceticism again — because it's easier and less impolite to turn down food at breakfast than at lunch.

And nobody drinks, or practically nobody. Aside from the familiar sales-meeting-cum-brunch, at which Bloody Marys are not uncommon, the only reports of booze with breakfast come from Los Angeles, and even there a wake-up glass of champagne is rare. (Probably some high-flier, up at 3 A.M. to play the eastern markets, for whom breakfast is more like lunch — a green salad, a little fish.)

To hear proponents of the new style comment on the old, you would think that lean and mean lunches are almost the patriotic duty of every right-thinking American businessman. Who can spare the time? How can anybody get any work done after a couple of cocktails? (What about all those Japanese managers who get blasted together at the end of the workday — probably their sole chance to talk freely — stagger home to their miserably subservient wives, and then show up the next morning with a hangover to begin another epically productive day?)

What the puritans in jogging suits overlook are the commercial purposes a civilized business lunch can serve, purposes that often can't be accomplished in the office. Lunch provides us a chance to get to know the other fellow's provenance, tastes, and values. Absolutely crucial are the breaks that naturally occur in a meal and the opportunities these afford for what anthropologists call "grooming talk." (Meetings are linear; lunch is not.) You've got him out of the office, far from ringing telephones and interruptive co-workers. You sit down, order drinks, lean back. Where are you from, Ed? (He seems plenty street-smart.) He asks you if the veal is good here — the chicken, the fish? (Finicky, is he?) The waiter clears away the plates. Well, what did you think of the President's speech? (Can his politics be as weird as that haircut suggests?)

Pearl Meyer, who heads the executive compensation practice of the Handy Associates headhunting firm, describes why the eddies and whorls of lunch are so important. "Suppose I'm negotiating and the other person says something I want to think about. If I'm in my office, I can't say, 'Excuse me, I think I'll make that phone call now.' At lunch, I can reach for my glass, take a sip, and say, 'Hmmm, would you like more wine?'"

The looseness of lunch makes it suitable for speculation, collective woolgathering, and the floating of trial balloons. Take a bite, chew a little — hmmm, what if we acquired that little company in the Southwest? The exact antithesis of such food-for-thought-and-body sessions is the typical board of directors' meeting — stone visages, everyone sensitive to a potential loss of face, no surprises, please, which is precisely why many boards have a meal together before the formal confab.

It isn't all freedom and touchy-feely — much of the old black

status-and-hierarchy magic still accompanies lunch. Louise Berni-
kow, author of a tongue-in-cheek guidebook called *Let's Have Lunch*,
points out, for example, that a definite pecking order informs the
businessman-host's choice of places to entertain. At the top of the
heap, probably because it's an option generally reserved for chief
executives (and one not available to all of them), is a private dining
area contiguous to your office.

Next comes one of your company's smaller dining rooms, then a
private club — a particularly exclusive club may even outrank the
corporation's executive mess hall — and last, a restaurant, preferably
one where they know and love you. In thinking about the commercial
establishments available to them, businessmen often unconsciously
employ the same taxonomy that undergraduates used to apply to girl-
or boyfriends: there's your regular, your fun, and your show.

Your regular is probably a neighborhood haunt with decent food
and reasonable prices, the kind of spot you typically frequent with
colleagues from work. Your fun may be a bit farther off the beaten
track and feature esoteric ethnic cuisine — a place to rendezvous with
co-workers who are also friends. (Just try feeding your favorite
blasting-cap-chilis-and-garlic Thai specialty to a visiting buyer from
Salt Lake City.) Your show has a big name, puts on a fuss, and is
suitable for customers you wish to impress or your wealthy and
exceedingly boring brother-in-law.

The choice, and even the manner of invitation, can get particularly
tricky if you're lunching with a subordinate or superior. If you're the
overlord, and thus usually the one empowered to pick the spot, go
easy on the dancing girls and prostrate waiter-slaves, at least if your
underling doesn't know in advance that this is to be a mostly celebra-
tory undertaking. He probably read too much into your casual
invitation — not understanding that you too sometimes end up with
white space on your calendar — and is already trembling in his best
managerial footwear.

If you're the subordinate delegated to select the restaurant, pick a
place with a variety of edible dishes, none too exotic, and tables far
enough apart so that you can all but hear one another think. Steak-
houses tend to be noisy; recently discovered hot spots, rushed and
crowded.

If your boss is a woman, and you're not, don't sweat it. Male-female business lunches may still draw the occasional odd stare—"I've concluded that most businessmen still eat with other businessmen," observes New York restaurateur Jim McMullen—but the greater problem for businesswomen may be the female-female business lunch. "Never go to lunch with another woman executive on matinee Wednesday," advises a female financial type in New York who has tried it. "First they sat us in the back room, where there were nothing but other women, right next to the noisiest baby shower in history. After we insisted on another table, they took two hours to serve us."

This by-now-wiser woman also exemplifies the purposiveness that many baby-boom managers are thrusting upon the lunching practices of their companies. If the boss says, offhandedly, "Let's have lunch sometime," the young newcomer to corporate management will call up his secretary to fix a date.

Lunch is, or should be, a mixture of business and merriment, a combination conducive to and benefited by friendship. Happy warriors in the corporate jousts know this and exploit lunch to its fullest. Some executives have two lunches a day, and a new breed of stoic souls, such as Hill & Knowlton vice chairman Richard Cheney, attend as many as three business breakfasts a morning.

One frequent double-luncher, admittedly a man of ample girth, reveals how it's done. "You make one date for twelve—there are people in New York who like to eat then—and another for one-fifteen at another restaurant nearby. At the first lunch you have a soup course and an entrée, at the second an entrée and dessert, so that both parties will think you're having a complete meal."

Perhaps the high point of this canny veteran's lunching career came when, on one inadvertently overbooked occasion, he managed to bring off two lunches simultaneously. He held one in the Oak Room of the Plaza, the other across the lobby in the Edwardian Room. Next time you're bolting down your fish-and-vinaigrette, pause for a moment and call his ample image to mind—a sort of Bacchus of lunch, tiptoeing gingerly from table to table, his smile reflecting the certainty that good lunch is good business.

35

In Praise of Office Gossip

It ties people together, gets out the word,
and lets underlings blow off steam. But don't do it wrong.

JUST TRY TO IMAGINE what a corporation devoid of office gossip would be like. Formal reports with all the spiciness of, say, a quarterly earnings statement march methodically up and down the ranks. Heads still roll from time to time, of course, but bystanders politely avert their gaze. No one knows anything about anyone else beyond a bare minimum strictly related to work.

Zombie Corp., in other words, and about as likely to materialize as the Night of the Living Dead. People, to the extent that they're interested in other people — which is to say, to the extent that they're fully human — love to gossip. Where two or three are gathered together in friendship, unofficial conversation about individuals and their doings is practically inevitable. Our society has begun to recognize these truths and accept the phenomenon. A Yale professor of literature, Patricia Meyer Spacks, recently published a three-hundred-page paean to wagging tongues; in it she noted that magazines as diverse as *Time* and *McCall's* have discovered gossip's virtues.

What might seem more surprising is that the business world, bless its little not-always-up-with-the-latest-trends heart, also appears to be embracing this new realism. The let's-not-be-coy attitude of Howard Bratches, an executive recruiter with the Thorndike Deland firm in New York City, is becoming more typical. Asked if there's office gossip at his shop, he replies, "Of course — we gossip about clients, internal organization, outside business, and people in the office." John R. Kiley, a broker with Drexel Burnham Lambert, says he, like other citizens of the small town that is Wall Street, gossips "at lunch . . . all the time."

While admitting that they gossip, most managers still aren't willing to see such an admission in print. They also may be a bit uncertain about whether gossip is a force for good or ill. But if these execs haven't thought systematically about the role gossip plays in their organizations, a few of their advisers — consultants and business school professors — have. These experts cite many ways that gossip makes the working world not only more interesting to its denizens, but also a lot more humane.

First, gossip supplements the official channels of communication, which often run dry indeed. As an early-warning system, gossip allows people to think through in advance what they will do if the rumors become the awful truth. Subordinates may get an inkling of what the boss is wrestling with, and this long before he can make a formal announcement; the boss may hear whispers of bad news that no one has the guts to break to him straightaway.

Management may even deliberately use what is sometimes termed the gossip chain to get out the word informally. A West Coast businessman cites the example of a huge corporation headquartered in San Francisco: top executives there, he claims, relay messages downward by filling the ears of select, certified-reliable gossips called pass-on-ers. At other companies, trial balloons may be floated on these hot winds.

Gossip can serve as a medium for forging a corporate culture, for handing down values and acculturating newcomers. The retelling of company war stories, exemplary tales of how this old-timer came up with a new product or that one moved mountains to serve a customer better — this, too, is a kind of gossip. Alan Wilkins, an associate professor of organizational behavior at Brigham Young University in Utah, has studied storytelling at such companies as Hewlett-Packard. He notes that at that company, managers practically force people to attend birthday parties and coffee breaks so the troops will exchange ideas. Does anyone seriously imagine, though, that at coffee breaks or those poolside corporate beer busts in Silicon Valley, all the troops talk about is how to make a better microwidget?

People gossip principally about other people, and what a raffish, insubordinate, utterly irresistible impetus it is. While managerial prudes may be loath to recognize the fact, companies can benefit even from the most unauthorized strain of talk — the kind that focuses on personalities, peccadilloes, and private doings. As Professor Spacks points out, such let-down-your-hair conversations usually foster a sense of closeness between the participants, who typically number no more than two or three. After all, the word gossip derives from the Old English *godsib* as in sibling — one's own godparent or a person close enough to serve as the godparent of one's child.

In chatting with fellow gossips, an individual can speculate on others' behavior, think through his or her response, and test out that response on others. The exercise is probably salutary: gossiping co-workers sharpen their powers of observation and, just possibly, refine their understanding of people. This may be particularly comforting, and educational, to folks who don't have much say in running things. Students of gossip note that it flourishes among the relatively powerless — secretaries? — partly because it affords an outlet for angry feelings toward higher-ups that otherwise might have to go unexpressed.

Managers have to be a bit careful about how they gossip. Adela Oliver, whose firm, Oliver Human Resource Consultants, helps companies with personnel matters, warns, "You want to have access to the gossip chain, but you don't want to be perceived as part of the chain." It's helpful to get the early warning, but if your fellow honchos see you as a hopeless blabbermouth, they might be reluctant to trust you with confidential information. What you need to get into the chain is a loyal subordinate or colleague who will share the news with you without trumpeting your interest around.

Harvard Business School professor John Kotter, whose books reflect hundreds of hours observing executives in action, notes that the best managers are selective in using gossip. Concerned not only about their ties to underlings but also about underlings' ties to one another, these paragons may pass along news likely to improve relationships in the organization or to burnish someone's reputation. On the other hand, they'll stamp out gossip that might be harmful to reputations or personal ties. These straight arrows also refuse to gossip ill of rivals: "The risk you take with talking of others that way," Kotter says, "is that some people will see it for what it is — a power tactic, a subtle attempt to lower the other person's prestige. They'll walk away thinking less of you."

Wise gossips, managerial or not, also know there's only so much truth in what goes around. An investment banker who says gossip is important in his business sounds a note of caution: "The main problem is the timing; the timing is usually all wrong"—either way ahead of a deal, or hopelessly late. Only a fool fails to weigh gossip against information available from other sources.

And if you find yourself being gossiped about? These days your best bet is usually just to ignore it. You are living in the late twentieth century—not in some closed-room Victorian universe where people worry endlessly about being thought respectable. There seem few areas left where a manager's reputation can be seriously undermined by gossip. One example, admittedly unfair: a woman executive can still be compromised more than a male by reports she's having an affair with someone else in the organization.

Remember, too, even in the face of the most salacious gossip, that a certain compliment, however backhanded, is being paid you. Folks don't gossip about people they deem unimportant, or don't care about at all. Oscar Wilde said it best: "There is only one thing in the world worse than being talked about, and that is not being talked about."

❧ 36 ❧

In Defense of the Office Party

*For all the dangers they represent, such gatherings
are a still-good idea. You just have to know what you're doing.*

PRUDENT BUSINESSMEN loathe and fear office social functions. They see in them the specter of careers ruined, marriages jeopardized, at the very least a lot of people thoroughly embarrassed the next morning. So why do they keep putting themselves through the drill?

For some very good reasons, it turns out, reasons that even the party-givers may not fully understand. True, there are dangers — alcohol-induced breaches of decorum, misbegotten liaisons — but for every danger there's a countervailing benefit. Properly managed, the corporate shindig can be a forum for communications not otherwise possible, a wholesome rite of passage, and a joy.

First the dangers, from the least threatening to the most. There's always the chance that the office social function, whether an ad hoc cocktail party in someone's office or a dress ball honoring the chairman on his retirement, will simply fizzle. Everyone stands about self-consciously, talking the same tired talk heard endlessly at the coffee machine. "I've never enjoyed myself at one of these things," laments an executive who owns his own company.

He may have been the major cause of the problem. The one seemingly universal law of office parties is that merriment tends to break out in inverse proportion to the number of organizational levels present. If it's the guys in the sales force by themselves, *well* (pronounced as a four-syllable word). Add a couple of vice presidents, and the proceedings become a tad more restrained. Add the chairman, or a board member or two, and you might as well hold this particular prom at the county morgue.

The inclusion of spouses can exercise a similarly chilling effect. It isn't just that the little woman, or man, prevents you from dancing on tables or making goo-goo eyes at the luscious Ms. LaBelle from employee benefits. The more subtle danger is that Herself will take the whole matter far too seriously. Fred, the office joker, chaffs you about where you rented the resplendent tux with the half-inch-wide shawl collar — she's massively offended. On the way home, nay, for weeks afterward, all you hear about is how the boss talked to Harry three times and you only once. Says Frank Beaudine of Eastman & Beaudine, an executive recruiting firm, "It's the spouses who may bear a grudge."

Not that you can't get into plenty of trouble on your own. Alcohol is usually the catalyst. Yes, in the real world as well as in cartoons, people do get drunk at office social functions, do go on to tell their exalted superiors exactly what they think of them, and do, sometimes, get fired on the spot by the equally inebriated higher-ups. Often the break is patched up in the morning, but the melody lingers on.

From such horror stories careful folk conclude that they should not drink to excess at these events. They sometimes forget that they should be equally careful to avoid others who have been, as the euphemism goes, overserved. Your boss knocks back a few, transforms himself from Dr. Jekyll to Mr. Hyde, and proceeds to clean your clock, denouncing everything from your job performance to your sexual preference. Can he remember, the next day? Can you forget?

Bacchus also has a habit of bringing Venus in tow, setting up the possibility of, if not love, what the British inelegantly call "a bit of slap-and-tickle." Accordingly, office parties can be especially difficult for women. Their concern may be heightened because they tend to get more excited about an office bash than men do. "Women will shower, change, put on new perfume — at a party, women, even if they're executives, become women," notes one female executive. "Men keep on their daily business suits for a reason — they keep their positions."

Enter the double standard, with a vengeance. "Nobody thinks badly of a man who gets drunk," the woman executive goes on, "but if a woman does it, it's blown all out of proportion. You see a woman dancing with an executive, and the next thing you know, everyone thinks she's having an affair with him — he isn't having one with her; she's having one with him." The lesson? Women, be circumspect.

Men, besides the dictates of gentlemanliness, bear in mind that Ms. LaBelle may be a walking dossier of current litigation on sexual harassment.

It all may seem enough to put management off parties forever, and indeed, some companies report that they're cutting back on social functions, or opting increasingly for the sedate variety — taking the gang out to lunch. The push for lean and mean doesn't exactly encourage lavish entertaining. But then again, it's precisely in these dark moments when the beneficial effects of a bang-up blowout may be most required.

First, the corporate social function is a way of saying thanks, a gesture of appreciation that goes beyond the cold cash nexus binding employee to employer. The element of gratitude should be made explicit, and not with "Acme Industrial Fasteners wants to thank you." "I want to thank you" from a real person makes all the more believable the message you're trying to convey to folks: somebody up there has feelings — even feelings about you, mailroom clerk Zywicki.

There may be far more to Zywicki than meets the quotidian office eye, which is another reason for staging a bash. Social events allow a person to present more sides of himself than he may display nine to five — "women become women," men, if they let themselves, become gallants, proud fathers and husbands, wits, or merely fools. To those concerned with their progress up the greasy pole, this possibility translates into catchphrases such as "A party is a great place to mix with the big boys," and "These things allow people to get to know the boss as a person." Less driven types in the company simply enjoy finding out that that quiet fellow Binkers in dispatching writes slightly kinky suspense novels in his spare time.

Paradoxically, it's such disclosures, together with shoptalk between people who wouldn't encounter one another in the line of duty, that forge a company's sense of itself. "Gee, we're both bright, good-looking, preppy M.B.A.'s, and we're both with Acme, and we're both having fun. What a bright, good-looking, preppy, M.B.A.-ish, fun kind of company Acme is." As John A. Miller, a professor of management at Bucknell University, points out, "This is especially important for 'messy systems'— research, high-tech, or entrepreneurial outfits that have trouble defining what they are." And you thought they were just having fun at those corporate beer busts poolside in Silicon Valley.

If social functions help the company understand its identity, they perform the same function for individuals embarking on some major career change — a transfer, promotion, or retirement. Take a promotion party. "The social function jars the person promoted to think like someone at the next level of management," suggests Leonard Greenhalgh, an associate professor at Dartmouth's Tuck School of Business Administration. "You also get it through everyone else's thick head that a change is coming about." Sometimes the message to others is the most important, particularly at a retirement party. Says Greenhalgh, "Losing a boss or favorite co-worker can produce the same generalized withdrawal reactions as losing a close relation — motivation goes down. A party helps you come to terms with it."

The right kind of party, that is. A properly planned office social function, experts agree, has a clearly promulgated beginning and ending time, the latter to prevent people from wandering off before the gathering's mission is accomplished. A Cinderella close — the band stops, the bar shuts down — also signals folks to go home, thereby helping weak souls avoid the really dangerous parties, those spontaneous soirées cooked up by mischief-makers after the ball is over.

The preferable site is off-site, away from dingy office halls — create that element of fantasy, bring people out of their workaday shells, give them a reason to change clothes. The location, like the other appurtenances — food, entertainment — gives away precisely how serious the company is about making its social point. At retirement parties, for example — where the honor paid is usually determined according to some calculus combining title, tenure, and esteem in which held — the presence of a shrimp bowl may signal sad farewell to a vice president who'll be missed, the absence of same, a heartfelt sayonara to a curmudgeonly one.

In general, food is a good idea — hot food seems especially to hearten merrymakers — but sit-down meals are not. Munchies tend to mitigate the effects of booze. Sit-down meals, on the other hand, invite speeches — instant audience passivity, party death. Folks appreciate a few words of welcome, but companies that truly are big, happy families don't need a numbing round of orations to remind everyone of the fact.

While the troops should not be permitted to get comatose listening to the chairman, they should be given something to do besides mingling. Music and dancing can fill the bill. So can bowling. Denizens of the Ogilvy & Mather advertising agency in New York note that one of that shop's all-time best bashes was a black-tie bowling party, with music, held in the lanes on the Port Authority bus terminal's second floor.

Most important, someone must play host. Even if the senior officer present is the shyest of wallflowers, he should make the effort to shake hands, start conversations, and generally set an example of conviviality. To do otherwise is just possibly to let the glums or the crazies establish the tone.

Finally, in case you're thinking of doing without liquor at the party this year, you might be interested to know that IBM, a company legendary for its dry celebrations, now reports that for about five years it has been serving "light alcoholic beverages"— that's beer and wine— at selected social functions. Who knows; maybe someday Mother Blue will even get up and boogie.

❊ 37 ❊

Executives on Retreat

*Taking the managerial team off to the woods
for a little soul-searching is all the rage. Be prepared.*

IT'S HARDLY A NEW IDEA. Shakespeare's characters are constantly put to crashing around in the forest, sorting out identities, gaining insights. In times of crisis North American Indians would retreat to out-of-the-way holy places for a vision. Roman Catholics have been doing it for centuries.

Heaven only knows why corporate America took so long to get the gospel of so-called off-site meetings, but having discovered the good news, managers are embracing it with evangelical fervor. In 1968, according to Theodore Mandigo, a partner in the accounting firm of Pannell Kerr & Forster, which specializes in the hospitality industry, the U.S. had two or three conference centers — facilities catering almost exclusively to business meetings. By the end of this year there may be three hundred, with total annual revenues of nearly $4 billion.

Why is everybody headed for the hills? The reasons are as diverse as the purposes and settings of off-site meetings, but can be arrayed along a spectrum from the traditional (let's play golf) to the avant-garde (strap on your life preserver and expect to be terrified — it will make you a better manager).

The granddaddy of off-site conclaves, still zany after all these years, is the company sales meeting. You probably know the drill. Assemble in some sunny place — Maui is popular currently — the men and women who during the rest of the year ply their solitary sales territories. In the morning elevate them with encomiums to their prowess, together with tales of wondrous new products. In the afternoons permit them to recreate themselves through sports and leisure. In the evening fete them with dress-up banquets or silly-costumed barbecues, pool parties, or luaus. Sometimes at such meetings there is drinking.

Of almost equally ancient provenance is an institution called the golf retreat. Some echelon of management will get together, usually annually, at a resort well south of Buffalo. General Electric, for example, has a yearly gathering for its top five hundred managers in Boca Raton, Florida, another for its top 115 near Phoenix, Arizona.

But what primarily accounts for the increase in off-site meetings — and probably represents the most common type nowadays — is the genuine training session. These gatherings can be about as much fun as your college calculus course. Accounting firms, you will be pleased to learn as tax time approaches, apparently take the prize for seriousness: conference center personnel report that the C.P.A.'s usually spend from 8:30 A.M. until 11 P.M. in the classroom, capping a bleary three or four days with a written examination on what they've learned. Management consultants and investment bankers are also known to be fairly intense about their self-educational efforts, though typically they'll end the proceedings not with a whimper but with a bang-up party.

Charting strategy is probably the second most common corporate use of conference centers. Such sessions come in two varieties: your "regular" and your "hot." Your regular occurs about the same time every year, maybe even in the same place, and usually contains about as many surprises as, say, the annual budget review. Your hot is an ad hoc affair, held because the heat is on in some respect: the old strategy isn't working; the company has made an acquisition and the two camps can't seem to get along; the chairman is suffering a crisis of confidence in himself or in his subordinates. In addition to the stated purpose of such a gathering — we're going to get together to talk about X — it often has unstated purposes. The conclave might be designed to serve as what human-resources types call a bonding session — the participants are to get to know, and, if possible, like, one another. Or it may be convened to scare the bejesus out of complacent troops. Hot strategy sessions are the most dangerous of off-site meetings, and not necessarily because of what goes on at them. They are signals that the gods atop the corporation have grown restive and may soon require human sacrifices from among those deemed responsible.

Far from the conference center and on the cutting fringe of the off-site phenomenon is "the wilderness experience." More and more companies these days, including Wang Laboratories, Polaroid, and Standard Oil of Indiana, are sending their people into the woods in the hope of changing not just managerial minds but hearts as well. The vehicle is typically a variant of Outward Bound, a program originally developed to instill self-confidence in adolescents by teaching them to survive in the wilds. In the corporate version, denizens of the office are dispatched — with guides, of course — to pilot rubber rafts through white-water rapids, or ride horses all day and sleep on the ground.

Anton Lahnston, a professor of organizational behavior at Boston University and the director of that school's booming Executive Challenge wilderness sojourns, explains why managers are taking to the woods: "The outdoor medium as a classroom offers the intersection of three learning experiences — cognitive learning; an emotional component generally lacking in traditional educational settings, involving such issues as fear, trust, and commitment; and the engagement of people's physical selves."

All the jargon comes alive in the experience of a group of Federal Express executives. The vice president of the company's western region took a dozen of his subordinates, not all of them exactly enthusiastic about the prospect, to a coastal town in Maine. When they got off the bus from the airport, they were put aboard an open thirty-foot boat and told to sail it to an island on the horizon. As described by Roy Yamahiro, Federal Express's vice president of human-resources development: "Twelve people couldn't sail this boat; they couldn't even get together enough to row to the island. They became angry, cursed each other and the situation, damn near threw two of the instructors overboard, and spent the night in the boat on the water. In the morning they finally figured out how to sail it." And what did the crew get out of their experience as galley slaves? "They came away a more cohesive unit," Yamahiro says. "They still get together socially, even though they live all over the West, and they all work much more effectively with the V.P."

If you're thinking of convening an off-site meeting, take guidance from the experts. The primary requisite, says David Coulam, a vice president of SCM Corp. who runs the company's for-hire conference center, is clarity. "Things tend to work out well if people feel there is purpose to the meeting," he says. Be clear about the purpose yourself, and then communicate it to participants beforehand. Tell them, too, about as many procedural details as possible. Time spent worrying about whether to wear the blue blazer or the Harry Truman–signature model Hawaiian go-to-hell shirt is time that might better be spent on company matters.

Once the session is up and running, conferees should be given enough latitude to do what you brought them there to do. This may mean — hold on to your swivel chairs, executive control freaks — letting them come up with answers to the questions you have posed and then listening to those answers. "Have in mind the general ideas, but do not be ironclad about conclusions or time frame," advises Richard Shepard, chief executive of Linclay Corp., a real estate development company that stages a biannual retreat for its managers.

For the wilderness experience, you'd better have expert professional help standing by to assist the participants in making sense of it all. The one significant change in Boston University's Executive Challenge program since its inception is that now counselors spend 60 percent of the time in the program debriefing the newly experienced, helping them figure out what went on and their feelings about it.

Finally — and most often neglected — make some provision for keeping the work of the meeting alive when everybody goes back to the office. This may be as simple as ensuring that everyone has three or four small items to act on the following week. Or it may mean — gulp — that you actually have to launch that grand project you dreamed up while collectively contemplating the pines. Begin immediately, before the bureaucratic routine can kill off the new thinking.

And if you're asked to go along on one of these little picnics? The first rule, directed at those who might be tempted by the freedom of the occasion to misbehave, comes from the director of a conference center: "Remember that neither you nor the boss will forget anything that happened at the retreat." The second rule: when it comes to the new experiences offered you, keep an open mind. The secret of many of those Outward Bound adventures is something that the people who run them call perceived risk — it looks scary as hell, but there are so many safety lines attached to you that you have to be truly creative to kill yourself.

The third rule: in applying the second rule, keep in mind that you can draw the line if you feel you're being asked to do too much. Yamahiro of Federal Express tells of a wilderness adventure he staged before he had mastered the art. He took a group of men and women from his then employer, Martin Marietta Aerospace, out for an eight-day white-water rafting trip. The folks laboriously hauled their gear down a canyon to behold the churning, rioting waters of the river. One hard-core nonswimmer promptly declared that he would never go down that particular torrent. Yamahiro patiently explained that short of dragging themselves back up the canyon, the river was the only way out. The group then rallied around the nonswimmer, hoisted their rafts, and beat a retreat up the canyon, leaving the river behind. Talk about team building.

38

The Managerial Dress Code

*The baby-boom generation, which said it would never put on
somebody else's uniform, has. Pull up your socks.*

DOES THE TIE that you picked out to wear this morning consign
you forever to the ranks of lower-middle management? Sorry, friend,
you've just run afoul of the managerial dress code in its latest, Draconian incarnation. After wobbling in the sixties, rules, usually unspoken, about what clothing is considered appropriate for office wear
are back with a vengeance.

The change has several roots. First, the Peacock Revolution died
aborning, without permanently placing a single Nehru jacket in the
boardroom. Next, beginning in the mid-1970s, a massive dispersal of
the relevant technology—how to dress correctly for business—
occurred, carried along by a growing horde of dark-suited M.B.A.'s.
Women joined the managerial work force in record numbers, found
there was no business uniform for their sex, and promptly adopted
one—and a grim little number it is. Finally, recession struck in the
early 1980s, curbing any surviving tendencies toward sartorial ex-
pansiveness.

If you don't believe in the importance of the right garb, just attend
to the views of the executive recruiters, those connoisseurs of managerial horseflesh—both its performance and conformation. Gerry
Roche, whose ultra-big-league practice with the Heidrick & Struggles firm has included, for example, placing Ed Hennessy at the top of
Allied Corp., states an opinion maintained almost universally in headhunting circles: "Dress is a very, very critical key one looks at in an
executive." He tells of sending a candidate for the presidency of a
multibillion-dollar company to be interviewed by the chief executive,
who was vacationing in Europe. The man arrived a bit disheveled
after the overnight transatlantic flight on the corporate jet, but went

directly to see the top dog. An hour later Roche received an irate call from his client, who began with the horror-struck expostulation, "You sent me a guy with sagging socks."

What makes all this a little hard for the untutored to figure out is that even though it goes on just about everywhere in the corporate world, few self-respecting businessmen will admit to any particular concern about what they wear. "Men are very suspicious about a man who is too interested in clothes," reports Lois Fenton, a consultant on business dress with Executive Wardrobe Engineering in Mamaroneck, New York. "A man who sits next to me on a flight may ask what I do. When I tell him he'll say, 'I'm not interested in clothes,' and then for the duration of the flight he'll pump me for information on how to dress."

In the benighted era before so-called wardrobe consultants existed —twenty years ago, say — precise, detailed information on the subject was more difficult to come by. If you were to the business milieu born, you could replicate what Papa wore each morning as he headed off to the office, or ape your prep-school classmates. Otherwise you were left to pick up on what your colleagues at work wore — a good idea even today. What you had going for you was a consensus, handed down from one generation to the next, about how middle-class folk were supposed to dress. As late as the Eisenhower years, it may be recalled, men wore hats and business suits to baseball games.

John F. Kennedy took care of the hats, the baby-boom generation dispensed with much of the rest. As they came of age, the love generation adopted their own standard of dress — jeans mostly — and even managed to insinuate an occasional bell-bottom into the office wardrobe of a forty-year-old envious of the youthquake's freedom.

But by the time economic reality closed in and the baby-boomers went scrambling for business jobs, much of the consensus and historical continuity in matters of dress had been lost. Middle-class kids had been wearing Sgt. Pepper outfits or collegiate-folkie-sincere so long that some couldn't remember how to tie a tie, if they had ever learned. In addition, thanks to a greatly expanded system of higher education, more and more children of blue-collar families were looking for white-collar positions, even though they didn't know exactly what to wear with the white collar.

And then, as if in answer to a baby-boomer's prayer, along came *Dress for Success*. First published in 1975, the book provided a detailed guide to correct business attire, complete with photographs, line drawings, even diagrams on how to tie a tie — Windsor knot, half Windsor, or four-in-hand. It was an immediate success, and has proved an enduring one. Over 1.5 million copies are in print, along with about 775,000 copies of a sequel, *The Woman's Dress for Success Book,* published in 1977. Compare these numbers with the book sales racked up by, oh, Peter F. Drucker — the management guru's most popular book, *The Effective Executive,* has sold some 300,000 copies over fifteen years — and you may get some sense of where, as they say, the managerial class's head is at.

What Frederick W. Taylor, the time-and-motion pioneer, was to scientific management, John T. Molloy, the author of both dress-for-success books, is to the managerial dress code. He put the choice of what to wear to the office on a completely new footing. Pick your clothes not on the basis of some fashion designer's current whim, he inveighed, nor even according to what you or your spouse thinks looks good. No, base your selection of a tie on solid, empirical research — research that Molloy, a former prep-school teacher, claims to have conducted over a decade consulting to individuals and corporations on matters of business attire.

According to Molloy's vocabulary of wardrobe science, a particular outfit doesn't look terrific; it tests well with a specific audience. A man's black raincoat, for example, proved in tests with almost every audience to convey a lower-middle-class image.

The look that tested best with senior executives was, not surprisingly, pretty much the old Ivy League standard: a blue or gray two-piece suit of conservative cut, a white or light pastel shirt with long sleeves, a neatly patterned tie darker than the shirt, dark over-the-calf socks, wingtips or other plain laced shoes. Molloy prescribed it as the standard uniform for managerial hopefuls. Minor variations could be worked on the basic outfit in order to avoid offending particular audiences or to exploit regional differences. In Detroit, for instance, brown suits for women came across as more acceptable than blue ones — but only in Detroit.

Molloy's basic message transcended regional or industry differences: use clothing as a tool to help you get ahead. Find out which outfits, according to the research, go down well with your relevant publics, and wear them — slavishly. Not without cause did Molloy style himself "America's first wardrobe engineer."

While academics had doubts about the quality of Molloy's research, the business community just ate up his prescriptions. M.B.A. candidates, their numbers swelling every year, embraced the gospel with the fanaticism of converted heathens. Business schools — Columbia, Wharton, and Carnegie-Mellon, among others — set up noncredit seminars in how to dress for you-know-what. Corporations, descrying an intersection of the employee's interest and the company's — he wants to get ahead; the company wants to set up a dress code informally — bought the books for their employees and brought Molloy in to give presentations. By his reckoning, Molloy has served as a consultant to 380 of the Fortune 500 industrial corporations.

Since the widespread dissemination of Molloy's message, enforcement of the managerial dress code has, if anything, tightened. "Five years ago," Molloy says, "when I talked to companies about how they wanted recruits to dress, the message was 'We'd like the young man to wear a suit, but won't hold it against him if he doesn't.' Three years ago, the message was 'We demand that the men wear suits, and would like the women to, but won't hold it against the women if they don't.' Today I hear 'We have so few jobs and so many qualified applicants, we're looking for ways to eliminate candidates. Those who won't dress appropriately we'll eliminate.'"

While the tightening has probably been most dramatic at the interview and entry level, it has had effects up the line. Indeed, now that everyone knows the rules, proper dress has become a sort of heraldic symbol of a young manager's dedication to the corporation, particularly the young woman manager's. Thus, according to the experts, if a recently promoted woman executive uses the occasion to trade in her suit for dresses and bangles, management may infer that she doesn't want to rise any higher.

It isn't just that companies have made the dress code more ironclad — individual men and women also took up the ball from Molloy and promptly ran with it toward even more conservative business attire. With respect to the men's uniform, which couldn't have become much more conservative anyway, about the only change Molloy has noticed is a move by senior management away from the button-down collar. "Button-downs have now become a sign of lower and middle management," he says.

Manufacturers and retailers of men's suits notice a few slight changes, though, all consonant with the general trend. Andrew Kozinn, the president of St. Laurie Ltd. of New York City — it makes suits for its own outlet and for men's stores across the country — observes that "four or five years ago, ninety-nine percent of our line was vested — now only twenty percent to twenty-five percent is." (Molloy's book said almost nothing about vests.) Kozinn also sees a trend to the natural-shoulder, less tight-fitting suit usually associated with Brooks Brothers. A representative of Brooks, the mother church of the dress-for-success look, seemed slightly amused by the suggestion that his company's business might be affected at all by trends in men's clothing. He did note, however, that the chain has expanded more in the last six or seven years than at any other time in its 165-year history.

Where the real changes have occurred is in women's clothing. In his books, Molloy decried the lack of a consistent, recognizable business uniform for females. He advocated a two-piece suit — skirt and blazer-style jacket — with a blouse analogous to a man's shirt. Pinstripes, he noted, while a status symbol for men, were a "strong negative" in a woman's suit — too much of an "imitation man" look. A scarf at the neck was not essential.

Was the fair sex, ever independent in matters of fashion, to be denied pinstripes? They were not. Women rushed out to buy pinstriped suits in such numbers that they just blew Molloy's stricture away. He concedes as much, adding that in the last three years the colors of women's suits have also become more conservative, more like men's.

The crowning glory took the form of a tie. When, about four years ago, the winds of fashion offered up first a ribbon to be worn as a bow tie, and then a scarf that more closely resembled the genuine article, distaff dress-for-successers quickly buttoned up their uppermost button and tied one on. It's now part of the uniform.

And how. Two marketing professors from New York University

asked the readers of *Savvy*, the self-styled "magazine for executive women," to rank twelve outfits on their appropriateness as office garb for the female professionals. According to the six thousand respondents, the clear-cut winner, with an overall score of 100, was a two-piece suit with a blouse and a neat little bow tie. In second place, with a humdrum score of 71, was a similar suit worn with a blouse open at the collar.

Since more and more folks these days have an eye for the niggling details, the greatest risk you run currently is likely to be overdressing — perhaps out of some pathetic attempt to distinguish the way you wear the uniform from the norm. It has always been possible to be overdressed for certain regions, industries, or functions within a company. A manufacturing V.P. who dressed like the chief financial officer, for example, might draw occasional stares, and not just from factory workers in greasy T-shirts. Now that everyone has been raised a little closer to the same blue-suited standard, however, the danger is getting too far out ahead of everyone in terms of the panache with which you wear your office dress blues.

Thinking of dabbing on a little cologne? Watch it. Asked about use of the aromatic, a headhunter replied, "Well, you can sometimes place those . . . uh . . . light types in jobs in the fashion industry." Considering a silk handkerchief for the breast pocket of your suit? "Affected and distracting," says St. Laurie's Kozinn.

The point, of course, is to blend in. In particular, you should avoid outdoing your superior. Indeed, for women, some experts recommend varying the basic uniform depending on where you are in corporate hierarchy.

But what, some Neanderthals might have the bad taste to ask, about femininity? Downplaying that, at least the traditional froufrou version of it, is part of what the woman's uniform is about. This comes out in phrases heard over and over again in talking with dress consultants: "Suits should be tailored to cover up any bumps or curves" (well bumps, sure . . .), "The more your clothes wipe out, the better," and the ubiquitous line "The look eliminates sexual tension" (who's tense? who's tense?).

Before giving up all hope, be apprised that there is one interesting, sneaky, countervailing trend. Sales of lacy, sexy, gorgeous lingerie are booming, fueled in some substantial part, apparently, by the purchases of so-called executive women. Pam Chadwick of Victoria's Secret Inc., a San Francisco–based retailer of expensive unmentionables, observes, "There are women who wear our lingerie underneath to take the edge off the uniform — it makes them feel alive and sexual."

It beats worrying about whether your tie is aligned at just the right angle. You laugh? You doubt that people really take these matters all that seriously? Well, perhaps you should be skeptical. Out in Silicon Valley, a host of entrepreneurs and engineers seem bent on giving American business a new lease on life, and this mostly without benefit of neckwear. (The dress consultants write it off as reverse snobbery.) For most of the rest of the corporate community, though, the prevailing attitude is better reflected by the questions at a recent NYU seminar on girding up your loins for success. Among the most urgently pressed inquiries was whether a woman should wear her tie with ends sticking out stiffly, like a man's bow tie, or allow them to flop down. Answer: it depends on the material; let the tie do what comes naturally. In matters of dress, it seems to be about the only thing that can afford to these days.

❦ Part V ❦

IN THE LIFE

39

The Happiest Executives

*They may not admit it, but some managers are actually
quite content. In a nonpeaceful sort of way, of course.*

AMONG THE ADJECTIVES routinely used to describe executives, "happy" barely places at all. "Hard charging" or "aggressive" probably leads the list; "happy" languishes somewhere near the bottom, in the neighborhood of "poetic" and "sensual." Most students of business simply don't think of managerial types in that light. Edward Bowman, the Reginald H. Jones Professor of Corporate Management at the Wharton School of the University of Pennsylvania, interviewed thirty chief executives for a research project on their concerns and problems. He talked with them about a lot of things, he says, but "whether they were happy or not just didn't surface in our interviews." He adds, "It never occurred to me that they were happy or unhappy people. It seems irrelevant."

Somehow, being happy seems incompatible with the fire in the belly that is supposedly standard equipment for any self-respecting executive. Daniel J. Isenberg, a professor at the Harvard Business School, neatly sums up the paradox: "Happiness, in a way, is a lack of striving — you're there. But what then is happiness to someone who enjoys the striving itself?"

More managers than you might suspect have found an answer to the question. Asked to name the happiest businessmen and businesswomen they know, executive recruiters and psychologists who consult for corporations first scratch their heads at the weirdness of the question, then quickly reel off a respectable list. Subsequent conversations with the people they name indicate that while some are loath to talk about it — particularly those at big companies — yes, the nominees are in fact happy. Moreover, in their accounts of why they are that way, a fairly standard pattern emerges.

As the fortunate ones themselves insist, the subject calls for a bit of definition at the outset. Their first question was, typically, "What do you mean by 'happy'?" They certainly don't claim to be constantly elated. On happiness as something akin to euphoria, Sigmund Freud probably put it best: "What we call happiness in the strictest sense comes from the (preferably sudden) satisfaction of needs which have been dammed up to a high degree, and it is from its nature only possible as an episodic phenomenon." What does seem possible as more than an episodic phenomenon is a generous measure of contentment with one's lot, a feeling of being generally pleased with how life is going and, truth to tell, pleased with oneself. Perspicacious observers of the happiest executives sometimes say of an individual example that he or she seems serene.

Not that he, or she, isn't also more or less constantly in motion. The happiest executives work hard and are happy in their work. Stanley Peterfreund, the avowedly happy owner of his own human-resources consulting firm in Closter, New Jersey, echoes a sentiment common among this crew: "I've been fortunate for most of my working life to be doing exactly what I've wanted to be doing." Specifically, these contented managers delight in three aspects of their work: the challenge it affords them, the clout inherent in their jobs, and the autonomy they have achieved.

In describing their work as a challenge, and most use just that word, these lucky folks typically weave together four separate threads. As Harvard's Isenberg notes, they view the issues that they wrestle with as complex, meaty, and full of significance. Though they're not quick to say so, they feel that the skills they bring to bear are unique, or at least distinctive. While new assignments may stretch them beyond what they've done before, they still sense that they are masters of the work they do. No matter how high the occasional flood rises, their heads remain above water.

And they manage to stay curious about, interested in, even enraptured by their field of endeavor. Ronald Gallatin, a managing director of Shearson Lehman Brothers, says of his encounter with the daily grind, "I'm excited to come in and excited during the day." They have fun on the job. Larry L. Cummings, a professor of organizational behavior at Northwestern University's Kellogg Graduate School of

Management, has been looking to uncover the traits that distinguish what he calls high-energy, high-contentment executives from their less ebullient brethren. Happy managers, he finds, "have the ability to take a playful attitude toward their work and themselves." They can keep at bay those carping, censorious adult voices built into each of us, the ones that whisper, "You can't do that" or "It will never fly."

At its simplest, the clout that happy executives exercise consists of being able to demonstrably affect matters for the better. Or at least so it seems to them. "What I do is improve things," says James Balloun, the partner in charge of the Atlanta office of the McKinsey consulting firm. In describing the beneficent effect they have, happy executives most frequently talk about people: customers helped, partners rewarded, subordinates encouraged and developed. Their efforts shouldn't be construed as purely altruistic, however. Happy executives are compensated well, and not just financially. Most would probably agree with Harvey Wertheim, a managing director of Harvest Ventures, a New York City venture capital outfit, who says, "Money doesn't matter a lot." Clearly they attach large importance to the recognition, and respect, of people who see them in action.

A happy executive typically runs his own show. He may own the business or serve as a partner in a firm. If he works in a large organization, he may not be chief executive, but he probably has carved out a territory in which he can act as if he were. Gallatin of Shearson Lehman Brothers makes the point nicely: "Once you reach a certain level, the key thing is to do what you do best without interference." As Richard Boyatzis, president of the Boston consulting firm McBer & Co., observes, it helps that in a senior executive position "you can pretty much design your own job," applying yourself to what interests you most, delegating the rest. If there's a boss lurking somewhere in the picture, you would rarely know it from talking with contented executives.

When it comes to describing how the happy honcho's work fits into the rest of his life, the experts repeatedly use the word *balance*. Management psychologist Harry Levinson, harking back to research done years ago at the Menninger Foundation, points out that the folks with the best mental health have "a wide variety of sources of gratification — they take pleasure in many different things." For the happy executive, sources of gratification beyond work typically include a spouse almost invariably described as terrific, children much doted upon, some fairly vigorous sport or avocation taken seriously, and in certain cases civic or charitable activities. The spouse, may it be noted, usually has talents and interests of his or her own.

If you need a quick and dirty test to tell whether a given hard-working executive is reasonably happy, Roderick Gilkey, a clinical psychologist and professor of management at the Emory University business school in Atlanta, proposes two touchstone questions: Does he take interesting vacations, from which he returns refreshed? And does he sponsor his children, to use Gilkey's term, encouraging their efforts but not setting punishingly high standards for them?

In the ranks of the happiest executives you will not find many workaholics, though you can get a good argument going on this point. The majority view holds that the workaholic's behavior is driven in a way that the contented manager's is not: It is compensatory, a more or less desperate effort to make up for something the victim feels is missing in himself or in his life. Executive recruiters say that such behavior doesn't often lead to the elevated positions that happier managers seem able to achieve. Says Barry Nathanson, president of the Richards Consultants headhunting firm in New York, "I've dealt with chief executives who look down on a guy because he's a workaholic. They get tired of seeing his gray face all the time."

The minority view, on the other hand, holds that many workaholics are both happy and successful. They love their work, this line of reasoning goes, and apply themselves to it to the exclusion of just about everything else. Good news for the company that employs them, bad news for spouse, children, or people who have to work for them.

Finally, there is in the makeup of the happiest executives a trait that might variously be ascribed to temperament, hard-won wisdom, or a successful upbringing. These men and women seem able to recognize themselves for what they are, and to accept what they see. Because they take a tolerant attitude toward themselves, they can accept others and work with them easily. All this gives the happiest executives a leg up in dealing with stressful situations, whether brought on by their own mistakes or the mistakes of others. They'll make a benign or self-deprecating joke, and then get on with the work at hand.

When it comes to the occasional mischances that can befall any business, "The two words I use most are 'It's over,' " says Stew Leonard, chairman of Stew Leonard's Dairy, a Norwalk, Connecticut, food emporium celebrated in a television documentary based on the book *In Search of Excellence*. Leonard doesn't just sit on his considerable executive happiness; he consciously employs it in managing his five hundred or so employees. "When I feel bad or frustrated," he says, "I stay away from people, because it's very contagious." Ah, but when he's feeling good . . . "Happiness is like perfume," Leonard proclaims. "If you wear it, you share it with everyone around you."

40

Looking Out for the Executive Alcoholic

She denies it. Her secretary denies it. Her boss denies it.
And every day she edges a little closer to disaster.

I'M SORRY, Mr. Bleaney is at lunch with a client; he said he may be late. Bleaney's been coming in at 7:15 in the morning — what can the sly devil be up to? Mr. Bleaney is in a meeting across town; I have a number where I can reach him. Boy, Bleaney can really handle the stuff. Bleaney's still terrific, of course, but maybe we should give this one to Jackson . . .

Mr. Bleaney is an alcoholic. His wife knows that something is wrong, but can't, or won't, put a name to it. His secretary just wants to help him through a bad time. Colleagues have seen changes in the way he acts, but after all, he's doing the job. And Bleaney himself? Sure, he admits to being a bit erratic, perhaps even that he hits the sauce more of late, but then he's under a lot of pressure.

One of the ironies of executive alcoholism is that you can live with it, and indeed die from it, without ever knowing the problem for exactly what it is.

Statistics on the incidence of alcoholism are a confused, often tendentious hash, but enough evidence exists to suggest problem drinking easily ranks among the top two or three threats to executive health. If managerial drinking merely keeps up with the national average — and no data suggest that it doesn't — then about one out of fourteen high-level types is struggling with the bottle.

Many observers suspect, however, that executive drinking exceeds the norm. They point to a 1979 Opinion Research Corp. survey in which 18 percent of top- and middle-management executives interviewed expressed concern about their use of alcohol. While this may simply argue that the managerial conscience is more developed than most, it may also reveal a hidden epidemic of booze-related difficulties, particularly so since the typical reaction of the problem drinker is to deny that alcohol is his nemesis. For every James S. Kemper, Jr., the insurance-company chairman who admitted he was a recovered alcoholic, or Ray Kroc, the late McDonald's founder, who, though not an admitted alcoholic, made news by checking into an alcoholic-treatment center, there presumably are thousands whose excesses remain largely under cover.

You know, I know, we all know what an alcoholic is. He's a Skid Row bum. Fewer than 5 percent of alcoholics are. He's out of work. People who treat alcoholics say that the job is usually the last thing to go, often five years after the spouse and children have checked out. He's somebody who drinks in the morning. Dr. Anne Geller, the head of the Smithers Alcoholism Treatment and Training Center of New York's Roosevelt Hospital, says few do that: "Everybody knows that means you're an alcoholic — so you take a Valium instead."

In addition to not knowing enough, people often refuse to recognize the executive alcoholic because a stigma still accompanies the label. Bruce Mansfield, a former president of Ohio Edison and a recovered alcoholic, recalls the president of another company: "For years people criticized his conduct and blamed his drinking. I never heard anybody call him an alcoholic."

The ignorance and denial extend to the alcoholic himself, with a vengeance. Charles Shirley, director of industrial programs of the New York City affiliate of the National Council on Alcoholism, recently studied twenty-five executives who had finally found their way to Alcoholics Anonymous. Most said they had not sought help earlier — on average they waited seven years — because while they realized their drinking had become troublesome, they didn't know they were alcoholic.

It's difficult to fault them for their confusion. If alcoholism is a disease, then it is probably the only one ever so designated by democratic process, specifically by vote of the American Medical Association in 1955. The doctors concluded, in effect, that the best reason to define alcoholism as a disease is that it's impractical to do otherwise. Calling booze a moral problem, and dealing with the afflicted accordingly, only feeds the guilt, fear, and anger that drive many a drinker deeper into the bottle.

It's a puzzling sickness, though. Why will Mr. Smith, who has two highballs before dinner every night, turn into an alcoholic, while Mr. Jones, with the same habit, does not? No one really knows. Nor is it easy to define and identify the alcoholic. Measures of consumption don't help much. If you wish to brighten your next business lunch, casually mention that the National Institute on Alcohol Abuse and Alcoholism classifies as a heavy drinker anyone who averages two drinks or more per day. In the NIAAA's estimate, 68 percent of such drinkers are alcoholics. (White-wine imbibers at the table need not smile smugly. A five-ounce glass of wine, about the standard restaurant offering, contains approximately the same amount of alcohol as a shot of whiskey. So does a twelve-ounce bottle of beer.) Probably the best definition was formulated by the late Marty Mann, a founder of the National Council on Alcoholism. She defined an alcoholic as a person whose drinking interferes in a *continuing* and *growing* way with the components of the person's life — self, family, friends, and work, usually in that order.

While no alcoholic executive is typical, a more or less representative case history can be sketched. It generally takes years for the disease to run its course, ten to fifteen between the onset of problems and eventual hospitalization being not uncommon. Some people, particularly women, can bring it off in less than five, though.

Most American males do their heavy drinking between the ages of eighteen and thirty-four, with perhaps the most intense boozing concentrated in the early twenties, before the lads settle down. As his contemporaries taper off, however, the alcoholic-in-the-making keeps on at the same level or drinks more. A Yale graduate who went on into management recalled his experience recently: "In my bachelor days, I didn't keep track much — you kept strange hours, were out on dates. I only began counting after I was married. That was the dry-martini-straight-up era. My bride and I would each have three before dinner on weeknights, four at the cocktail hour on weekends. When I started having four on weeknights, I began to wonder."

Soon there are problems at home, and the family rallies round in ways that will subsequently be replicated at the office. The spouse may be engaged in what experts on alcoholism term "enabling," unwittingly helping her mate to go on drinking. She spreads a blanket over him when he passes out in the living-room chair, or makes excuses for him. The children assume some of their alcoholic parent's responsibilities — taking out the trash, mowing the lawn, talking to Mom. The family's circle of friends changes and grows smaller. No more evenings with the Martins, who serve only one cocktail before dinner and are chary with the wine at table.

As the alcoholic's self-esteem at home begins to plummet, his work — heretofore perhaps largely unaffected — becomes all the more important. If he feels that his efficiency is beginning to slip, he may compensate by coming in before everyone else, or by staying late. "I was always in early," reports an executive alcoholic who later recovered, "knowing that I had to get done before lunch what I used to have all day to do. In seven years, I was absent maybe seven days."

Often the company continues to reward the problem drinker for such diligence. Charles Shirley's study of twenty-five executive alcoholics found that not only did most of them keep their positions until the final stages of the disease, many were steadily promoted. In some cases, this may have owed something to the drinker's bonhomie. One of Shirley's subjects, a diminutive woman who shot upward through the ranks of an advertising agency while abusing both alcohol and drugs, found that her male colleagues enjoyed drinking with her enormously, indeed encouraged her to drink. "They thought I was cute," she recalls acidly.

The alcoholic frequently ends up carrying geniality too far. Shirley suspects, and other experts agree, that the first widely visible signal of an executive in distress many times comes from his misbehavior at an event "off campus" — the party after the regional sales meeting, at a high-level weekend retreat, or on a business trip. The normal wraps are off; sociability is at a premium. A large Wall Street brokerage firm had no idea that its hottest young salesman was an alcoholic, not until Harvard Business School called to say he was running amok, even by the standards of its executive programs.

The boss is often the last to know. Because of the nature of managerial work — unsupervised, hard to define, blending business with the social — indications of falling productivity that often give away an alcoholic on the shop floor don't apply. The executive's secretary will notice, though — his coming back late from lunch, or not, or not coming back at all; increasingly frequent bouts with "flu" or "tooth-ache"; taking more time to get work done.

Typically, she'll attempt to conceal his problem from others, doing a bit of enabling of her own. Twenty of the twenty-five executives in Shirley's study said that their secretaries covered up for them. She does so out of loyalty, or for fear of losing her job or, rather perversely, because she gets a kick out of the enhanced authority that his dereliction affords her.

Over time, the executive's behavior changes in ways that can't be hidden. To illustrate his belief that such changes are the best indication of a manager's drowning, Dr. Harry Brownie, a psychiatrist, tells of an alcoholic executive, a lifelong straight arrow, who suddenly took up with a woman from the typing pool. Periodically, the two would leave the office and check into a hotel across the street, to the great merriment of the rest of the clericals, who would time their assignations.

At this stage the alcoholic's physical symptoms begin to increase in number and severity. He may already have had blackouts, episodes of alcoholic amnesia. While to everyone else he'll appear to be acting normally — striking deals, plotting corporate strategy — later he'll remember nothing. "I'd phone the guy I had lunch with the day before," confesses a former corporate vice president, "fishing, trying to get him to reconstruct what we had talked about." The alcoholic's capacity, the amount he can drink before getting drunk, stops increasing and begins to decline.

By this time, too, what the experts call job shrinkage has started to set in. The alcoholic executive can probably still discharge the duties he's had for years, but he doesn't add to them as he used to. His peers or subordinates, sometimes with the kindest of motives, may take on work that he would have picked up before. Higher-ups, who now know that something is wrong, feel that they can't count on him anymore, particularly for assignments dealing with outsiders. They trust him with less and less.

Why don't they just fire him? Frequently because of the "halo effect"; a nimbus of glory from his past accomplishments persists. Moreover, when sober he may still be damn good. Or he may have risen so far, and amassed such power, that it would be embarrassing, and tricky, to push him out. The second most likely person to cover up for an alcoholic executive, Shirley found, is his immediate superior.

In the final stages of the disease, the alcoholic can no longer predict what will happen when he drinks. If the corporation goes along, and the conspiracy of silence is maintained, he may simply imbibe his way toward eventual hospitalization or death, appearing increasingly sporadically at the office, an office that few call or visit.

Alternatively, he may go out in a burst of ignominy. "My company always made a big thing out of plant openings," recalls a former executive whose specialty was public relations. "We were opening one in San Antonio, and I was in charge. I met the corporate plane — with the chairman and president aboard — dead drunk. That was the end of my career."

A fairly standard regimen is prescribed for the alcoholic executive who gets treatment. First, four to seven days of medically supervised detoxification if necessary — sedatives relieve the discomfort of withdrawal. Next, three to five weeks of rehabilitation in an alcohol-free setting. Finally, back at home, abstinence and continuing participation in Alcoholics Anonymous or a similar group — a recovering alcoholic may go to an AA meeting every day. He need not find himself with the midnight choir from the Bowery — in some cities around the country there are AA groups that cater exclusively to executives, just as there are ones for pilots and judges.

The catch is getting Mr. Bleaney to seek treatment. Oddly, and perhaps cruelly, the company has something potent going for it here that worried family members don't have — the executive's fear of losing his job. Many counselors think this the single most powerful inducement to self-referral. While statistics on recovery are as bad as those on the problem itself, most observers believe that over 70 percent of alcoholics who get help under this spur recover, a rate well above average.

It's dicey giving him the message, though. If the executive alcoholic is your superior, the experts agree, you're almost certainly better off not confronting him yourself. Go to someone in personnel, or the company medical director, and tell him that *you* have a problem. You do: your boss's drinking.

If Mr. Bleaney is your peer, or subordinate, you still can run into trouble. Offering him your layman's diagnosis will call forth all the rationalization, and lies, that he can muster. You probably need an expert, one who knows more about alcoholism than the drinker himself and who won't be talked out of the problem. Many companies — including General Motors, ITT, J. C. Penney, and Morgan Guaranty — have employee-assistance programs, a euphemism for counseling to deal with the corporation's alcoholics. But if he's a heavy hitter, you probably should turn to an outsider.

One of the most flamboyant is Dr. Joseph Pursch, who as a navy commander treated both Betty Ford and Billy Carter. Now with Comprehensive Care Corp., a company that makes a business out of helping problem drinkers, he specializes in what he calls "the VIP alcoholic," including chief executives.

Pursch himself leads the confrontation. And what a confrontation! After being called in, typically by the top corporate lawyer or president, Pursch talks by phone to the alcoholic's wife, children, chauffeur, bodyguard, and pilot of the corporate jet, and company officers — all this without the subject's knowledge. He then manages to gather everyone involved, including the drinker, at some out-of-the-way place — perhaps the executive's summer home.

With the surprise confrontation set for 8:15 A.M., one of the children is delegated to keep the executive from drinking that morning. (A pregnant daughter-in-law works even better, Pursch claims.) After the members of the posse have an 8 o'clock meeting among themselves to get rid of butterflies, the still-unaware executive is brought in and surrounded. The participants tell him how concerned they are about his well-being, then each peppers him with examples of his misbehavior, stressing facts, not feelings, and makes a threat that he or she is prepared to carry out.

From the wife: I'll go ahead with the divorce. From the chauffeur: After twenty-six years with you, I'll quit. From the company president to, say, the chairman: I'll go to the board and do everything I can to get you fired. The alcoholic is then told that he must go for treatment, not at some future date, but today. The group explains to him how the company and his personal affairs will be run in his absence.

Usually he cracks in less than half an hour. He's then given a drink — you can be sure that he needs one — and driven to the plane. On the flight to the treatment center, he can imbibe all he wants. Once the plane touches down, though, that's all.

It's a dramatic, even elegant way to say good-bye to alcoholism. But there's no bad way.

41

The Narcissistic Executive

This type of manager has something electric about him.
Stand by for a few shocks.

IN THE EARLY 1980s, a new strain of strange behavior became apparent among big-time executives. John DeLorean represented the best example. And, on a different plane, Bill Agee — leaving aside the personal stuff, what was this business of riding roughshod over board members to consummate a questionable deal, then going to every arm of the national media to explain that, gosh, we only did it for the shareholders?

Minor weirdness abounded. Ted Turner, continuing to lose large sums on his loudly trumpeted challenge to the networks, plunged again on a noisy, unsuccessful venture to televise pickup professional football games. David Mahoney, back in those days chairman of Norton Simon, took to the television screen to hawk the services of his troubled Avis subsidiary — an okay thing, perhaps, for Lee Iacocca (an old hand at carmaking, reassuring the customers) or Frank Borman (astronaut/celebrity in his own right), but Norton Simon was a conglomerate, for heaven's sake.

Was it something they were putting in the water in those executive carafes?

No. It was, instead, the manifestation of a new executive style, or at least a style we're seeing more of these days in the corporate world. To be specific, call it the narcissistic style.

In the last ten years professional observers of the human animal — psychologists, psychiatrists, sociologists — have become intrigued with the notion that certain aspects of contemporary behavior can best be understood by reference to a syndrome that they label *narcissism*. This isn't just your garden-variety vanity or swelled-headedness. It's a particular psychological condition, with a distinct — if much debated—etiology, associated ways of acting, problems, and benefits. Some experts have even gone so far as to assert the existence of a "narcissistic personality type," though the details—like the whole proposition—remain controversial.

While the clinical concept does seem to have explanatory cogency beyond the analyst's couch—see, for example, Christopher Lasch's best-selling jeremiad against contemporary civilization, *The Culture of Narcissism*—two considerations should be borne in mind before applying it willy-nilly to the goings-on in the executive suite. First, most students of the phenomenon would agree that this isn't a sort of bug that you either have or you don't. Different people affect the style to different degrees. "Every successful manager must have some element of healthy narcissism," notes Manfred Kets de Vries, a psychoanalyst and professor of management at Montreal's McGill University.

Second, assessments that anyone is far along on the narcissistic spectrum, much less a narcissistic personality type, can only be made by an expert with access to the subject's inner life. What a layman can do is to understand the drives and behavior that go to make up the style, then see whether this understanding helps illuminate a puzzling managerial action. Probably the best route to such understanding is to follow the career of that creature who never was: the pure, unalloyed, thoroughgoing corporate narcissist.

How did he get that way? Psychoanalysts generally believe that the condition begins with a fierce inner struggle early in childhood. Faced with an unbearable disappointment—Mother doesn't love me enough, or at least not in the right way—the child also finds that his sense of self-esteem isn't sufficient to keep anxiety at bay. As a result, he starts to indulge in fantasies of grandiosity—"I'm not just all right, I'm the greatest"—thereby setting in motion the psychological motor that drives the narcissist: grandiosity opposing, trying to keep submerged, impaired self-esteem.

Drive him it will. Throughout his youth he will strive mightily to marshal support for his grandiose yet fragile image of himself—this by cultivating whatever good looks he has, learning to charm, and oftentimes just by working hard. All of which isn't, of course, a bad recipe for success.

By the time he's ready to look for his first job on the road to management you'll be eager to hire him. He's well groomed, nicely dressed, articulate — indeed, he may talk a little too much — and confident, even cocky. Romantics around the office will say that, aah, there's just something electric about the guy.

A year after bringing him on, you'll probably congratulate yourself heartily. He's such a worker, it seems. Yes — because he needs a succession of triumphs to keep his idea of himself afloat, and he digests those triumphs quickly. "Not all workaholics are narcissistic," observes Roderick Gilkey, a professor at Emory University, "but a lot of better-functioning narcissists are workaholic." Moreover, the man is creative. How better to set yourself apart from, and above, those around you than by doing things differently?

Two years after you hired him you may not be so pleased. He has trouble holding on to good people. Predictable — it's in dealing with others that the narcissistic sort often first run into difficulty. They can seem warm, ingratiating, but, as the people who work closely with them rapidly figure out, it's a pseudo-warmth, operative only as long as it serves the purpose of their self-aggrandizement.

The narcissist, you see, is quite alone mentally. A key aspect of the condition is the inability to see others as anything but part of the background, furniture on the stage set of Numero Uno's success. Gilkey tells the story of a young businessman who had been in treatment for a narcissistic disorder for two years. One day, in the course of a session with his analyst, he suddenly became agitated and began to perspire. "My God," he blurted out, "there are two of us in this room."

Such behavior can tend to alienate folks. Another young hotshot, rising fast on the financial side of the entertainment business, went around announcing his engagement and accepting the congratulations of his colleagues. The only problem: he hadn't bothered to pop the question. It never occurred to him that his intended might refuse or that she might be offended by his trumpeting the marriage before she knew of it. He's still single. Corporate underlings who have the boss's latest Fabulous Project popped on them in a meeting with the big brass can understand her reaction.

As he enters the middle passage of his career — from age thirty on, say — the future courses open to the narcissist become more clearly defined. There are the individuals who have gotten away with it. None of their dramatically risky ventures bombed. They changed jobs, or companies, frequently enough to avoid being exposed as Attila the Hun. ("Oh, he's arrogant, but . . .") The spouse was complaisant, or venal. Such men often persist, climbing the corporate ladder, perhaps expanding their arena — they're always onstage — to include café society or money-intensive sports. They may even, heaven help them, begin to curry the press's favor.

Others aren't so lucky. Their employers, valuing the creativity but deploring the inability to play on the team, build a sort of cocoon around them. They become "our brilliant art director" in an advertising agency or "our favorite mad scientist," heading up the company laboratories — coddled, flattered, not trusted, unlikely to rise any higher. "You know how those guys are . . ."

Still others end up finding their large corporation too small a theater for them to play out their grandiosity in. They leave, sometimes to start their own company. And what do they call it? "Naming the company after yourself is almost a pure giveaway that there's narcissism at work," observes Theodore Millon, director of clinical psychology at the University of Miami. It was, you may remember, the DeLorean Motor Co. The car was known simply as "a DeLorean."

Whatever his career situation, for the hard-core narcissist the progress through middle age usually represents increasingly tough sledding. Inclined from the beginning to be what clinicians term "sexually exhibitionistic" — no, not flashing in the park; preening, and taking care to be seen squiring beautiful women — he can be devastated by any deterioration in his looks. One narcissistic executive realized how troubled he was — troubled enough to seek treatment — when he mistook someone else for himself in a group photograph. The shock came because the other man was considerably uglier than he.

By this time, too, the hollowness of the narcissist's emotional ties begins to tell in his personal life. His wife may leave — to him, inexplicably — in search of warmth. Or she may come to seem less than perfect in his eyes — crow's-feet and all that — prompting him to, as they say, trade one forty for two twenties.

At work, even if he has attained a top job, he's a prime candidate for feelings of "Is that all there is?" Faced with midlife wounds to his continually imperiled self-esteem, his insatiable grandiosity seeks all the more urgently after confirmation, support. His deals become bigger and riskier. Colleagues begin to question his business judgment. "A problem with narcissists is that they don't get anxious when they ought to," suggests Professor Abraham Zaleznik of the Harvard Business School. "Civilization depends on people feeling anxious."

In a sense, the narcissistic style is setting him up for what might be called The Big Mess. Something goes wrong—his latest venture gets into financial trouble, his current bold corporate stroke hits a snag. Grandiosity fights all the more visibly with dark feelings. His highs get higher, his lows lower. People around him are buffeted by the flipping back and forth.

Because his grandiosity can't permit him to seem a loser, he embarks on a quest for smashing victory to redeem the defeat. By this time, however, his grandiose feelings may have gotten so far out of hand that his "reality testing"—the technical term for being in touch with the real world—becomes impaired. His never very strong regard for others, their values, laws, and sensitivities, slips even farther. "I'm the greatest," he tells himself. "I can do whatever I want, things that other people can't do." Bingo—he gets himself into The Big Mess.

Is the narcissistic executive style actually on the increase these days, or does it merely seem so? Years ago, it may be recalled, insurance mogul W. Clement Stone used to give out special silver coins that bore his face on one side.

Clinical observers aren't certain whether the incidence of narcissism is growing, or whether, having developed the concept, we simply find more of it about. Most do suspect, however, that the style is, as they put it, overrepresented these days in the population of business executives. Not necessarily at the very top, where sound judgment and a capacity for team play are still at a premium, but probably in the echelons just below.

If you go looking for examples of the style in the chief executive's office, the experts think you're most likely to find them—aside from companies where the guy's name is on the building—in conglomerates. Dealmaking, takeovers, the dramatic corporate coup are much more to the narcissistic taste than building a career in machine tools over thirty years.

The danger posed to American business, if one is posed, may not be from too much of the style, but from too little. "I don't think corporations should overreact to DeLorean, or the few instances like this," suggests James A. Wilson, of the graduate school of business of the University of Pittsburgh. "Companies have been excessively seeking after the stable, even dull, executive, and haven't allowed themselves the flamboyant or expansive one." It's right to value the creativity and excitement that accompany the style.

At the same time, bear in mind the fate of the original, mythological Narcissus. Entranced by his reflection in a pool, oblivious to everything else around him, he fell into the water and drowned, still clutching after his own image.

42

How Executives Think

A growing body of research suggests that managerial minds work differently from everybody else's.

THE PEOPLE AT THE TOP put their pants or skirts on just like you and me, right? Sure, they may draw down those fancy salaries, but for what? For politicking their way up the ladder and then taking the heat on all those big decisions, right? Okay, so some may be a little smarter than the average Joe, but when it comes down to it, they don't think any differently from you and me, right?

Wrong, on every count but the pants and skirts, about which there isn't good research. After years of studying the subject, certain path-breaking behavioral scientists have concluded that there is indeed something distinctive about the workings of the executive mind. While the researchers don't agree on all the particulars, their findings overlap enough to suggest rough consensus on what it is that those high-priced noggins do differently. A near-genius I.Q. by itself doesn't guarantee superior managerial thinking.

The expert who has probably toiled longest in this particular vineyard is Elliott Jaques, the director of the Institute of Organisation and Social Studies at Brunel University in Uxbridge, England. To call Jaques a polymath rather understates his qualifications: he holds a Ph.D. in social relations — sociology, psychology, and anthropology — from Harvard and an M.D. from Johns Hopkins; trained as a psychoanalyst, he is a Founder Fellow of the Royal College of Psychiatry; more to the point here, he conducted what may be the longest-running research project ever done on a corporation — a study of Glacier Metal Co., a British metals engineering outfit, that lasted from 1948 until the late 1970s. These days Jaques is working with clients that range from the U.S. army to an Australian mining company.

At the heart of Jaques's findings is a concept he calls the time frame of the individual. His research indicates that individuals vary radically in terms of the time periods they can think out, organize, and work through. It taxes some folks to figure out what they have to do today, and in what order. Others — namely, executive types — can see a long way, identifying the steps necessary for some move that will take years to complete, envisioning the consequences of each step, and then taking the measures to set the juggernaut in motion.

Over a lifetime a person typically becomes capable of handling progressively longer time frames. This development isn't smoothly incremental, though — it's discontinuous, occurring in spurts that carry the individual from a one-day time frame to a three-month time frame, and thence, after a decent interval at each stage, to one-year, two-year, five-year, ten-year, and twenty-year time frames. The statistical distribution of people capable of the different time frames is also discontinuous: most of the population is never capable of more than a three-month time span; a smaller group is capable of envisioning an entire year, and so on; only one individual out of several million, Jaques estimates, is ever capable of a twenty-year time frame.

What makes this stuff dynamite in a corporate context is Jaques's additional finding that there is a sort of natural structure to organizations engaged in work, wherein most jobs can be classified according to the time frame required of the incumbent. An unskilled shop-floor worker can almost always get by with no more than a one-day time horizon. A person holding down the lowest-level managerial job, if he's to be any good at it, must be capable of at least a three-month time frame.

Jaques's research shows that the best organizations, in terms of morale and productivity, are those whose structure follows what might be called the natural hierarchy: one-day-time-frame workers report to a foreman who can organize at least the next three months; he follows the dictates of a manager who can plan a year or longer; he reports to a general manager with a two-year time frame; he answers to a vice president capable of charting strategy over five years. Atop it all sits a chief executive who can cast his mind forward to encompass the next ten or more years. In common parlance this ability, much sought after in executives, is called vision. For a rough handle on where you fit, think about the most distant deadline you feel comfortable with.

Jaques believes that time frame is the best indicator of the broader mental capabilities that psychologists call cognitive power. Cognitive power is not I.Q. — it reflects not raw brainpower but how someone's perception and thinking are organized, how he operates. Jaques concludes that an individual capable of thinking out a year ahead has one level of cognitive power, someone capable of thinking out two years, the next level.

Each level, Jaques hypothesizes, has a characteristic mode of thinking, but his descriptions of the different modes remain a bit murky. For example, an individual working with a maximum time frame of up to one year is capable of something called reflective articulation — he can stand back from the work he supervises, articulate what is going on, form ideas about it, and then play with these ideas. A person capable of thinking out ten years can "shape whole systems" — he can understand how a large organization like a corporation fits together, imagine how its boundaries might be expanded, say by charging into completely new markets, and reason through the second- or third-order consequences of such a move.

The conclusions drawn by other students of executive intelligence are less cosmic. While each researcher is quite willing to point out how his findings differ from everyone else's, to an outsider's eye most of the work appears to support the proposition that executives' thinking differs from others' in at least three ways.

Senior managers display a greater capacity for what Siegfried Streufert, a psychologist at the Pennsylvania State University College of Medicine, calls differentiation. For several years Streufert has been putting executives and others of approximately equal I.Q.-type intelligence through complicated decision-making exercises. He has compared the performance of good managers, as judged by their companies, and lesser ones from the same companies. Streufert finds that successful managerial types can see distinctions between similar-appearing phenomena better than laymen do, and that good managers are also more prone to consider the same fact from different perspectives. In particular, managerial adepts are capable of seeing a matter from someone else's point of view. Wallace Stevens, who besides being one of America's foremost poets was a vice president of the Hartford Accident & Indemnity Co., wrote a poem entitled "Thirteen Ways of Looking at a Blackbird"—just routine cognition for vice presidents, apparently.

Along the same line, in comparing the cogitation of executives with that of bright undergraduates, Professor Daniel J. Isenberg of the Harvard Business School observed that the students were much more likely to consign a particular fact to some larger category in an effort to understand it — executives weren't nearly so ready to categorize. Yale psychology professor Robert Sternberg and one of his graduate students, Janet Davidson, have done research that suggests that managers have a cognitive ability that they label "selective encoding": the executive brain can quickly sort the relevant from the irrelevant. This gives them an edge in recognizing and defining a problem where others see only a jumble of business as usual.

Executives display a distinctive talent for what Streufert calls integration, which is somewhat similar to what Sternberg and Davidson term selective combination and selective comparison. Having picked out the salient facts, managers put them together in ways that other folks don't, positing a causal connection here, speculating on a possible analogy there. To use Streufert's term, good managerial thinking is multidimensional. Isenberg found that managers were much more willing to draw inferences than were the students he tested. The business types would proceed with their thinking while the students were still asking for more information. Executives were also more adept at jumping from abstract levels of thought to the particular, and back again. Isenberg suspects that managers may, in fact, pay less attention to isolated pieces of information than others do — the big thinkers have learned it's more effective to spend their time putting everything together. All the researchers noted a managerial knack for dredging up from their memories solutions to past problems to see how those solutions might shed light on the problem at hand.

Managerial thought is, apparently, distinctively flexible. Isenberg found, for example, that executives began to plan the actions they would take to solve a problem much earlier in the thinking process than the students did. The executives would do some analysis, plan, look at the world and do more analysis, and then plan some more.

Streufert and Sternberg have detected a similar willingness to modify plans in light of emerging reality. Based on his observation of execs in action, Isenberg speculates that often managers simply take the minimum action possible that will still keep their outfit in the game and then wait for the unfolding play to present what looks like a better opportunity.

In other respects, the findings of the different researchers still need to be reconciled. Jaques, for example, believes that Streufert's research results support his own more sweeping conclusions. Streufert sees big differences. He agrees that executives can put together elaborate strategic plans, but he finds that only the immediate steps are thought through in detail — the later parts are left unclear, awaiting further information — and the plans need not cover any particular period of time.

Resume normal breathing, managerial types — the era of a standardized college-board-type test to determine your executive thinking ability isn't at hand quite yet.

43

The Care and Feeding of Contacts

Immanuel Kant would have called the practice sleazy.
A lot of practitioners say they're just being realistic.

MENTION CONNECTIONS or the old-boy network to the aver-age red-blooded American businessman, and you may get a grimace. The words can connote low deals, back scratching, bumbling relatives eased onto the payroll . . . *we don't play the game that way.* And yet, as the still, small voice of reality whispers, contacts *are* important. Prod the average executive a bit and he will admit as much. From a corporate vice president in Minnesota, who had just finished a long peroration on how little such ties meant to him and his colleagues: "Well, of course it is true that in fifteen minutes in the lobby of the Minneapolis Club you can see everybody you need to talk to in a week."

Who's kidding whom? Perhaps for the betterment of us all, per-haps only as a measure of how brazen we've become, the subject of connections is coming out of the closet. The old-boy net as tradition-ally understood is still functioning, notably in the selection of corpo-rate directors, but it's rapidly giving ground. Taking its place is a new, deliberate, and relatively above-board pattern of contact formation, sanitized by feminists and others under the name "networking." While not immune to the old questions — is this or that use of a contact strictly ethical? — the new approach also brings novel prob-lems, including the emerging, trendy danger of being overnetworked.

The cynical definition of a contact is "someone you can get in touch with who can do something for you." The practical definition adds, "and for whom you can do something." We are not talking about the pleasures of friendship. People maintain a contact to achieve some other purpose, often one that has nothing to do with how the parties feel about each other.

In the world of commerce, three such purposes predominate: obtaining information, getting business, and finding someone a job. Of these, the first, and most innocuous, clearly consumes the vast bulk of the time devoted nationwide to riding the Rolodex.

Research on how managers actually spend the day suggests that, if anything, we probably underestimate the extent and importance of brief, intelligence-grubbing encounters. Professor Henry Mintzberg of McGill University found, for example, that the top executives he studied devoted about 80 percent of their working time to talking with people. Fully 44 percent of the verbal give-and-take was with individuals outside the executives' organizations.

Dope from a contact is thought to be up to the minute — it hasn't had time to wilt in everybody's in- and out-baskets. It seems more reliable — from the horse's mouth; no subordinate with an ax to grind translating it into bureaucratese; unsullied by the P.R. boys' fog machine. And it certainly carries more cachet — for your ears only; insider stuff. Any clown can go through channels.

While using contacts to gain information is ubiquitous, their power to drum up business varies dramatically from industry to industry. It would take a very dim bulb indeed, or a corrupt one, to place his company's order for 50,000 256K RAM chips with Whamloc Corp. solely because Whamloc employs his college roommate. But when the product in question is less easily specced out — accounting and legal services, management consulting, executive recruiting — who-knows-whom may become crucial, at least for giving the service firm a crack at the job.

As a result, consulting outfits such as the Management Analysis Center of Cambridge and Cresap of New York provide their newly hired junior consultants with explicit guidance on the discovery, care, and feeding of contacts. It's hardly of the diabolical, put-LSD-in-their-drinks order, though: keep in touch with your business-school classmates, perhaps by occasionally sending them one of the firm's think pieces; entertain clients as much as your liver and spouse will tolerate. Other firms encourage consultants to fly first class, to rub elbows with decision-makers.

Certain executive recruiters, dependent on contacts for both the business coming in the door and the product going out, are assiduous in their cultivation. Max Rugger, the co-chairman of TASA Inc., a headhunting tribe with offices in twenty-one cities around the world, sends out over 1,200 Christmas cards a year, writing on each a short personal note. A. Robert Taylor, the firm's former chairman, recommends unearthing your acquaintance's nonbusiness interests and then catering to them. To a man concerned about high blood pressure, for example, he routinely sends snippets from his own reading on the subject.

Experts on what is euphemistically termed "business development" make two other points. Quite often it isn't your contact who ends up giving you an assignment, it's a contact of your contact. The same buyer who would be loath to ask, "Are you guys any good?" may feel that he has really shopped around after putting the question "Do you know any good accountants?" to two or three acquaintances. Also, no matter how carefully tended your contact may be, if your firm botches the work, expect no more chances.

The old-boy network has always been most visible in finding the old boy gainful employment. How else could the British, who coined the term to describe the favoring of fellow Etonians and Harrovians, have come up with Kim Philby, the old Cantabrigian who became Moscow's best connection in British intelligence? Or how could New York's Morgan Guaranty Trust Co. find itself with so many alumni of Harvard's snouty Porcellian Club — a porker's head adorns the club tie — that the bank is sometimes called the Bay of Pigs?

Typically, the company reliant on old boys will have a "talent spotter" on the faculty or staff of, say, Yale. When a person of the right ilk comes along, phone calls will be exchanged and just-our-sort-of-guy invited in for a chat.

Increasingly, however, your school or country-club decal alone won't get you into the managers' parking lot. Equal-opportunity guidelines account for part of the change. But if you believe the executive recruiters — the main beneficiaries of the trend — it may also be because of the more demanding nature of managerial work, which causes companies to set tougher standards in hiring.

It does appear that corporations are calling on headhunters with ever greater frequency to fill upper- and middle-level management positions — as opposed to bringing in somebody's friend of a friend.

According to surveys by the recruiting firm of Heidrick & Struggles, approximately 47 percent of executive job openings were filled by headhunters in 1981, versus 37 percent in 1976. Only the old-director network remains untouched. Heidrick & Struggles says search firms played a role in locating just 5 percent of new corporate board members in 1981, and then the assignment was often to find women and minority-group representatives — precisely the folks that the traditional arrangements couldn't turn up. The best way to get on a board, more important than your business success or a high profile in trade associations and philanthropic activities, is to already be on another board.

Even this last citadel may give way eventually, however, under the onslaught of a new breed — the straight-out, self-aware, no-hemming-or-hawing-about-it networkers. The genus has two over-lapping species, those interested in "career advancement" in a general sort of way, perhaps with a dash of solace thrown in, and those looking for a J–O–B.

The first species is predominantly female. Stumble into a meeting room in almost any American city and you're likely to find yourself in the midst of a Women's Forum, Women in the Media session, or a confab of the Women's Aquaculture Network. Participants will be sharing experiences, being supportive, and trading business cards. Toward the end, a verbal "bulletin board" may take place — I have this job opening and need a woman with marketing experience; I know a brand manager who might be interested.

According to Catalyst, a feminist group in New York City, over one thousand women's networking organizations exist in the U.S. Since their purpose is in part to compensate for exclusion from the old-boy network, until now no men needed apply for admission. This may be changing, though. If men have all the power, some bright souls are beginning to ask, what am I doing spending all my time talking to women? Catalyst's Jean Clarkson argues that the effort has been good for women's self-esteem, but she does concede that "we still don't know whether women's networks really work in helping women get ahead."

Whatever the worth of existing networks, sometimes a man or woman actively seeking a job must build anew. One expert on the design of organizations, Professor Joseph Weintraub of Babson College, tells of a student who spun a web of eighty-four contacts, at least a few of whom finally helped her land the place she wanted at a major Boston company. There are even step-by-step instructions available. Outplacement firms — those counselors to executives "between opportunities" — and guides to career change such as the best-seller *What Color Is Your Parachute?* prescribe a networking regimen that has become so ubiquitous that potential networkees may be starting to catch on.

Begin by making a list of all your contacts — it's probably longer than you suspect. Pay special attention not just to those who might be able to offer you a job, but also to those who might know someone who could. Call each one up to ask if you might get together to talk about his business, or industry trends, or almost anything except your crying need for work. Once you're in the contact's office, there'll be plenty of time to shove a résumé down his throat. Besides, he'll have the pleasure of nattering on about what he knows best, not to mention the Santa Claus thrill of helping another.

So common has the technique grown these days that certain prominent practitioners report being overnetworked. Alice Sargent, who some years ago set up the first network of female management consultants in Washington, D.C., laments that she now receives a call whenever a new girl interested in the business hits town — let's have lunch; tell me everything you know about launching a consulting firm. One response is to refer the caller to someone else in the network — that is, network 'em on down the line.

If you think you're immune to overnetworking, you may be surprised. Graduates of various prestigious colleges ought to be aware that the old-boy net has gone electronic. Their names are being added to computerized data bases that will be used to match them with job-hungry undergraduates. Bryn Mawr, for example, generates computer lists of its alumnae cross-tabulated by business and location. Along comes a young woman interested in selling heavy machinery in Juneau, Alaska, and, bingo, instant connection.

But what about the woman who graduates from Southwest Missouri State, just as bright and energetic as the Bryn Mawr alumna but with no one to speed her résumé past the personnel director's secretary? "She'll just have to work harder," says Dolores Brian, director of career planning at Bryn Mawr. Nor is Brian worried about the possibility that an employer's use of such networks may result in an awfully uniform group of employees.

Such questions are only part of the rub the morally tender feel in thinking about contacts. Isn't it wrong, they ask — taking their lead from that notorious solitaire, Immanuel Kant — to treat a person as a means, rather than as an end?

No, answer the self-declared networkers, not as long as three conditions are met. First, both parties must consent to the transaction. (Isn't there something somewhere, anywhere, that's still wrong for two consenting adults to do to one another in private?) Second, the use to which the contact is put, the end in mind, must be unexceptionable. Finally, confidences must not be betrayed.

It all makes getting a job and advancing a career sound a bit like what goes on in a singles bar. Which perhaps it is.

44

On the Charity Circuit

Executives don't do good works quite the same way
everybody else does. Their motives are complex.

"FRIENDS OF THE SKRONK," the after-dinner speaker intones, "we are here tonight to honor Fred Beasley, chairman of Amalgamated Propylene, for the great work he has done on behalf of skronks living and dead." Actually, Fred's contribution consisted entirely of agreeing to be honored tonight, turning over his list of contacts to the Friends, and having Amalgamated pony up a few thousand dollars for the cause. "You all know Fred." Sadly, no; many of the folks in the audience are corporate underlings present because their companies, headed by Fred's contacts, bought tables and had to fill them up. "You all share his passionate dedication to the skronk." What's a skronk?

It's easy to be cynical about much of what executives do in the name of charity. For one thing, a lot of contributions come out of the shareholders' pockets and not the executives', and there are endless arguments about whether company funds should be used that way. But more is going on here to benefit both charities and executives than meets the eye, especially the cynic's eye. The dinners, United Way chairmanships, and service on nonprofit boards must be seen in their true Proustian complexity.

One thing the cynic fastens on is the discrepancy between the face that participants conspire to put on these activities—we all turned out tonight because of our genuine admiration for Fred and his cause—and the rather less saintly motives often at work beneath the surface. Consider, for example, how a big-league charity dinner is put together. Robert Williams, director of public relations for the Boy Scouts of New York, describes his organization's method, which is fairly standard: "There is always someone to be honored with the Good Scout Award—the honoree and the chairman are selected a year in advance. We explain to the honoree that we want to present him the award and we ask him to help us raise money. Then there'll be a discussion of how to do that. Usually the honorees give us a list of their vendors." Companies that sell goods and services to the honoree's company will be asked to buy tables at $2,500 apiece. Williams goes on: "Sometimes the man will say, 'Okay, I'll accept the award and ask my friend to be chairman.' Sometimes we get someone who will be the chairman and then he asks a friend to get the award." The charity gets lists of vendors from both of them.

A few fine points of this particular art form: in deciding whom to invite, organizations don't usually limit themselves to vendors. If the honoree sits on any corporate boards, the charity will invite the chief executives of those companies. Also the bigwigs who serve with him in the trade association, and any he plays golf with. In selecting an honoree, prestige is important. The executive director of another big New York City charity notes, "One hard thing is picking the guy who is going to be the hot man in town next year — we're looking hard at John Reed of Citicorp now." And what's the worst thing that can happen? Having the honoree get fired a month before the event, the experts say, or die.

Such dinners are not universally popular. Robert Beggan, who's on the professional staff of the national United Way organization in Washington, D.C., maintains that they're big in only a few cities — mainly New York, Miami, and Las Vegas. Asked if the national organization itself puts on such affairs — after all, executives such as James Robinson III, chairman of American Express, are active on its behalf — Beggan replies: "Bite your tongue. Most of these guys hate them." Why? "Because there are so many," Beggan says, "and because the focus is on the act of giving, not the reasons for giving." John R. Lane, director of the art museum of Pittsburgh's Carnegie Institute, observes, "The honoree gets pushed into it and all his friends, both social and business, feel a pressure."

Why not just solicit contributions in honor of old Fred, award him his laurels in a small private ceremony, and let the rest of the movers and shakers have a rare night at home with those beings they faintly recognize as their loved ones? "It's been done," reports Penny Stoil, who, together with partner Fran Liner, helps charitable organizations in New York stage the more conventional type of bash. "They're called phantom dinners." The problem, Stoil says, is that you can probably get away with a Banquo banquet only once. She argues that, by contrast, a properly done conventional dinner will beget still a bigger dinner for the same cause the following year. "Properly done" means that the guests gain some exposure to the sponsoring organization, enjoy themselves, and leave thinking of the evening as something they'd like to repeat.

Diverse motives impel execs into good works. This holds true whether the good work consists of serving on the board of a nonprofit organization or showing up for the twentieth banquet of the season —"Not filet mignon, new potatoes, and green beans *again*." The mix of motives also governs an executive's choice of causes to tie up with; typically, a myriad present themselves for his consideration. In a speech last May to the National Conference of Boys' Clubs, the uncommonly forthright Minot K. Milliken, vice president and treasurer of the big textile company that bears the family name and president of the Boys' Club of New York for nineteen years, listed several of these motives.

Predictably, the desire to do some good heads Milliken's list. But executives also get involved, he says, because they want to show what they can do beyond their workaday endeavors. Some "seek a different kind of social acceptability or social mobility." Some want to meet "prospective customers or clients" or even competitors from whom they might learn something. Another reason for serving on a nonprofit board, he says, "is the desire to control—other people, or ideas, or programs." In short, to exercise power. And for some, he concludes, "It makes them feel less guilty about having more when they are helping people who have much less."

The awful truth in all this: good works benefit not only the charity on whose behalf they're performed, but also the worker. Roderick Gilkey of the business school of Emory University notes that studies of male development—there aren't yet comparable studies of women—show that particularly for men in their forties and older, some form of public service helps fulfill the developmental task of achieving "generativity." A generative individual passes on to others some of what he has learned and been given, thereby achieving a smidgen of immortality for his accomplishments. This link to development may help explain why baby-boom executives sometimes don't seem as interested in charity work as their elders.

Fred Hoar, now an executive of Raychem, a maker of high-tech chemical products based in Menlo Park, California, and for a long time a moving force in the United Way effort in Silicon Valley, notes that the young people he worked with at Apple Computer in the early 1980s, including that company's leaders, didn't seem all that interested in conventional good works. They were too busy developing a technology they thought would change the world. But, he adds, neither did Gordon Moore, chairman of Intel, nor Charles Sporck, C.E.O. of National Semiconductor, do much for charity when they began building up their companies twenty years ago. Now that they're in their late fifties and have arrived, they both devote lots of time to public service. Who knows? Steve Jobs may yet turn out to be the Andrew Carnegie of his generation.

45

The Importance of Being Visible

To get ahead, some experts argue,
you have to insinuate yourself into the spotlight.

THE MORE WOMEN AND MINORITIES make their way into the managerial ranks, the more they seem to want to talk about things formerly judged to be best left unsaid. The newcomers also tend to see office matters with a fresh eye, in the process sometimes coming up with iconoclastic analyses of the forces that shape everyone's experience in the organization.

Consider the startling views of Harvey Coleman of Atlanta on the subject of getting ahead. Coleman is black. He spent eleven years with IBM, half of them working in management development, and now serves as a consultant to the likes of AT&T, Coca-Cola, Prudential, and Merck. Coleman says that, based on what he's seen at big companies, he weights the different elements that make for long-term career success as follows: performance counts a mere 10 percent; image, 30 percent; and exposure, a full 60 percent. Coleman concludes that excellent job performance is so common these days that while doing your work well may win you pay increases, it won't garner you the big promotion. He finds that advancement more often depends on how many people know you and your work, and how high up they are.

Unmeritocratic heresy? Not to many people, especially many women and members of minority groups who, like Coleman, feel that the scales have dropped from their eyes. "Women and blacks in organizations work under a false myth," observed the late Kaleel Jamison, a management consultant who helped corporations wrestle with these issues. "They think that if you work hard, you'll get ahead — that someone in authority will reach down and pluck you up." In her view, "Most women and blacks are so terrified that people will think they've gotten ahead because of gender or color that they play down their visibility." Her advice to those folks: learn the ways that white males have traditionally used to find their way into the spotlight.

What might be called the official majority view hasn't disappeared. "You're going to be noticed if your performance is good," says Arthur Brown, director of employee development at General Mills. But some companies seem to be questioning that notion; at least they have decided to bring the issue of visibility out into the open, even in instances taking a stab at managing it. At Sun Co. in Radnor, Pennsylvania, for example, the human-resources types are trying out ways to make an employee with potential visible to someone besides his boss. Among the possibilities they've tested: getting up to ten people who routinely deal with an individual to report on how he's doing; singling out those in low-visibility jobs to give briefings to managers higher up; and assigning a rising star to a project team in the hope the other team members will informally coach him on what he's doing right or wrong.

If you are prepared to entertain the idea that visibility is important — just for argument's sake, of course — and if you do not work at a company like Sun, then you may be wondering, for argument's sake, "Is there any way that, for example, oh, say, someone like me could increase his visibility?" The question gets back a resounding yes from denizens of the corporate world, many of them — surprisingly or not — white and male. It's important to do it correctly, though. The president of a Fortune 500 company voices a widespread sentiment: "I hate to see a guy running for office."

For starters, if it's in your power, choose to work for a high-growth company in a high-growth industry, preferably a company renowned for heaping responsibility on junior managers. If no such M.B.A. fantasy offers itself to you, or if you already have a job, at least attempt to end up in the functional area that drives your employer's business — manufacturing, maybe, or sales. Even majority-view proponent Brown admits that this counts at General Mills: "In consumer foods, with its traditional product-management system, you look to your marketing people to provide the real leadership downstream. People in manufacturing, sales, finance, or administration tend to be lost in obscurity."

When you move into a new job in unfamiliar territory, leave the take-charge guy or gal Superperson suit in the closet for a while. Heed the advice of John Clemens, now an associate professor of management at Hartwick College in Oneonta, New York, in former incarnations a marketing man with Pillsbury and an executive with a San Francisco ad agency: "Start by being invisible. Shut up and become eyes and ears; learn the lay of the land, the politics of the place."

Once you know where at least most of the land mines are buried, begin wandering around. That's right, biz sports fans, the famous Management by Wandering Around technique, popularized by *In Search of Excellence,* is a top-flight visibility-getter. Be careful, however, not to get it mixed up with the Meddling Fool routine also standard in some managerial repertoires. What you must be seen to be about is tactfully, indeed engagingly, asking questions that clearly relate to work you've been assigned—a relationship you will take pains to explain engagingly if it isn't obvious.

What you should be doing at the same time, of course, is looking for genuinely broken things to fix. Not big deals, mind you, or political hot potatoes—just small, orphan problems that have been annoying everyone and that you can solve. Alternatively, devise improvements that can be worked without offending anyone. Observes Alan Bennett, a thirty-four-year-old Armstrong Rubber Co. general manager cited by that company's president as a model of visibility, "The key is what you do when you see a problem on your job. It's one thing to report it, but another to work through the different people concerned to come up with some sort of game plan. Give the guy in charge a chance; say, 'Here's your problem, but here's a way out.' "

Counsels John Clemens, "Associate yourself with innovation, not the routine." This probably represents the single best answer to the "But how?" that logically follows most boilerplate advice on gaining visibility—injunctions such as "Get on a special task force" or "Get your name on reports."

If all else fails—and sometimes even if it doesn't—volunteer. While jobs on a special task force typically don't get handed out this way, positions as floor captain for your company's United Way drive or chairman of special events for the local chapter of your professional association typically do. You will at least get to know, and be known by, more of your peers, and you may end up rubbing shoulders with some higher-up who might remember you another time.

Who knows, through one or another of these efforts you could catch the eye of, gasp, a potential mentor. The question then becomes, do you actually want one of these fabled beasts? As recently as five years ago, when the phenomenon was starting to be written about, having a mentor — someone high up in the company to teach you the real ropes and watch over you — seemed the royal road to visibility. More recently, however, a wave of revisionism has begun to form. Yes, a mentor can put your name forward for plum assignments, and riding upward in his slipstream makes it easier to handle organizational wind resistance. But what if he goes off the track? Says a sadder-but-wiser ex–Union Carbide man: "Years ago when I worked for the company, four rising M.B.A.'s were known as the Four Horsemen and were obviously going places. Three did rise, and one fell by the wayside — my mentor. When I needed help, he couldn't give it." Even if nothing dramatic happens, being identified as someone's protégé can cut you off from salutary relations with others in the organization, especially your peers.

The underlying point: being mentored, like every other strategy for gaining visibility, entails risk. Your innovation may bomb, the United Way drive may fail to come up to last year's mark. While smart visibility-seekers attempt to manage their efforts so that failures don't fall on them alone — "We were all working together on this on behalf of the company; in the larger sense, isn't it the company that failed?" — sometimes the chickens come home to roost in just one person's office. Be prepared for that when you send them out clucking your name.

46

Is a New Male Manager Emerging?

The feminist movement is changing men as well as women.
But just try to take four weeks' paternity leave.

THE NEW MAN. You probably have read about him in the annals of contemporary pop sociology. He is, to use the patois, more in touch with his feelings, better able to relate to women, and just all-round supportive. The married version recognizes that his wife's career is as important as his own, makes a point of attending the birth of his children, and tries to be as unremote a father as possible. The unmarried version, while reluctant to commit himself meaningfully to others, at least is a gourmet cook.

It may come as more of a surprise that some experts think this new paragon has a place in the ranks of management. Alice G. Sargent, a consultant to the likes of Du Pont, argues that the most effective managerial style these days incorporates behavior that some used to regard as feminine — listening attentively; endeavoring to make sure that everyone's feelings are considered; getting one's thrills vicariously, from the achievement of others. Feminist ravings? Not to read the blurbs offered up by gurudom for Sargent's book *The Androgynous Manager.* From John Naisbitt, author of *Megatrends:* "The eleventh megatrend is the shift from a machismo to an androgynous society . . ." From Kenneth Blanchard, co-author of *The One Minute Manager:* "One Minute Managers are clearly androgynous . . ." Foolish you, thinking all that one-minute praising entailed was a mere pat on the shoulder.

Somewhere in all the hype exists a kernel of truth. Men are changing, at least in the sense that some act differently than their fathers did. While the rate of change in the executive suite seems positively glacial, it may be picking up speed. What has changed men, most students of the phenomenon agree, is the feminist movement. Not many men joined up, but legions have had to accommodate themselves to it. Along the way women raised some disturbing questions. Why do most males appear to think that the only feeling they can express at work is anger? Why do so many big strong men die of stress-related illnesses? Might not you guys, putting all that energy into maintaining the John Wayne front, be missing out on something?

Oversimplifying a little, one can array men along a spectrum from old to new manhood depending on how much they have been rained on by fallout from the feminist movement. Men in their late forties or beyond have probably felt it least. Men forty or younger, on the other hand, have in all likelihood had to cope with a so-called significant other who works outside the home, or yearns to. These are the worthies who have found themselves negotiating, sometimes end-lessly, what Gerda McCahan, chairman of the psychology department at Furman University in South Carolina, terms the third job in any dual-career household: keeping home and hearth running com-fortably.

At the radically new end of the spectrum, according to some ob-servers, reposes a type that the poet Robert Bly calls the soft male. This man, probably in his twenties, has taken the feminist message to heart. He tries hard to please both his mother and the woman he lives with. Indeed, he sometimes deliberately links up with a strong woman. She seems to know what she wants; for himself, he hasn't a clue. While he's clearly in touch with his feelings, you almost wish he weren't. Bly has joined in many workshops on what the participants call men's issues. After one he told an interviewer, "Often the younger males would begin to talk and within five minutes they would be weeping. The amount of grief and anguish in the younger males was astounding."

Please take note, Neanderthals among you who would blame women alone for these unhappy young men: the traditional male failed them as well, perhaps more than anyone else did. He failed to find good answers to the feminists' tough questions, failed to elucidate and defend the virtues traditionally thought of as masculine, and, most critically, too often failed to be around enough to provide any kind of example at all.

To put the matter in the jargon in which it's inevitably cast, men seeking to change haven't had many role models. To the extent that older males offer much guidance, it tends to be along the lines of "Real men don't talk about such stuff." Nor has the society managed to agree on what men are supposed to be changing into. Just when you thought it was safe to splash on a little cologne or to let a woman pick up the check, along came that word *wimp*.

The resulting confusion can generate discomfort bordering on dysfunction, even within business organizations. Samuel Osherson, a Harvard psychologist and author of the book *Finding Our Fathers,* says that in his clinical practice he sees men whose resentment of their fathers' remoteness gets played out in their work lives. "They complain, 'I was unsupported by my boss, I kept waiting for him to help me out,'" he says. "They want father to come save them, but they're still enraged at him. They end up ambivalent, moving from job to job, leaving behind an impression of competence but also a reputation for having interpersonal problems." In other instances, the results can border on the comic. Bly relays the observation of a friend who works for one of the largest money-center banks. Young men there are supposedly so hungry for the instructive attention of older males, and have so little sense of themselves, that they end up slavishly aping the boss down to the smallest details of dress and mannerism.

Companies are beginning to accommodate some of the changes affecting their male managers. The example most often cited: corporations have learned to put up with greater resistance from executives asked to relocate. It used to suffice for an employer to serve as buyer of last resort for the relocatee's old house; now, increasingly, the employer must help find another job for what folks in the relocation trade call the trailing spouse. IBM, a trailblazer in enlightened human-resources management, provides a questionnaire for employees that helps them think through the pros and cons of a potential move. Employees complete the form with their families and keep it. All they tell IBM is whether they'll make the move.

Employers may even be picking up on the value of the androgynous manager, or at least certain aspects of him/her. Executive recruiter Jonathan E. McBride, who runs his own firm in Washington, D.C., voices a thought echoed by other headhunters: "I sense a subtle shift away from the control-oriented, autocratic type to more of a facilitator. When I ask my clients what they want, a lot of them say, 'A good listener.' You used not to hear that a lot." Even Wall Street, that bastion of male chauvinism, appears not to be immune. From the human-resources director of a big brokerage outfit: "Most of the people—make that some of the people—we've brought in over the past few years have been a bit more concerned about the people dimension of the business." He concedes that his company is starting from "a very low base."

What corporations don't seem prepared to accommodate is the desire of some male managers to take a more active part in the lives of their children. What statistical evidence there is suggests that these days more men want to do that, and from the start. Ronald Levant, director of Boston University's Fatherhood Project, maintains that the percentage of fathers present in the delivery room for the birth of their children has risen from about 25 percent in the 1960s to 80 percent.

The percentage of companies offering paternity leave—time off for father to help settle the baby in its new home—has increased as well. According to the people who put together statistics on the subject, however, there's less there than meets the eye. Catalyst, a New York City group that studies how women and families are faring in the corporate world, found that of 384 large corporations that responded to a survey on paternity leave, 114 offered it, although the leave was always without pay. When Catalyst asked those 114 companies how much time off they judged reasonable, however, over two-fifths said that they didn't consider any time off reasonable. Phyllis Silverman, who ran the study, concludes that many companies offer paternity leave only for legal reasons. Those that offer maternity leave, beyond disability benefits, fear discrimination suits if they don't provide some equivalent for men.

Most new fathers would probably feel great reluctance to take the time off, anyway. We are still largely creatures of the traditional wisdom: you provide for your family by working hard and getting ahead. The boss, who smoked cigarettes and read magazines in the waiting room while his children were born, and who hasn't seen much of them since, wouldn't countenance anything else. These days, though, there's new wisdom abroad: father, you too can hold, feed, burp, diaper, and make cooing sounds to this latest indication that God wants humankind to continue. Also to romp, stomp, and generally play with the kids as they get older.

Play may be more important than most grown-ups thought — to the father, not just the child. Christopher Lasch, author of *The Culture of Narcissism*, holds that joyous, unself-conscious activity represents the best way out of self-absorption, the baby-boomers' trademark and nemesis. Many fathers love playing with their kids. Says one, a forty-one-year-old corporate lawyer with two young children, "Nothing in the world matches it." He adds, though, that because of his work, he sometimes goes five days without seeing his children when they are awake. "I live in a fair amount of pain day to day," he says, "because I'm not living up to my own standards for how I should be caring for my children." Spoken like a true new man.

47

How to Relate to Nepotism

The practice is widespread, sometimes good, mostly bad,
and harder on the nepotee than anyone else.

IT'S THE SUBJECT of many jokes. The company chairman, addressing the assembled employees: ". . . And so, in closing, I give you our new president, a tall tree in the forest of executive timber, a person of the strictest probity, a man with the vision to lead us into the twenty-first century." Polite applause. The new president: "Thank you, Dad."

Nepotism isn't really funny. While no one keeps statistics on how many people hire their relatives, sociologists and business school professors estimate that perhaps 96 percent of American corporations are family-owned or -dominated, in the sense that these businesses couldn't be taken over without the acquiescence of a particular clan. We're not just talking about your corner dry-cleaning establishment, either — perhaps 35 percent of the Fortune 500 companies are family-dominated, or at least have had successive generations of the same family somewhere in top management. Everyone has heard of the Watsons of IBM and the Fords of you-know-where, but there are also the Clarks of American Express, the Stuarts of Quaker Oats, the Houghtons of Corning Glass Works — the list goes on and on.

If you own a company or a controlling interest in one, the temptation to staff it with kin can be tremendous, particularly if you're the founder. Consider the example of Kaypro Corp., the Solana Beach, California, manufacturer of portable computers, which went public in 1983. Founder Andrew Kay employs his wife as secretary of the company; his son David as his right-hand man in running it; another son, Alan, as head of the administrative staff; his father to superintend the maintenance staff; his brother to run the company print shop; and a daughter as a consultant. Do family members feel open to criticism or sensitive about the subject of nepotism? "I put all that behind me when I decided to join the company," says son David. "I came to work here because I wanted to help my father."

If many of a corporation's top executives are related, it becomes difficult, and downright hypocritical, to forbid hiring down in the ranks of people who, while not related to the company's royal family, are related to one another. This policy of permitting blood or married kin on the payroll persists even after a company has grown large or the role of its founding family has been diluted. At Hewlett-Packard, Levi Strauss, and Adolph Coors, about the only restriction on family relationships is a rule against a person reporting directly to his relative. At most companies the stricture is waived only for members of *the* family.

One happy result of having a clan sitting atop the organization and others scattered throughout is an almost familial feeling that binds folks together. Managers who have come from nonfamily companies to work at the likes of Levi Strauss or Coors say they sense a big difference: "Here there's a concern with individual people," reports one such executive. "It's not just a matter of dollars and cents." Employees also speak enthusiastically of other managerial virtues — for example, a corporate ability to act quickly. A senior, nonfamily executive at one big family-dominated company observes, "When there's fifty-one percent of the stock sitting at the table, you don't have to wait long for a decision."

So what's wrong with a little nepotism? Plenty, it often turns out. Family ties can wreak havoc on the company, on the nepotee — the person who got his job through Dad's or Uncle's good graces — and on anyone who has to work with, under, or over this chip off the old block. Witness the gyrations caused not too long ago by a former Getty Oil employee named Gordon P. Getty.

Most trouble arises when the imperatives of the two very different institutions, family and business, come into conflict. Or at least so say the experts — professors of organizational behavior such as Paul Thompson at Brigham Young University and Ivan Lansberg S. at the Yale School of Organization and Management. (Lansberg, a native of Venezuela, uses the initial of his mother's maiden name after his surname.) The purpose of the family, the academics say, is to care for and nurture family members. The purpose of a business, on the other hand, is to produce goods and services as efficiently as possible, maybe even at a profit.

The most obvious conflict occurs when management hires or promotes an incompetent with ties to the family. The company needs good people, particularly in its executive positions. But Junior — in nautical terms, not packing a full seabag — needs a job. Taking care of him wins out over the business imperative. The word for this is injustice, at least in the eyes of employees who expect a modicum of fairness from their companies — which is most employees.

If you don't think that nepotism can cause a company to lose valued executives and to be unable to attract new ones, just ask anyone who was at RCA when Robert Sarnoff got the top job his father had held. "He never won the confidence of the technical people," says a former executive vice president of the company. Of young Sarnoff's tenure, the RCA man comments, "It's what set the company on its present course"— a none-too-happy course that ended with its purchase by General Electric.

Trauma can also occur when business considerations triumph over family. Thompson at Brigham Young University recounts the case of a company, dominated by the same family for eight decades, that after losing money for two years decided to bring in a new president from outside. His first act was to fire 30 percent of the workers, who thought they had lifetime tenure. Some family members were horrified and fell to squabbling over what had happened. Today the company is making money, but its veteran employees, in Thompson's description, "are still shaking in their boots, wondering if they'll be the next to go."

At the center of such dramas is the nepotee him- or herself. The role isn't enviable, but there seems no shortage of applicants. A study at Harvard Business School and MIT's Sloan School found that M.B.A. candidates who had come from families that own businesses almost invariably said on matriculation that they weren't going to join the family firm when they graduated. When they got their degrees, however, most promptly went to work for the ol' home enterprise.

"The opportunities really are phenomenal," notes Barbara S. Hollander, a Pittsburgh-based organizational consultant and family therapist who's also in the fourth generation of a family with its own business. "The person who goes into the family business has a ready-made lab in which to learn." She adds, however, "Family members pay heavy emotional dues for participating in the business."

Indeed they do. According to the experts, the psychological problem that most commonly bedevils the nepotee is precisely what you would expect: a nagging need, in some cases lifelong, to establish himself as a competent, worthwhile person in his own right. While the typical nepotee can't or won't articulate this feeling, it shows up in managerial moves that look pretty bizarre. A son or daughter, on taking over a business, will suddenly push it into products about which the company knows nothing; three brothers will decide to mince the business into three autonomous divisions that make no organizational sense.

Nepotees may be especially prey to other forms of psychological malaise. Roderick Gilkey of Emory University says that some feel an underlying ambivalence toward the family business. They may experience the "prince-pauper syndrome" — they got every material thing they wanted, but were emotionally deprived. Dad was too busy with the company. As a result, Gilkey says, they come to feel smoldering anger or depression, feelings all the more inexplicable to them since, after all, they've been given everything. It's a dandy recipe for alcoholism.

Virtually all the experts agree on one piece of advice to the potential nepotee: don't do it, at least not when you're just getting out of school. Go to work for some other business, or form a rock band, or join the Foreign Legion — whatever will allow you to develop your own sense of competence. It helps, of course, if the skills you develop are useful to the family firm and of the sort that will impress your co-workers. If you have taken a job with Daddy too early in life, think of leaving for a while. One nepotee who did says, with obvious relief, "I wanted to do my own thing."

For someone not of the blood who works at or is thinking of joining a nepotistic company, fully understanding how the business really works is vital. Accept as almost a certainty that you won't become chairman; if it's the worst type of family-dominated enterprise, be forewarned that you may well be passed over someday in favor of a nincompoop son-in-law.

As for getting along with your nepotee co-worker, treat him just as you would anyone who desperately wants to make a point, isn't sure he has the wherewithal to do so, but just may have the power to get you fired. If you're in the delicate position of being Junior's boss, and if he shows some promise and doesn't seem a complete beast, probably the noblest thing you can do for him is to give him a fairly straightforward — and friendly, and incredibly tactful — appraisal of what he's doing well and what not so well. Perhaps the biggest managerial problem that family members have is getting honest information, which may be just what they need to develop a sense of their own competence.

Be careful, though. In the tricky world of corporate nepotism, where few people are ever completely sure where they stand, the mailroom clerk you chide or confide in this afternoon may be having dinner with the chief executive tonight.

❋ 48 ❋

Getting Aggressiveness Right

Shouting at people is no longer acceptable,
but then again, nobody loves a wimp. What's a manager to do?

OKAY, LET'S RUN THROUGH IT one more time — maybe this time we can finally figure it out. Managers are supposed to be aggressive, right? Brenda L. Ruello, a big-league executive recruiter with the firm of Heidrick & Struggles, says, for example, "I've never seen a specification from a client of what it wants in a candidate that didn't include the word; it's always there along with 'bright' and 'articulate.'" But if someone remarks of a particular executive, "He's an aggressive guy," images of boorishness spring to mind as readily as any others. A woman executive must never be aggressive, of course, at least not if she's to avoid unkinder labels. No, she's supposed to be assertive. And the difference is . . . what?

The confusion goes deeper than the merely semantic. Serious students of contemporary corporate folkways — consultants, headhunters, and real live managers — report almost invariably that displays of screaming, table-pounding pushiness are no longer deemed acceptable behavior. While there may be a few industries where executives haven't yet got the word — the garment business, cosmetics, perhaps a few atavistic enclaves within investment banking — the more general understanding seems to be that a good manager doesn't shout. Indeed, as the research of Harvard Business School professor John P. Kotter and others attests, he may not even give orders. Instead he asks questions, makes requests, and permits himself an occasional observation.

At the same time, the most admired executive in America today, at least according to one search firm's 1984 survey, is Lee "I-gotta-tell-ya" Iacocca of Chrysler. Also up there in the rankings: GE's "Neutron Jack" Welch — like the neutron bomb, he leaves the building standing but eliminates the people. It's not just that we want strong leaders to revive our flagging companies and fight off the threat from abroad. We also seem to think that they have to be of a more aggressive, tigerish stripe than, say, Reginald Jones, the corporate statesman who headed a list of the most admired chief executives of large industrial companies compiled by *Fortune* in 1981.

The more fenced-in the farmer, the more he takes cowboys for his heroes? What does seem clear, at least to some experts, is that the typical middle-aged, middle-level, white male manager is going to have an abundance of temptations to become angry and aggressive in the years to come. Gordon L. Lippitt, a professor of behavioral science at George Washington University, lists a few: "Computers, to the extent that a manager feels unable to use them and sees them passing crucial information up the line; fewer promotions, due to business cutbacks; an influx of bright, capable women armed with M.B.A.'s; young managers who want to be V.P.'s in three years; the perception that there are limited resources to get the job done with; and limitations on his decision-making authority, as decisions get pushed downward or pulled upward in the organization." Make my day.

If a resort to Clint Eastwood tactics is proscribed in corporate circles, then how is an executive to manage his or her aggressiveness? One unpleasant possibility is that we'll be seeing more passive-aggressive behavior. A passive-aggressive manager eschews open hostilities, in part because he feels distinctly uncomfortable with them. Instead he hides his considerable aggressive feelings beneath a manner that may be agreeable, even charming. The feelings get expressed, though, with a vengeance, in his manipulation of co-workers, especially subordinates.

A passive-aggressive boss constantly sets others up to get zapped. He will have difficulty describing what he wants, but when the Munchkins come forward with their attempt to satisfy him, it almost certainly won't do. He will assign a project, but withhold a piece of information crucial to completing it. He will set impossibly high standards or change the rules midway through the game.

Robert C. Bleke, whose Atlanta consulting firm, Bleke & Boyd, helps companies handle psychological problems, describes a real-world example of the games passive-aggressive execs play: "In meetings with his senior vice presidents, one chief executive I know will periodically ask a question like 'Did you know that our competition is doing so-and-so?' In fact, there's no reason why they should know it, or care about it. The V.P.'s sit there without an answer, embarrassed, shown up. The boss may think he's just trying to keep them on their toes. What he's actually doing—whether consciously or not—is causing them to feel inadequate and himself to feel superior." Bleke adds, "The more intelligent the executive, the more middle- and upper-class, the greater the chances for this kind of behavior to show up as a means of expressing aggressiveness."

As the beer commercials all too seldom say, come on, America, let's get it right for a change. In this endeavor, it's helpful to consult what seems the only body of serious thinking on the subject—the lore of assertiveness training. Assertiveness training, it turns out, is not what you probably think it is. Born in the women's movement of the late 1960s—at least, according to some of its apostles—as a way of getting females to speak up for themselves, it has broadened its appeal and relevance. Malcolm E. Shaw, who for fifteen years has taught assertiveness under the auspices of the American Management Association, notes that far more men attend his course than women. Not just ninety-seven-pound weaklings, either. "A lot of the people sent by companies are there because they're too aggressive," Shaw says. "It's not a course for shy, timid people, but for the people who run over others."

In such training, students are coached to distinguish aggressiveness, which puts others down in pursuit of a goal, from assertiveness, which does not. Shaw, for example, teaches trainees to recognize a spectrum of aggressive behavior ranging from the patronizing ("You must be new here") through the contemptuous ("A woman doesn't have the temperament to do this kind of work") to the palpably attacking, wherein bad motives are ascribed to others, names are called, and abuse is heaped.

Shaw also lays out a hierarchy of assertive actions, from giving information ("I noticed you mutilating the houseplants in the reception area"), to expressing a need or want ("I want you to leave the plants alone"), to persuading or pointing out benefits ("Being kind to the foliage will increase your chances of promotion"), to pointing out dire consequences ("If you don't stop messing with the greens, you'll be subject to disciplinary action"). Apparently a modicum of assertiveness is required to make any communication palatable to the recipient. Research indicates that listeners are about as put off by so-called nonassertive behavior — "I'm really sorry that I have to say this to you, I know that I don't have any right to, but . . ." — as they are by ranting and raving. Don't whine on, harvest moon.

Properly done, assertiveness training places as much emphasis on getting the student to recognize how his own manner comes across as it does on helping him deal with aggressiveness in others. Says the chairman of a small electronics firm, who has been trying to rein himself in a bit since taking the course, "People don't know how they appear to others; people haven't thought about it."

The managerial objective here goes well beyond making sure that one person doesn't abuse another. The ultimate goal is to keep communications flowing back and forth between people, even in the face of strong feelings in one or all. "If an executive behaves aggressively in a meeting with his people," Shaw avers, "it cuts off the flow of information and stifles, demeans the participation of the people who will have to carry out whatever decision is made."

In ticklish situations, assertiveness trainees are counseled, whether you're giving or getting, start at the low end of the assertiveness hierarchy — limit yourself to making statements or asking unloaded questions, at least until the information you need is on the table. If the stuff coming back at you is uncomprehending, defiant, or downright nasty, you may have to escalate. If you do, keep always in mind what you hope to accomplish in the interchange, whether it's getting your point across or finding out why the other person is so upset.

Watch for visual clues from the other's bearing and mannerisms — his body language, to use the pop-psych term — and listen, listen, listen. Robert Gal, a senior vice president of Wakefern Food Corp., which buys and distributes products for the Shop-Rite grocery store chain, says he never lacked aggressiveness but that he's still glad he took assertiveness training two years ago. His conclusion, echoed by other trainees: "Listening — that's the key."

In the course of a career, you will almost certainly run afoul of managers who seem to have received their only training at Thug U. In dealing with them, the basic principle remains the same: try to keep the lines of communication open, if only so you can indicate to them —maybe not while you're both red-faced with anger, but later— precisely how counterproductive their behavior is. At least with your superiors, it's probably the only way you can get them to change the way they act.

The tactic can work even with those passive-aggressive smoothies. Psychologist Bleke, who has successfully confronted such types, recommends the following: after being zapped, arrange to see the perpetrator in private. In the most friendly manner you can muster— remember, these aggressors hate open conflict—go over what's happened, pointing out how it causes you to perform at something less than your best and is bad for the whole organization. The predictable result, according to Bleke: the miscreant won't stop hassling others, but he will stop doing it to you, leaving you free, as they say, to fight another day.

49

Chairman of the Bored

*Most are loath to admit it, but businesspersons do get bored.
Here's why, and what to do about it.*

ASK THE TYPICAL AMERICAN EXECUTIVE whether he's
ever bored on the job and you're likely to get a hearty response of the
following sort. From Roy L. Ash, formerly chief executive of troubled AM International: "I never encountered the word *boredom* in my
career. You have to look to yourself—I think boredom is a self-
generated condition."

Right on, as Horatio Alger might have said. The only problem is
that not everyone in the legion of managers seems to have gotten the
message. Indeed, if one promises the speakers anonymity, quite a few
discouraged words can be heard on the subject. From a young banker
at one of the biggest money-center institutions: "I'm bored to tears"
—so much so that he's thinking of jumping to, if you can believe it,
the insurance industry, "because it's changing so fast." A woman
executive, to contain her ennui, sits in her office and reads vaguely
job-related books. She, in turn, tells of an acquaintance, a $100,000-
a-year man, who took to writing plays during his not particularly
stimulating hours behind the big desk.

Even top canines will occasionally admit to suffering dog days of
the spirit, though somehow these admissions end up sounding like
paeans to capitalism and its opportunities. Arthur Levitt, Jr., chairman
of the American Stock Exchange, says that it was in part tedium that
impelled him to change jobs four times. David A. Norman, president
of Businessland, a nationwide, California-based chain of computer
stores, confesses that restlessness drove him from his job as president
of another company to start the Businessland venture. "It just wasn't
quite as exciting as it used to be to jump out of bed at five-thirty in the
morning," he recalls.

If the condition afflicts even the dawn patrol, how much more widespread must it be among lesser business mortals. On the incidence of executive boredom, eminent management psychologist Harry Levinson says simply, "I think there's a good deal of it." Other observers of corporate life agree — not to mention businesspersons themselves. Some, in fact, think that tedium is increasing: at companies that are growing more slowly or eliminating whole tiers of management, the argument goes, there are fewer opportunities for promotion or for changing jobs. The ruts in which managers are stuck become sloughs of despond.

The commonsense explanation of boredom — that it arises from having too little to do, or from doing the same thing over and over — doesn't fully account for the managerial variety. A bored manager may complain that not enough is hitting his in-box, but he will move on quickly to cite something else also, along the following lines: "I don't feel that I'm using my real talents . . . The organization is so structured that it stifles your creativity . . . Abilities aren't recognized here." And the ubiquitous "There are no opportunities in this job." The common theme is frustrated ambition — no one is paying attention to me; I'm not going anywhere.

Often all that's needed to crystallize these frustrations into the glassy-eyed blahs is a bit of time on one's hands. As the bored reader of books puts the matter, "For boredom to set in, you have to have time to realize you're bored." Managers who never have such time may simply not notice their own symptoms. They have fallen into what some experts on executive behavior call "the activity trap." A sudden hiatus in activity may leave them with the realization that on the job they're a bit stale, flat, and, yes, even bored.

All this helps explain why boredom is more of a problem for some groups in the corporate world than for others. In general, the phenomenon seems to strike staff executives more than it does line types — a corporate planner, say, just seems to have more time to fill than someone running a division, and less chance of becoming chief executive. People who work at companies that have grown large and bureaucratic over many years feel more tedium than folks employed by smaller, faster-growing businesses. Reports a vice president of one of the largest U.S. retailers, "Everything here is done on the basis of teamwork. Unless you actively carve out a niche for yourself, you can be lulled into feeling like part of an ant army."

One gets an impression that women executives are more commonly bored than their male counterparts. Again, it's a matter of expectations. Says a senior woman, "I never expected to spend my life in a nine-to-five job. I keep finding myself working for a company that doesn't get as excited as I do about certain issues." Partly as a result, she has changed jobs six or seven times. Boredom also affects a surprising number of younger managers, even those on the fast track. Observes a thirty-three-year-old vice president, "The me-generation — my generation — expects to be fascinated all the time on the job." This woman says she has learned better.

Whatever their situation or sex, most of these executives offer similar accounts of what it feels like to be bored at work. You don't want to come to the office in the morning. It takes you twice as long as it should to do the simplest task. You phone your broker so often he stops returning your calls. Most maddening is the self-torturing inertia — you know you should be doing more, that there are lots of things you could do, but then, what's the use?

Not that you're just going to sit there — no indeed: spurred by ennui, you'll probably soon be out there driving your subordinates crazy. A young manager at a big oil company confesses, "When things get slow" — when he's bored, in other words — "I start to bug people." It's a common response, and potentially disastrous. J. Stephen Morris, a psychologist who has done a lot of outplacement work, tells of the president of a small company who, whenever the doldrums hit him, would go down into the organization to chat folks up. This jumping of the chain of command had the unintended effect of starting rumors and setting people at one another's throats. Morris's conclusion: "A bored executive can really make your company into a playpen."

He can also cook up some mighty strange deals. The chairman of a large corporation recently gave a confidant two reasons why his company was contemplating a major acquisition. First, he thought the deal would benefit shareholders in the long run. Second, the new business would give him, the chairman, something to do.

For workers lower down in the ranks, an enlightened employer can take several steps to help alleviate the problem. The one place in corporate America where you'll probably find all of them being tried out is Silicon Valley, a laboratory for new management techniques.

The most radical measure is job rotation—taking a finance guy, say, and putting him in marketing, which he then presumably learns. This defies the conventional wisdom that you should have trained specialists working in their specialties, and would seem a bit costly. "Yes, it is expensive," says Harry Postlewait, vice president of Raychem Corp., a Menlo Park–based manufacturer of high-tech plastic products. Postlewait adds proudly, "We do it all the time."

A less extreme countermeasure to managerial ennui is job redesign —a euphemism for giving the bored employee something more, or different, to do. This doesn't necessarily entail rewriting the job description. The trendier tactic these days is to assign the ho-humming so-and-so to a task force concerned with coming up with a new product or solving some problem. "One of our biggest problems is marketing people who've worked with only one product, or one *part* of a product," notes an executive at a very large Valley company. "We'll put them on a task force, and while they may not contribute that much at first, they do learn new skills."

Poor bored you probably do not work in Silicon Valley, however. Indeed, you may even be reluctant to confide the full extent of your tedium to your employer, whose attitudes toward the subject may be somewhat more conservative than those of Neanderthal Steel Corp. What can you do on your own to lighten the heavy hours?

The first step is to figure out whether it's truly boredom that weighs you down. Do you really suffer a lack of stimuli at work, great yawning gaps between when the telephone rings or anything interesting arrives in the interoffice mail? Or are you perhaps pretty much uninterested in everything, on the job and off? If the latter is the case, and you're feeling down, and the condition persists, then—you will be happy to know—you're not bored at all. You're depressed. If this continues for a couple of quarters, particularly a couple of quarters when sales and profits are up, in contrast to you, then you may want, as the phrase goes, to seek professional help.

Okay, so you have decided that it really is the job. Are conditions so bad—the routine so unvarying and locked in, the opportunities for advancement or recognition so limited — that you should take your-self elsewhere? Be realistic.

While you're thinking about it, try a little job redesign of your own. Look for a project that will be sufficiently different to interest you, but sufficiently in accord with corporate purposes to interest your boss too. If moving your brain to that extent is just too hard, then do an easier thing — move your body. Take up some kind of exercise; travel somewhere new on business; at the very least, get out of the executive dining room and go somewhere novel for lunch. The point is that if the stimuli don't come to you, you should go to them.

Among the best stimuli, successful survivors of managerial bore-dom report, are other people. Too commonly a bored person with-draws from contact with his colleagues, which may be all right with them since few individuals are more boring than someone afflicted with you-know-what. Mingle, mingle, mingle, you tedium sufferers. You'll know you're coming out of it when you stop being interested in treatises on, yawn, boredom.

50

When Executives Crack

A trivial event may trigger the crisis,
but the problem has probably been gnawing away for a long time.

SOMETIMES IT'S PERFECTLY OBVIOUS to everyone in the
office: we found him cowering under his desk. She came to the
reception thoroughly drunk and told off two of our most important
clients. He threw a typewriter at his secretary. In other instances—
probably the more dangerous ones—the change is barely apparent: he
just never seems optimistic anymore. She didn't use to have this much
trouble making decisions.

Another executive has cracked. Inside him, a problem pulsing with
energy has broken through his customary inhibitions and defenses.
Now it threatens to disrupt his work. What is his company to do,
assuming it has the acumen to find out?

Such crises occur more often than you might think. The Human
Resources Group, a New York City firm that helps companies assist
employees with problems, recently did a computer analysis of some
1,700 cases of troubled employees brought to it in 1983 by eight large
U.S. corporations. Almost 10 percent of the cases turned out to be
executives or managers who considered themselves to have serious
personal problems. Since most executives are loath to tell their employers about this kind of difficulty—if they seek help at all, they
seek it outside the company—the figure of 150 or so troubled managerial types at eight companies may in fact understate the number of
executives in turmoil.

The nature of their problems doesn't lend itself to easy or precise
categorization. In the Human Resources Group's study, of the 154
cases that involved managers or executives with serious problems, 28
were attributed to alcohol, 10 to drugs, 25 to marital problems, and 34
to that catchall of difficulties besetting the manager, stress—leaving

57 consigned to the category labeled "Other." Some counselors to executives in crisis report that depression and anxiety are more common than alcoholism. Just about everyone dealing with fissuring managers comments on the ubiquity of problems with adolescent children. Don't underestimate the damage that parental heartache can do: the president of one Fortune 500 company, distracted by the emotional problems of his daughter, ended up acting so strangely that he was forced to forfeit both his job and his status as heir apparent to the chairman.

Whatever their cause, executive crises show surprising consistency in the way they build slowly and then play out dramatically. Managers who will end up cracking lay the groundwork with a long history of neglect — sometimes neglect of their families or co-workers, but almost always neglect of themselves. As an advertising executive who is still recovering from a drug problem puts it, "We make our jobs so important. But what about caring for ourselves?"

In the phrase of psychologist Robert McLaughlin, who consults with corporations on executives in trouble, "They will have tried to finesse a lot of the problems of development in human life." They may, for example, disregard symptoms of physical distress — those nagging stomach pains, say, or those headaches. Or they let someone else — perhaps a housekeeper — raise their children. Or they leave a crew of disappointed, hostile people at home. "Executives live in harsh, self-punishing ways as a matter of course," McLaughlin concludes.

Probably the most self-punishing habit, according to McLaughlin and other observers, is the manager's tendency to bottle up his emotions. Executives seem particularly reluctant to express feelings that smack of discouragement or, worse yet, panic. "It's not appropriate in a corporation to admit your concerns or problems," notes John DeLuca, director of the medical department of Equitable Life, ruefully. Says DeLuca, "I think that's *the* major executive crisis — their inability to have one."

And then something happens. It may be an event of obvious importance — a spouse, unattended to for years, finally walks out; a parent or a sibling dies; a major investment goes sour. Or it may be something that to the outsider might seem fairly trivial — the executive is bumped in a minor traffic accident; a son or daughter gets into a youthful scrape. What hits the executive is a sense of loss — the loss of someone, or the loss of control, or the loss of a carefully nurtured illusion.

Typically, his response, because he has neglected thinking or feeling on the subject for years, goes way overboard. Not "My marriage is on the rocks," but instead "I'm incapable of loving or being loved." Not "I'm going to die someday"; instead, "In light of my eventual death it's all worthless."

Strange behavior may ensue. At one company, for example, the chief financial officer became obsessed with the plight of the world's poor. Rather than resigning to do relief work in the Sahel, he began to divert corporate funds to charities concerned with the problem. The company didn't really catch on that something was askew until, in the words of the psychologist brought in to deal with the case, the executive "began neglecting his personal hygiene" — he stopped bathing. More common indications of psychological trouble include withdrawal, unexplained absences, missed deadlines, wide swings in mood, seemingly inexplicable emotional outbursts, and dramatic changes in appearance.

For the company to acknowledge that there's a problem, the afflicted individual may have to come in dressed as Napoleon and proclaim that he's marching the entire marketing department to Moscow. It makes the psychologists shake their heads in dismay: even at companies with well-established employee-assistance programs to help the troops, the typical reaction to an executive acting strangely is to deny as long as possible that anything is wrong.

After all, managers are supposed to be tough — they can get a little weird at times, but they're tough. Both underlings and superiors may be a bit afraid of offending this recalcitrant character, particularly if he still seems to be doing his job, more or less. It's often very hard to tell that he isn't. Says an executive who used to come to work still feeling the effects of cocaine, marijuana, alcohol, and other mind-altering substances, "The thing that really amazes me is that no one noticed." If they do notice, co-workers may cover for the troubled manager. And besides, as Rowland Austin, the head of employee assistance at General Motors, notes, "If you look at the record, you see that these people have probably been performing at two hundred percent of capacity compared with everyone else. So when their performance deteriorates, it goes down to one hundred and seventy-five percent."

Eventually, though, after the troubled exec has lost a major account, or grossly abused a colleague, or become catatonic, the company may be forced to conclude that something has to be done. But what? One favorite option of yore — firing the guy — seems less attractive with every lawsuit that's filed alleging wrongful termination. And, besides, think of the cost of replacing this former high performer.

This is one area where, believe it or not, the corporation just may be better off bringing in a consultant. "A crisis for an executive is a crisis for the company," observes Dr. Harry Brownlee of the consulting firm Brownlee Dolan Stein. "The company often needs as much help as the executive."

The consultant, presumably a so-called mental health professional, can probably size up the situation fairly quickly. Robert McLaughlin, for example, who likens his role in dealing with executives in crisis to that of Red Adair in capping blown-out oil wells, says that he can usually make a diagnosis after one day of interviews with the troubled manager's colleagues.

Once the company has a good idea of what's wrong, it can take appropriate action. If the problem is acute, the troubled executive may have to be hospitalized right away. The consultant will know how to go about it and where to put him. As one counselor notes, referring to New York City's last-chance facility for the distressed, "You don't send a six-figure-a-year person to Bellevue."

If the situation isn't at the somebody's-about-to-jump-out-a-window stage, then the company people in charge will be able to think through precisely how to confront the individual so as to ensure that he'll seek treatment. This may not be hard; the experts say that quite often the manager's reaction will be relief — "Thank God somebody finally noticed and wants to help me." If, on the other hand, the executive wants to continue denying reality, the company may have to muster its evidence — stressing how the individual's performance has deteriorated, rather than any psychological diagnosis — and put the choice squarely: accept help or be fired. The boss of one alcoholic manager went so far as to lock her out of her office until she went for treatment. Later she thanked him.

Will the company ever get the executive back? Evidence on the point isn't encouraging. One expert estimates that only one out of three executives hospitalized with severe emotional problems returns to the same position — the rest decide to leave the company or never recover enough to hold down their old job. Perhaps surprisingly, the success rate in bringing back alcoholics appears to be much higher.

If the formerly troubled manager clearly has worked through his problem, the question of taking him back finally comes down to a test of the company's wisdom: are the decision-makers irretrievably locked into a manager-as-tough-guy ethic? Do they confuse illness with weakness? Forget all the lofty pronouncements about the corporation's social responsibilities and the annual-report talk about how employees are the company — it's in the answers to those two questions that management goes a long way toward determining whether theirs is to be a humane corporation.

51

The Guilt-edged Executive

*Feeling guilty about neglecting your family to stay late
at the office? Stop whimpering and learn to cope.*

IN THE BLINK OF AN EYE the dark bird of managerial guilt
sweeps down upon you, tearing furiously at your executive innards:
Oh, my Lord, I completely forgot about that 3 o'clock meeting. All my
subordinates gathered in the conference room, waiting for the guidance I was to supply them, and here I sat, tied up on the phone. I forgot
to tell my secretary about scheduling the thing, and then those simple,
trusting folks didn't even feel they could call to ask where I was. I've
got myself overbooked. I've let the team down, I'm letting everybody
down these days. How will I ever make it up to them?

Managerial guilt is not, admittedly, a threat to corporate America
on the order of, say, the Japanese challenge. Psychologists who counsel businesspeople say that only a few are actually immobilized by it.
But the rest feel its beak and talons occasionally, and it can be mighty
unnerving. The good news is that the best tactics for coping with
managerial guilt, if not always obvious, are fairly easy to learn.

First, what is it? Not the feeling, mind you — unless you're completely devoid of shame, you presumably know what that's like. No,
what is it that's going on psychologically when you feel guilt?

The simplest explanation is that guilt consists of the thud-in-the-
gut discovery that how you are behaving doesn't measure up to how
you think you ought to behave. Students of the subject take the
analysis a bit farther, however, differentiating two kinds of guilt, the
first springing from sins of commission, the second from sins of
omission.

In the first case, nasty you does something your conscience — or, if
you are a Freudian, your superego — tells you that you shouldn't do.
You stay out late, drinking and telling lies to that attractive new

person in the marketing department, instead of going home to your long-suffering spouse. Roderick Gilkey of Emory University notes that what gives this behavior its guilty sting is the pleasure it affords — if you didn't enjoy it, you wouldn't feel guilty. You love to stay out late, you devil.

In the second case, you fail to do enough to live up to your internal image of what you should be, that never-quite-to-be-attained benchmark that psychoanalysts call the ego-ideal. You were not courteous, kind, trustworthy, brave, clean, and reverent in that sales meeting this afternoon. For most executives, this represents the more pernicious type of guilt — it's generally easier to change one's behavior, to stop doing all those terrible after-hours things, than to soften the demands of ego-ideal cobbled together in childhood from the example set by parents. In the real world most managers seem perfectly capable of combining both kinds of guilt: you love your children and want to be a good parent. You also want to get ahead. So you miss your daughter's school play, choosing to stay at work instead. You feel terrible, partly because you're thoroughly enjoying your dizzying rise through the ranks.

All this helps explain not only what executives feel guilty about but also what they don't feel guilty about. Perhaps the biggest surprise here is how little remorse most managers experience over bad business decisions. Gosh, we thought we were doing the right thing launching that new product; who could have guessed that it would bomb as completely as it did? It's a rare ego-ideal that requires the right call every time.

What the conscience does require is that the individual act like a good parent, even to those surrogates for children, employees. Executives caught up in mergers or takeovers sometimes agonizingly dream that they're losing their children. Gilkey tells of the chairman of a company about to be taken over who dreamed that he was abandoning a child by the roadside for someone else to pick up. Another guilt-racked executive in a similar situation confessed, "I have sixty little hearts pounding back at the plant, and I feel a need to protect them all." No comparable dreams are reported about shareholders.

If he feels that way about the employees, you can imagine how the typical executive suffers over the folks actually left behind — the family. The No. 1 cause of managerial guilt in America, hands down, is the manager's perception that he's neglecting the people back home. Even successful, otherwise well-adjusted executives are not immune. Consider Robert Huff, the president of Bell & Howell. He says he usually works from 7 A.M. to 7 P.M. and every other Saturday, and that he travels two days a week. "What bothers me," he admits, "is that the family doesn't have dinner together." But it also bothers him a bit, apparently, when he takes time off during the workday to go watch his son play ball — he calls such excursions "sneaking out."

Sometimes managers devise strategies for coping that let them get away with more work. Hard-toiling Thomas Shelton, the manager of market research at Deere & Co., tells of his wife saying to their four-year-old daughter, in anticipation of a visit from Grandmother, "We're going to have a visitor, and it's someone you haven't seen in a long time. Can you guess who it is?"

"Dad?" the little girl said eagerly.

Wince. Shelton now leaves work around dinnertime, eats, and then returns to Deere. "By going back to the office, I can put the family thing out of my mind," he confesses. Executives also delude themselves and sometimes their families with the notion that when they rise just a bit higher, they're going to start spending more hours at home. By that time, of course, the habit of working long hours is thoroughly ingrained, and often the children are grown and gone.

Just about everyone agrees that the executives hardest hit by family-related guilt are women. "It's rampant among them," notes Bill Meyer, president of Rohrer Hibler & Replogle, one of the oldest and largest firms of psychologists to management. Despite changing societal values and norms, he observes, women still feel a greater sense of responsibility toward the kids than men do. To make up for the time they spend at work, they often overcompensate when they are home, smothering their children with toys and attention. This actually makes the situation worse — the kid just wants to go on watching TV and living his life.

The next most common cause of managerial guilt is failure to get control of one's work. In this case, the executive typically beats himself on the head for failing to live up to what is, in fact, an unrealistic managerial ideal. "Many general managers have been trained to believe they should rationally 'plan, organize, lead, and control,' " observes R. Jack Weber, an associate professor of behavioral science at the University of Virginia's Colgate Darden Graduate School of Business. "Yet my research shows," he goes on, "that the work life of most of them is characterized by fragmentation, discontinuity, inadequate time for reflection, and relentless interactive demands" — all those people who keep calling or coming by to bug you. At the end of a day of firefighting, the executive looks at the mess on his desk, concludes that he hasn't accomplished anything, feels guilty, and vows to do better the next day.

Other causes of guilt: you finally get some time free to spend with your family, but instead you go out and play golf. According to the experts, this syndrome afflicts mainly middle managers, who may feel they have to spend more time building rapport with their colleagues.

In the damned-if-you-do, damned-if-you-don't category is the guilt certain executives experience when, after they've arrived on high, they start taking it slightly easier. "They're relaxing and justifying going off to exotic places," notes one astute observer of this Olympian sport. "They take advantage of their position when there are serious problems to be dealt with. These executives know they're goofing off, and they feel guilty about it." Less explicable — probably because it's fairly neurotic — is the guilt that a very few high executives feel simply because they've got to the top.

Your occasional bouts with the bird are, in all likelihood, more mundane. What can you do about them?

First, pay attention. Guilt, like physical pain, is a signal that something is wrong. At the same time, don't blow your paltry sins out of proportion — contrary to what the guilt-prone typically conclude, the fact that you acted badly in this instance does not necessarily mean that you are a bad person through and through. You might also examine your heart for evidence of anger. Resentment you haven't expressed directly to the resentee sometimes gets turned inward and becomes guilt.

If that doesn't take care of the problem, you may have to do something about the way you behave. Should that prove impossible, you can try to educate that toothy ego-ideal of yours — feeding it information on how most managers in fact spend their time, or maybe getting it to reflect on where it picked up its highfalutin' notions. How much of what you do can you control? It also helps immeasurably if you know precisely how you're doing; ask your company for more of what is popularly known as feedback.

When neglecting the folks at home is getting you down, try working on their understanding of and reaction to how you behave. Putney Westerfield, formerly the publisher of *Fortune* and now the chief executive of the Boyden Associates executive search firm, finds that the managers who feel the most guilty about traveling a lot are those whose spouses suspect them of being unfaithful on the road. Try to convince your better half that it ain't so, maybe even by making sure that it ain't. Let your family in on the immensity of what you're up against on the job — all the fires you have to put out, all the crazies you have to put up with. At the very least, this may make them feel slightly guilty about making you feel so bad.

52

What to Do with the Children

*Experts maintain that executives often make
particularly poor parents. But it doesn't have to be so.*

THEY ARE so finally and ineluctably *there* — a combination of your last, best hope and Banquo's ghost, little boats you launch upon the dark water, wondering if they'll return as clipper ships, corsairs, or merely scows. But return they will. As Harry Levinson, the renowned psychologist to management, notes, "You can change wives, but you can't change kids."

Not that you won't be tempted to at times. Levinson again: "The single topic that probably comes up most frequently in my discussions with executives is adolescent children." For managerial women of the baby-boom generation, the worry — and the guilt — typically begins even earlier, about the minute they first leave the wee one to go back to work. The slightly anguished comment of an officer at a New York bank, the mother of an infant boy, seems representative: "I hope and pray that the woman taking care of my child will give him the same sort of love and care that I would."

What do we do with the children? We try, often we make mistakes. At least one psychoanalyst, Professor Abraham Zaleznik of the Harvard Business School, suggests that executives just may be the next-to-worst parents going, second only to politicians. But then there are so few hours in the day, and so much misinformation circulating about what we should do. "It's not the quantity of time, it's the quality" — a notion woefully incomplete, if not simply wrong. "Even if the mother works full-time, the child will develop just as well so long as a consistent, nurturant care-giver is provided" — mmmh, the experts have a few doubts about that one.

What *do* we do with the children?

The little bundle arrives, borne on clouds of glory and joy, leaving a

paper trail of diapers. And the juggling begins. Because of changes in
the law, these days most corporations treat maternity like any other
disability. For new mothers who have been working at managerial
jobs, this policy typically translates into a total paid leave of some six
to eight weeks. Some enlightened corporations — AT&T and Levi
Strauss, for example — also permit employees to add on unpaid personal leave, extending their absence to many months, after which the
employer "makes every effort," as the phrase goes, to give them back
their original job or one just as good. It's the impression of benefit
supervisors at many big companies, though, that women managers
today usually spend shorter periods away from work becoming
mothers than heretofore.

This is manifestly not because they're able to place their infants in
employer-run child-care centers. While a few companies did start
such centers in the early 1970s, many subsequently closed them
down — in part because employees didn't use them enough. (Students
of the day-care phenomenon suggest that part of the problem was that
parents hate to take kids along on their commute — O cherished
American freedom to crawl along the freeway, alone in your car!)
Nowadays it's a rare corporation indeed that provides child care for
its workers.

Most managerial women, it seems, end up leaving the little nipper
with the best individual care-giver they can find. Said mothers, as
concerned a group as you'll find, take comfort from what appears to
be the emerging consensus, buttressed by some studies, that a child
cared for by an unchanging, kindly outsider develops no differently
from one tended by his or her parent.

The heartache is, not all the authorities are so sure. "The studies
speak to the cognitive development of the child," observes Lee Salk,
the psychologist author of several books on child rearing, "not to his
affective development." The kid is great with blocks, but how are his
ties with his parents and others? Moreover, the most caring, smiling
nanny may not be nearly as stimulative as a souped-up managerial-
class parent — full of questions for the little one, inventing games —
particularly if Nanny barely speaks the language.

Salk and others who question the advisability of a mother with a
child under three going back to work offer one overriding piece of

advice: if you have to return to the job, move heaven and earth to try to be with the baby for breakfast, lunch, and dinner. This may mean trundling home at noon; it may mean having a fractious infant brought to you. Welcome to the first installment of the quality-of-time *versus* quantity-of-time dilemma. Two observations from the experts, sauce for middle-aged executive ganders as well as young managerial geese: you probably have to put in at least a minimum quantity to get those occasional quality moments; such moments have a way of coinciding with when the kid needs you, which is sometimes difficult to schedule on an after-work-only basis. When the child is very young, he seems to need a parent most when he's hungry.

Note the use of the sex-blind term *parent*. One bright spot for proto-executive families aborning is the increasingly active role taken by Dear Young Dad. Baby-boomers-become-fathers are discomfiting obstetricians in the delivery room, learning to change diapers — it isn't exactly tantamount to defusing a nuclear weapon — nibbling small pedal extremities, and even resisting the temptation to pass the young potatokin at the first sign of a cry. Older males, schooled in a different style of fathering — cigarettes in the waiting room, walking proudly *beside* the baby carriage — are a tad bemused by this, but they don't disapprove. Some, in fact, admit to being envious.

True, even new-style fathers still aren't doing enough. Most of the child-care and housework burden remains planted squarely on managerial mommy. Hearken, though, to the voice of change. An AT&T spokesman reports that a few male employees who have taken unpaid paternity leave for economic reasons — the little woman was making more money than they were — now find they have other, more compelling, reasons for staying home. They have apparently become absolutely besotted with their kids.

From about age three, when the tyke is dispatched to preschool, until the storm clouds of adolescence begin to form, a deceptive quiet may reign in the relations of child and parent. The chip or chipette off the old block is being socialized. Other forces — school, the Brownies, the ominous and powerful peer group — take over from the parents at least part of the task of teaching the kid what's what.

Therein lies the potential for two mistakes manager-parents frequently make. In the parlance of executive performance appraisal, the first would be tagged "excessive delegation." Chief executive (father, in the traditional view) delegates this messy little matter to the vice chairman (mother), who hands it off to the labor-relations staff (teacher). And everyone ends up wondering why the workers lack discipline, much less the animation that a shared corporate vision affords.

It's a question of, pardon the expression, role models. The little girl may find one in the home (later we'll tell her that certain disabilities attach); the little boy often won't. Failing to discover a suitable adult candidate at school or in the Cub Scouts, he'll turn to a slightly older boy, from whom he'll learn that it's all quite simple, black-and-white really.

Put bluntly, the parent, even the overbusy executive parent, has to be there, teaching the child by example how to put together broken toys and busted situations. For high-powered managerial types in particular, this entails avoiding the temptation to take the problem out of the kid's hands and solve the damn thing yourself. To understand the difficulties likely to arise in the nipper's day, experts recommend popping into his school on occasion (he can show you off proudly; the teacher will get over it). And vice versa — bring him to the office some Friday (you can show him off proudly; your secretary will get over it).

Such advice in part accounts for the growing number of little so-and-so's appearing now and then in the corporate halls, especially around holidays. That and the episodic failure of our system to provide adequate day care — the baby-sitter got sick.

The other common mistake made while outside forces are beginning to shape the kid up is to yank him repeatedly from them — that is, to move again and again. Father arrives at his new outpost to find other folks from the company waiting to greet him. For mother, there just may be a network of corporate wives. But what about the child, who may need outside supports far more than either adult?

Dr. Derek Miller, now a professor at Northwestern Medical School, was for a while, he thinks, the only American-trained psychiatrist in England. He treated many families of peripatetic American managers, frequently because the kids were seething with hostility over being uprooted. "Moving constantly can produce children who are superficially very charming," he observes, "but they have trouble forming deep attachments and they're often quite miserable inside."

For many executive parents the first signs of trouble with their children come when the kid hits the obstacle course of adolescence. The initial challenge: survive puberty. Youngling is pulled and pushed by forces within, seeking on the one hand to become independent, tempted on the other to scream "help" because of the weird things happening to his body. As a result, father and mother must play a deft, vigilant game — cheerleading when appropriate, standing back from time to time, demonstrating how to cope with feelings, most of all watching and listening.

Mr. Big may not be up to the task. It isn't just the matter of time, though managerial careers have a nasty way of taking off and consuming still more hours of the day precisely when El Kiddo is 'twixt twelve and twenty. The tougher problem is the psychology of the executive. Harvard Business School's Zaleznik sees executives spending their work lives in a world where the values of power prevail. You have to develop defenses; you get few opportunities to be nurturant. It becomes difficult to take off the armor when you're back at the castle. Zaleznik worries that managerial mothers, as more of them rise higher, will also end up buckling on the three-piece steel suit.

For executive fathers of adolescent sons, the trouble may be particularly acute. James Wilson, professor at the University of Pittsburgh who in his private psychotherapy practice counsels a number of businessmen, observes, "As a group, senior managers hate to be confronted. They're assertive, aggressive. They hate to lose, but in a sense they have to be confronted and lose at home for the succession of generations to continue."

This doesn't mean throwing tennis matches with that hulking adolescent ape across the net. It does mean letting down your guard to let him find out what is probably the truth — you are neither omnipotent nor omniscient. Also that you don't mind, indeed revel in, the fact that he's better at some things than you are.

But where do you get the time to have him find you out? Think about taking the heir apparent along on the occasional business trip — nothing like a touch of the slight humiliation airlines impose to crack the facade of even the most composed executive. Scramble, too, for some unstructured time together with your kids at every age. "Here in Silicon Valley," notes Jerry Kroth, a psychologist at the University of Santa Clara, "you constantly see men jogging by themselves, women jogging, men and women jogging together. What you rarely see here, but do every weekend in Germany, is a family walking hand-in-hand through a park."

At the end of the day, consciously and deliberately make an effort to change hats. According to the experts, this may be as simple as reserving to yourself the first fifteen minutes home. Attempt to arrange your domestic affairs so that you're not clobbered with "The washer's broken" the minute you walk in — no mean feat for working women. Take a shower, change clothes, mix and take a first sip of that blessed martini — you'll be much better prepared to listen, to share, and to coopt small revolutions.

53

What Your Vacation Says about You

Some folks climb mountains, others sleep late.
And some wait desperately for a call from the office.

THE PRESENTATION BOMBED. Your last trip proved a bone-wearying, thirty-six-hour scrape of bad business, bad food, and bad time on airplanes. The acid-quick analytical insights for which you're well known somehow just didn't materialize in the conference this afternoon. And a small voice begins to whisper, "You need a vacation."

I do, I do need a vacation. I need to get close to the kids again, to really talk with them, to share something. I need a vacation. I ought to be out there on the river shooting the rapids, soaked to the skin and yelling my head off. I need a vacation. I want to be there in a big double hammock strung between two palm trees on the edge of a lagoon, with my arm cradling the one I love, the two of us watching the sunset become the night sky, lying there, laughing, giving strange constellations new names. I need a vacation.

But what do you do about it?

The answer may be more telling than you realize. Anyone who has ever vacationed successfully knows the restorative effect the experience can have, restoration that you presumably take back with you to the office. In addition to this, though, a growing body of thought, mostly by psychologists, suggests that how you vacation says quite a lot about what kind of person you are, on the job as well as off.

One of the findings of a thirty-year study of the lives of Harvard College graduates was that the capacity to take and enjoy imaginative vacations was an indication of good mental health, according to *Adaptation to Life*, a book by George Vaillant, who became director of the study in 1972. Psychologist Marilyn Machlowitz, in the research that led to her book *Workaholics*, found that for the soul driven by internal demons to give more time and thought to work than is objectively necessary, vacations are fraught with anxiety. If he's finally compelled to take time off by a spouse on the way to divorce court, the workaholic won't enjoy the vacation much, may sneak a little work on the side, and will wait desperately for the call from the office that gives him an excuse to cut the whole thing short.

In the last few years, other psychologists have devoted considerable effort to trying to figure out the connections between work and free time. So far, according to Barbara Gutek, associate professor of psychology and executive management at Claremont Graduate School in California, they have come up with two competing hypotheses. The first, called the spillover model, holds that individuals tend to act at play much as they do at work. The hard-charging, exacting manager would thus be expected to plan a complicated vacation itinerary down to the last detail, and then whirl methodically through it, arriving at the last stop with a solid sense of accomplishment. In Gutek's view, most high-level executives fit the spillover pattern — because they enjoy their work so much, they look for the same sort of satisfactions in their time off.

The second hypothesis, known as the compensation model, posits that leisure is used to satisfy needs that aren't fulfilled at work. The office Milquetoast who cowers before superiors and subordinates alike will, as soon as he goes on vacation, don a safari jacket and go gunning for the most ferocious endangered species he can track down. He then promptly runs into the company's macho chairman, of course — the top guy is out there spilling over berserkly.

In a sense, both hypotheses boil down to the same insight: vacation is when you show your true colors. It's a time to make dreams realities. This isn't as simple as it sounds, which is why vacations speak volumes about the vacationer. First, you have to be able to divine what it is you dream of, want, and enjoy — this without the discipline provided by having to make a living and to act a certain way in the office. Second, you have to somehow come up with the wherewithal — financial and emotional — to go questing after it.

With this perspective in mind, it's instructive to look at the current folkways and fashions in managerial vacations. One phenomenon observed by students of the subject — psychologists, benefits managers, and travel agents — is that early in their careers, managers often seem reluctant to take vacation at all, particularly if it entails being away for more than a week or two. With most of their dreams bound up in their work lives, they don't want the organization — or themselves — to think that they're less than indispensable. The feeling, or the fact, of indispensability sometimes persists even after the manager reaches the top of the ladder. Charles Pilliod, who not long ago retired after ten eventful years as chief executive of Goodyear, reports that during the entire period he took perhaps four weeks off.

What makes the junior executive's reluctance ironic is that the more senior you become, the less you can count on taking a scheduled holiday as scheduled, at least until you reach Olympian levels. The most sacrosanct vacations in the company, to be juggled only in the case of nuclear war or a hostile tender offer, are the five weeks that the chairman takes at Lyford Cay every winter and the three weeks your secretary spends on the Jersey Shore with her nieces each August. The moral: the more valuable you become to the corporation, the more it will tend — if you let it — to coop up and undernourish your extracorporate dreams, which might otherwise have an inclination to go wandering: it does this in part by grabbing hold of your time, often in the most unpredictable way.

Calculating the proper time to take time off requires a delicate balancing of the exigencies of corporate and personal life — when will the company be busy, when will the kids be out of school. William Sanders, vice president of personnel at Sears, suggests just how careful the calculation of at least the corporate side of the equation has to be at his company. "If you're in a retail store," he says, "Christmas is obviously the worst time to be away." This, presumably, no matter how many wee ones are waiting for you by the family hearth. He continues, "But if you work in a staff job at headquarters, Christmas might be okay. You certainly don't visit the stores then — they're full of customers."

The conventional wisdom maintains that it's unwise to be on vacation when your new boss, whom you don't know, arrives on the scene. And what if your protean boss is a new man every day, some of them not very nice? When David Mahoney was running Norton Simon, some of the people working for him at corporate headquarters would go on holiday only when the mercurial chief executive was himself on vacation.

What the individual chooses to do with his vacation time is even more telling than when he chooses to take it. For American business-persons on a frolic and a detour, visiting Europe was all the rage through much of the 1980s. These folks understood the value of a strong dollar. They did not go for the standard tour of the big cities, however. Instead they meandered from château to château in France. This may simply have been the exhausting-the-exotic syndrome that travel agents notice — if you're used to visiting Paris on business, why return for pleasure; if you climbed Kilimanjaro this year, about the only thing left for next year is Nepal. Or it may have been bound up in the aspiration to live, however briefly, as wealthy, civilized Euro-peans do — less constrained by the Protestant ethic.

In vogue these days are so-called wilderness vacations, particularly among male executives: bankers go rafting down white-river rapids that nineteenth-century explorers would have thought twice about attempting; accountants hang from the sides of mountains. Jerome K. Full, a vice president of ITT Community Development Corp. and a man whose mountain adventures range from Wyoming to the Pyrenees, is representative in his view of the relation between work and leisure: "If you have a rigorous vacation that challenges you physically and forces you to operate at peak efficiency, it suggests the attitude you bring to bear at work. And you want to be identified with those who demonstrate a strong sense of initiative." Pure spillover, in other words. The operative dream here appears to be proving yourself just as competent in the world of nature-red-in-tooth-and-claw as in the conference room or over the telephone.

A large number of the most senior executives have still another dream. Andrew Harper publishes *The Hideaway Report*, a guide to mostly undiscovered luxury retreats. Recently he surveyed 2,500 of his readers — 70 percent of the sample were chief executives, presi-dents, or owners of companies — to discover their vacation prefer-ences. He reports, "When I asked, 'What was the most important factor that helped you decide where to vacation?' by far the most frequent answer was 'privacy and seclusion.' Second, but by no means as popular: 'resort setting, type of accommodation, food, and personal service.'"

For the top guy, who's onstage all the time, the anonymity of a small, exclusive resort affords a bit of gentle license. "There's an unwritten rule that what you do there is your own business," says Harper. "So you can do things you might not do back home with your colleagues. Within limits, of course." Another observer suggests that the principal naughtiness consists of staying up after 11 and then sleeping in the next morning. The object the chief executive has in mind is not to replicate what he does at work — taking action, talking endlessly with people — but rather to give rein to a part of himself that he normally keeps somewhat secret. The slugabed part, for instance.

While the experts don't have a formula that every manager can use to get in touch with that inner, dreaming, secret self that should be given a workout on vacation, they do offer some hints on how to structure the experience so as to make it more likely that the little fellow will get some air. The first principle is that on vacation, you should try to avoid doing things out of a sense of obligation. Obligation you got plenty of at work.

Does this mean that taking the kids to visit the grandparents is necessarily a bad vacation? No, particularly if you're lucky enough to actually enjoy being with your children. The encounter may turn out to be something out of *On Golden Pond*— preferably from the end of the movie, not the earlier parts: you settle some issues, effect reconciliations, and just may learn about yourself and others.

Kicking over the clock is the first step toward freeing yourself of managerial obligations. "See the fantastic Correggio fresco at 11, have lunch at the best restaurant in Parma at 12, catch the train at 1:30" can rapidly come to seem just like "See the vice chairman at 11, have lunch with a client at 12, get to the meeting by 2."

Nonscheduling takes some time to get used to. The second principle is to allot enough time off to make the adjustment. Dr. Ralph Hirschowitz, a psychiatrist with the Levinson Institute in Boston, makes the point more cogently: "The first few days of vacation usually require a kind of passivity simply to build yourself up for the more active interests that follow."

The third principle of vacationing is that more active interests should follow, though not necessarily active in the four-sets-of-tennis sense. Leisure isn't idleness. If it's done correctly, you should rapidly find yourself with a heightened receptivity to the world around you — which means ready to look at, muse on, and learn from things around you. Go out and feed your head, your eyes, or your other senses.

Finally, do whatever you can to set free the child within yourself. This is not to say you should build model airplanes, though if the model-builder is the only vestige of your happy, childlike self, you could do worse than to cater to it. This is to say, "Be silly, spontaneous, playful." Give full meaning to the phrase *goofing off.* When you're asked what you're doing, say you're engaging in regression in service to the ego — Freudian jargon for going back in psychological time as a holiday from the whips and chains of the conscience. That'll keep 'em guessing, and you goofing.

54

What Your Office Says about You

The old rules are giving way to new ones.
Watch for the telltale giant inflatable plastic banana.

YOU TAKE THE ELEVATOR to that special floor, emerging to step into the deepest carpet in the world and an almost funereal quiet. Proceeding down the long cool corridor, you enter his secretary's office, itself large enough to amply house three or four of your co-workers. She appraises you with a glance, makes a brief but unhurried phone call, and announces that Mr. Big will see you now. You walk right in.

There, somewhere at the end of the room, he sits — lost for a moment in an aureole of light from the wall-size windows, then descried behind a desk as big as a car. My God, he must be forty feet away. You approach gingerly, gestured to a visitor's seat all of eight inches above the floor. He smiles. Sit down, Smedley, he suggests, sit down — make yourself comfortable and grovel a little.

As kings, high priests, and courtesans have always known, the surroundings in which one works say a great deal about one. In the past the message communicated by most executive offices has been fairly straightforward: rank and authority. This seems to be changing, though, in ways that may affect even the junior manager faced with positioning his desk.

It isn't just that the power office, or its near ally, the drop-dead office, is giving ground to the more welcoming executive-work-area-cum-living-room. (Indeed, the *extremely* trend-conscious now spot a shift away from the latter toward a relatively bare-bones alternative they call the Theory Z executive office.) No, the fundamental change is a dawning realization on the part of people in corporations that offices and their contents should be arranged to fit the work done there, even when it means that the company president ends up with the same space as a purchasing agent, or that for certain individuals in certain departments, a clean desk may signal not orderliness but stagnation.

Part of the problem in getting the form of managerial offices to follow their function, and a reason for past excesses, is the difficulty of defining precisely what a manager does. Consider the office-design spectrum posited by Douglas Nicholson, the chairman of Building Programs International, a subsidiary of the New York real estate firm Cushman & Wakefield that consults with corporate clients on building needs. At one end is the single-task worker — a file clerk, say — whose environs must be organized around his equipment, the files. At the other end is the chief executive, whose function, in Nicholson's view, is mostly role playing — father figure, final decision-maker.

"The C.E.O. isn't concerned with equipment," Nicholson says. "He needs a stage set." Like something out of *The Wizard of Oz*, perhaps? Ted Ashley, the chairman of Warner Bros. until his retirement not long ago, played the mogul in Jack Warner's old office, as restored by the same man who did the sets for *The Wiz*. Through a foyer guarded by silvery doors from an Art Deco skyscraper, embellished with copper borders to make them larger, one entered an inner sanctum containing a fireplace, gray-flannel walls, and a desk with stainless-steel top and glass base. Drop very dead, you munchkins.

According to Nicholson, design confusion becomes most pronounced in the middle of the spectrum, where you find the majority of managers. Each performs many different tasks, but also does some role playing. How then to decide what space, furniture, and equipment are called for, much less how to situate the desk vis-à-vis the couch and visitors' chairs?

In the absence of serious thought about what an office is to be used for, companies typically fall back on the hoary conventions of status — to determine who gets what space, and power — to govern the arrangement of furniture. With respect to status, the Buffalo Organization for Social and Technological Innovation (BOSTI) — a nonprofit group studying office productivity — surveyed four thousand white-collar workers at twelve U.S. companies and thirty government agencies. BOSTI identified these indicators of prestige, in descending order of importance: space, location (not just on a corner or with many windows, but also according to proximity to higher-ups), amount of furniture, controllable access (is there a door to close?), quality of furniture, quantity of "devices" (phones, computer terminals), and personal display (artworks, plants).

On the subject of how to arrange your movables, for a long time about the only explicit advice available came in those cheery little guidebooks on power, how to get it, how to flaunt it. Place your desk so that the visitor has to walk as far as possible to reach it, even complicating his passage with strategically situated pieces of executive furniture. Use your mahogany lifeboat as a barrier, forcing the quaking supplicant to sit directly opposite you, preferably in an uncomfortable chair.

That was the old cliché. Gradually, however, as the corporate world increasingly held up openness as a value, power-office arrangements came to be viewed as a hindrance to the one managerial task that everyone agreed on: communicating with others. Some dirty minds even began to suggest that having your desk perched atop a raised platform reflected "power needs" or, worse yet, insecurity.

Hence the new cliché—the managerial office as conversation pit. Replace that hopelessly squarish desk with a round table, which visitors can draw their chairs up to. There's no hierarchy here—though, as BOSTI president Michael Brill points out, most managers immediately reestablish one by having a slightly different chair for themselves or by staking out the choice spot, back to the window or to the nearest wall. Have to be within arm's length of the old credenza, you know— the phone and all that.

While few managers have completely given up desks in the interest of achieving living-room ambience, the vast majority of offices of any size now make at least a nod toward parlor informality. Indeed, the office layout most frequently sought by senior executives today consists of a space divided into three areas: a work-surface area (where the desk is, usually), the informal conversational area (the couch and visitors' chairs), and the conference area (a long table with a place for Papa Bear at the head). Might not two areas to gather in be redundant? No, say the experts, you need the more hierarchical ordering of the conference table for when the factory hands come to visit; they'd be horribly ill at ease if invited to sit down with the senior V.P. on his crewelwork divan.

The only problem with this layout is that it requires a minimum of

300 square feet, 170 more than are found in the average managerial office. These square feet don't come cheap. Just fitting out an executive office can cost from $40 a square foot to over $100. Accordingly, the three-area work space may well turn out to be the 1976 Cadillac of American business offices — the acme of bigness. The trend is running toward less private space for everyone, including the top guys.

To make this downsizing palatable, a number of companies are instituting the standard-size office — everyone in the top echelon gets a Category A–size work space, the next tier Category B square footage, and so on. Hierarchical distinctions within categories can be made via the quality of the furnishings. Combine this with a policy of setting aside the choice locations — those corners with spectacular views — for conference rooms available to all, as, for instance, Atlantic Richfield does, and you have a halting step toward what Cornell professor Franklin Becker calls the "democratization of work space."

For partisans of the Theory Z office, any move that way is overdue. Taking their lead from Japan — where only the highest-level executives have private offices — they advocate a managerial work space situated in the midst of everyone else. If it's closed off at all, the walls should be glass. And since a Louis Quinze escritoire and matching love seat are going to look a bit odd when everybody else has a gray metal desk, the furnishings should not vary too much from the norm — that is, the place should look like an office.

So far, about the only Theory Z spaces around are right where the cutting edge slices first, in the offices of design firms. Probably a more likely next step for corporations will be to what the Houston architectural firm 3-D/International terms the "cockpit office" for executives and managers. (Others speak of "hideaway offices.") Mr. Big is allotted a relatively small private space for his work surface; he performs his more public functions — meeting with the troops, greeting visitors — in conference areas or living rooms that he shares with others of his stripe. A tough sale to status-conscious corporate mandarins? "It's a very easy sale," reports 3-D/I's president, Jack M. Rains. "You only have to sell the chief executive on a cockpit; after that, it's remarkable how fast everyone else decides they want one."

For the middle manager befuddled by where to put visitors' chairs, the flux in office-design trends may not help much. There's some heart to be taken here, however: the general direction is toward a more careful calculation of what each individual needs to do his job.

Within the four walls, say the experts, how you arrange things is largely a function of your personality, which determines the precise manner with which you attack your work. (If you don't have four walls — that is, are in an open-plan office — you may soon. The tax law has been changed to make floor-to-ceiling dismountable walls every bit as quickly depreciable as the shorter jobbies, an alteration welcome to the many, many managers who've found open plan too noisy and insufficiently private.)

At the Facility Management Institute — it's a division of the Herman Miller furniture company — psychologists and designers tend to assess offices according to several different ways of psychologically profiling the occupants. Extraverts, the folks at FMI believe, are likely to position themselves so that they can see out of their work space — desk chair facing the door — but the skillful extravert will do this in such a way that visitors will sit at the side of his desk, or, if he's truly extraverted, on the same side that he does. Introverts position themselves so as not to see out, to help them focus on their current project better. (Beware placing your chair with its back to the door, however — some people take this as almost a hostile act.)

Detail-oriented individuals, who tend to have more orderly offices, will also personalize them less than others do. More intuitive types, described by the FMI pundits as generalists, seers of the big picture, will have all sorts of detritus about, to remind them of other things. Ditto for extraverts, who nibble on one project, then another, then back to the first. These visual stimuli — they may be just separate piles of paper, one for each project — are important. Anyone who cleans them up in a fit of hygiene does so at the peril of losing some new ideas.

People who make decisions in a logical, systematic manner will have mostly clean desks, with work laid out in a precise, linear way. Folks who decide "according to what is personally meaningful" — less the organization's values than their own — tend to decorate their desktops and other surfaces with evidence of those values: photographs, mementos, cat posters. More data-oriented brethren — believing that if they get enough information a decision or conclusion will automatically issue from it — will keep heaps of the stuff around them, sometimes forever.

If psychological self-examination isn't your bag, just look in the mirror. Karen Crane, senior vice president of the Mutual Benefit Financial Service Co. and an industrial psychologist who coaches insurance salesmen, teaches that different office arrangements reflect the different personalities of the three basic somatotypes.

Your ectomorph — thin, sharp-featured, analytical — will inhabit neat, logically organized space, visitors' chairs arrayed across the desk from his or her own, abstract art on the walls. Big, broad-shouldered mesomorph — hearty, competitive, with a pitiably short attention span — will have lots of items scattered around, bright colors, maybe even a few show-off design risks: Daffy Duck mobiles, giant inflatable plastic bananas. Security-seeking endomorph — big-gutted, warm, a bit sappy — will have an office arranged for comfort, somewhat sloppy, and festooned with knickknacks and representational art: pictures of the family, pastoral scenes with cattle, Keane drawings of waifs with huge sad eyes.

Endomorphs, in particular, are fond of decorating their warrens with green plants. According to Professor Robert Sommer of the University of California at Davis, "Plants allow the employee to be nurturant, a feeling that corporations don't provide many opportunities to express." Watch out for company-owned foliage, however. One corporation installed acres of greenery in response to an employee survey, only to find that productivity did not noticeably improve — the workers wanted their *own* plants.

If you're an intuitive, data-oriented, extraverted endomorph at a clean-desk outfit, you may be prey to similar misunderstanding. Know, however, that the company has both the weight of corporate opinion and some psychology on its side. To quote the self-assured language of *Executive Style,* a picture book of drop-dead offices, "Nothing undermines authority more than a mess of last week's memos." (The tome further suggests that "you can also trumpet your lack of taste" with a display of awards and diplomas — "the best people, we've found in our tours of hundreds of offices, display the fewest.")

Personal-image consultant Donald D. Anderson explains the psychological rationale: "If you go into somebody's office and the desk is cluttered, it signals that he has other work to do. A clean desk says you're the most important person in the world, in that you have his undivided attention." It's a nice, modern thought—an office arranged so that your visitor will be at ease. Anderson goes on, "When the visitor is most comfortable—not distracted by the surroundings—*then* you can manipulate and control him."

The more that things, including offices, change . . .

55

Executives Ought to Be Funnier

Every manager's bag of tricks should include a sense of humor.
But you'd better know how and when to use it.

HEARD THE ONE about the three executives? Probably not. Executives aren't funny. At least, they're not supposed to be. Ask the person on the street, ask the corporate underlings, ask the wives of senior managers — they'll tell you that the people at the top, while perhaps admirable in other respects, are hardly a barrel of laughs. Work is work, after all; let's get serious.

In his sneaky heart of hearts, the intelligent executive knows better. Not that it's all giggles in the corner office, but the potential for mirth is usually there, frequently lurking just below the surface, sometimes erupting into the light of day. Indeed, people who hire executives look for a sense of humor. But canny execs also realize that humor can easily backfire, that its application has to be carefully calculated.

Just how widespread is this kept-under-pinstriped-wraps humor? David Baum, a teaching fellow at Temple University in Philadelphia who also consults on the managerial uses of humor, offers an instructive story. In a workshop for sixty executives from a bank, he asked how many of them felt they had a sense of humor. Each of the sixty bankers raised his or her hand. "When the hands were up," Baum reports, "everyone was looking around at his neighbors with shock on his face. You know, like 'What the hell, what do you have your hand up for?' or 'I know you, forget it, get your hand down.'"

The way the bankers were expected to act at work — what social scientists, with their customary light touch, call the behavioral norm — effectively prevented underground springs of laughter from bubbling to the surface. Norms vary from industry to industry, of course. Banking tends to be on the somber side — "When you're dealing with people's money," comments one observer, "the clients don't want to see the spitballs flying." In advertising, by contrast, if all the folks in an agency come on like church elders, you just might wonder how creative their product is likely to be.

Being funny seems most acceptable in industries and companies that are relatively new, growing fast, and innovating a lot. In Silicon Valley, it may be noted, employees at all levels commonly come to work on Halloween in humorous costumes—the receptionist as a ghoulie, say, the computer engineer as a ghostie, the executive V.P. as a long-legged beastie.

While one can't quite envision that happening in the steel business, most experts on managerial horseflesh—executive recruiters, business-school professors, and the high muckety-mucks themselves—regard a sense of humor as essential in an executive, whatever the industry. William Gould, a headhunter with his own New York City firm and an officer of the Association of Executive Search Consultants, explains why he would never offer a client a humorless job candidate: "What companies are seeking is someone who can see issues clearly. If a person can laugh, particularly at himself, he can probably step back and get the right perspective on things."

Academics, noting research that shows managers get things done mostly by working a network of contacts, point out the usefulness of mirth in building such networks. Other experts call attention to the similarity between making a joke—yoking two utterly disparate things—and that much prized managerial attribute, vision, which at least partly consists of seeing unexpected connections.

More visceral benefits to the humorist include the chance to relieve himself of aggressive feelings in a more or less acceptable way, reduce stress, even display philosophical composure. Renn Zaphiropoulos, co-founder and president of Versatec Inc., a manufacturer of computer printers and now a Xerox subsidiary, is thought by many to be the funniest executive in Silicon Valley. That may be an overstatement, but the man does have refreshing views on certain subjects. For example, he defines business as providing a service for a profit. "If you provide the service and make no profit," he goes on, "it's philanthropy. If you make a profit and provide no service, it's thievery." When asked recently what his sense of humor had done for his career,

Zaphiropoulos replied simply, "It has given me the courage to go through the rough times."

The trick, as Zaphiropoulos admits, is knowing when and how to use it. Being a clown — compulsively responding with a joke to everything that comes up — won't get you to the corner office; it'll keep you from it.

The first proper managerial use of humor is to defuse tense situations. When he was president of Chrysler, Eugene Cafiero traveled to England to meet with workers at a troubled plant there. Ushered in to meet the burly unionists, he was confronted with a man who loudly proclaimed, "I'm Eddie McClusky and I'm a Communist." The Chrysler executive extended his hand and said, "How do you do. I'm Eugene Cafiero and I'm a Presbyterian." A burst of laughter clears the air, all can focus anew on the tasks at hand. The tension-dispelling effects of humor lead some experts to conclude that it's particularly important for female and minority-group managers to cultivate their funny streak. By their very presence, these executives may, in certain benighted quarters, generate a bit of awkwardness.

A second use, so near akin to the first as to be almost identical, is to create rapport. Here's where perhaps the most admirable form of executive humor, the self-deprecating jest, comes in. Research indicates that in encounters between people of different status, the high-status individual almost always initiates the joshing. If Mr. Big uses his prerogative to mock himself in a genuinely funny way, then for a moment differences in status are eclipsed, and high and low have a better chance of really talking. Sandra Kurtzig, the founder and president of ASK Computer Systems Inc., a California software company, has a gift for just this technique. A typical Kurtzigism: "When I started this company, my long-range planning consisted of figuring out where I'd go to lunch." Asked if she'd serve on another company's board, she has replied, "I don't do boards or windows."

Somewhat paradoxically, certain types of humor can, by contrast, serve to reduce rapport and heighten status differences, or at least endow the joke maker with a slight nimbus of power. Jacqueline Goodchilds, an associate professor of psychology at UCLA, has found that in small groups, people who make sarcastic witticisms at the expense of others are seen as powerful. Before you sign up to take

Don Rickles lessons, however, be aware of two caveats. First, the sarcasm has to be funny. As Goodchilds puts it, "If the humor falls flat, the power dissipates too." Second, no one in the group likes the sarcastic so-and-so; they're merely afraid of him or her. Given a chance, the jest-whipped worms may turn.

You're much better off using humor to make difficult messages more agreeable to the recipients. You don't want to couch reports of tragedy in a joke — "I've got bad news and good news; the bad news is that we're closing your plant and laying off all the workers . . ." But putting a humorous face on less serious ill tidings can help in two ways. First, it softens the blow. Second, it protects the messenger by creating a we're-all-in-this-together bond.

Even if the news is good, the lubricant of humor can assist in avoiding potentially sticky situations. Suppose that twenty-eight-year-old woman M.B.A. you hired has been working like a demon. If you, her male boss, stand up at staff meeting and announce, "I wish to single out Ms. Crinziki for special attention — congratulations on your Herculean efforts," approximately the following will happen: three middle-aged males will have strokes; everyone will conceive undying enmity toward the object of your attentions; Crinziki herself will be pleased for a moment, but mostly embarrassed; and they'll all wonder just what *is* your relationship to this tyro. So much more politic to simply let drop "Well, I guess we'd better get the energy conservation boys in again — with the long hours Crinziki has been putting in, our light bill is going to be obscene."

Humor is also a perfect accompaniment when you want to let the troops know that you're aware something's up, and that you're concerned, but you don't want to hammer away at the point. "Gosh, guys," you might say, "I just figured out the message in your latest inventory figures — you want a new warehouse for Christmas." Enough said. Research on presentations shows that people most clearly remember points driven home with laughter.

Almost all these managerial uses of humor are elements in perhaps the most important use: building team cohesion, spirit, and performance. Jim Kouzes, the director of the Executive Development Center at the University of Santa Clara, sees many Silicon Valley managers who use laughter to, in his lovely phrase, encourage the heart of their workers — to help them get through a routine sixteen-hour workday. Zaphiropoulos of Versatec sums the matter up nicely: "I use a sense of humor to produce an informal situation, and I do that primarily because informality encourages communication," he says. "A person who doesn't laugh may be a ruler, but he would get only what he asked for — nothing more. In high-tech companies you can't survive by having people do merely what you ask them to. You hope for pleasant surprises."

Perhaps the most secret thing about executive jocularity is how easy it is to achieve: if you indicate the slightest willingness to laugh, jokes will walk right up to you, delivered by subordinates, peers, maybe the boss. Look for humor, expect it. Soon you'll probably see its laughing face everywhere, even smirking from behind the solemn, workaday visages of your fellow managers.

Who knows — you may even learn the answer to that timeless question, "How many executives *does* it take to change a light bulb?"